THE HUB OF HELL

THE HUB OF HELL

**A True Story of a Nineteenth-Century
Neighborhood, Murder, and Trial**

BEVERLY J. PORTER

credo
house publishers

Published in the United States by Credo House Publishers,
a division of Credo Communications *LLC*, Grand Rapids, Michigan
credohousepublishers.com

ISBN 978-1-625861-38-2

Cover and interior design by Sharon VanLoozenoord
Editing by Donna Huisjen

Cover image, "Birds-eye view of Minneapolis, Minnesota, seen
from the west," courtesy of *Minneapolis, Minn./Hoffman; Chas.
Shober & Co. Props. Chicago Litho. Co.* Minneapolis, Minnesota,
United States, ca 1874. [Chicago: Published by Geo. H. Ellsbury
& V. Green] photograph. https://www.loc.gov/item98509722/.
Used by permission.

Printed in the United States of America

First Edition

For Ron, Eric, Darcy, Bryan, John, and Dan.

CONTENTS

FOREWORD

THE REFINEMENT of the Victorian Era left its mark on American culture, etiquette, architecture, fashion, and thought in varying degrees, but for Minneapolis, Minnesota, it was also a time of modernization and growth. As one of the first cities with electricity, its active city life drew crowds, and people often traveled about the angular roadways via one of many streetcars of the Minneapolis Street Railway. Trains connected the city to Chicago, Omaha, and various other places across the state's borders, carrying numerous patrons, including Buffalo Bill's Wild West traveling shows. (Originating in 1883 near North Platte, Nebraska, the shows became so popular that the entire troupe even crossed the sea to perform for Queen Victoria in London.)

Thanks to the ingenuity of Atlanta pharmacist Dr. John S. Pemberton, by the mid-1880s Americans enjoyed their first bubbly taste of Coca-Cola and it likely refreshed many new fans of Sherlock Holmes while they read Arthur Conan Doyle's first novel, *A Study in Scarlet*, or possibly soothed the nausea of those who had read about Jack the Ripper. America's Great Plains endured weather extremes, from that of a severe summer drought to a deadly blizzard.

All were newsworthy events, yet in Hennepin County a murder story dominated the local headlines. Information found in those newspapers, combined with courtroom transcripts, was used to develop the plotline of the following true story.

**Birds-eye View of Minneapolis ca 1885,
created by Isador Monasch.**

MINNEAPOLIS, MINNESOTA.   1885 A.D.

Source: Library of Congress, Herancourt, W.V. and I. Monasch. *Minneapolis, Minnesota.*
Minneapolis, I. Monasch, 1885. Map. https://www.loc.gov/item/75694644/.

Introduction

NORTHERN MIDWEST winters are often as harshly bitter and confining as the iron bars of the old Hennepin County Jail in Minneapolis. Punishment was certain and guaranteed in an atmosphere that was intentionally uncomfortable and dismal. In the fall of 1887 the Barrett brothers were inmates there. This was an era of notorious outlaws, but unlike the legendary gangs of Jesse James or Cole Younger, the story of these brothers has been lost in history—until now. Theirs is a complex story of passion, betrayal, danger, heartbreak, and tremendous loss.

Trials ensued. Convictions followed. Sentences passed. Justice would be served . . . but was it?

A brief article on the front page of an old newspaper planted a seed and curiosity took root. Intriguing trails were barely traceable, and slow, methodical on-and-off research spread out well over a dozen years. Time passed, and other projects and life chapters commanded my attention, but this story was imbedded in my mind and heart. It had me. The deeper I probed, the more I discovered of a story much bigger than I expected or ever imagined.

Come along—I'll show you. Let's reflect on a series of events, with the clear understanding that this is not a work of fiction. Each of the people you will find between these pages walked, labored, loved, and hated a century before many of us were conceived. They have since turned back to dust, and only their long quieted voices remain—if only we will listen . . .

Hennepin County Jail.

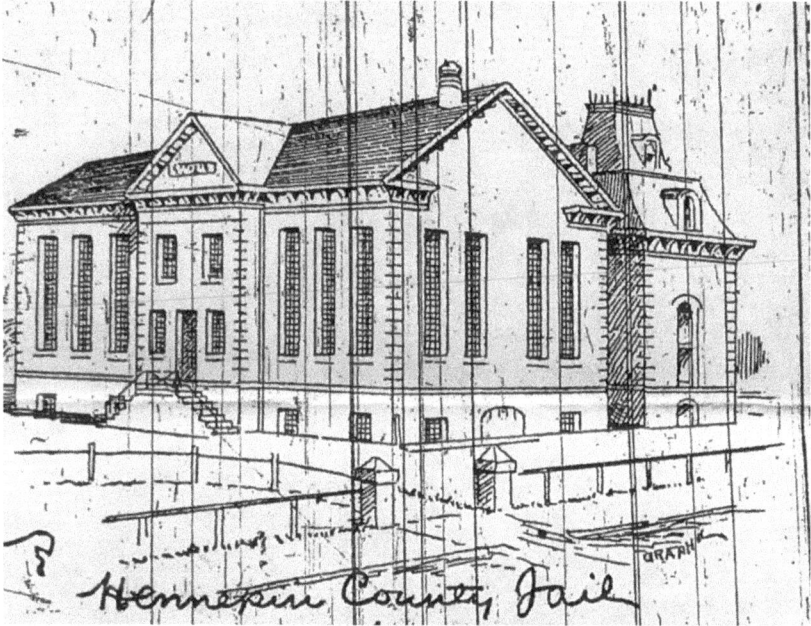

Source: *St. Paul & Minneapolis Pioneer Press*, March 23, 1889, p. 2,
Minnesota Historical Society, St. Paul, MN.

THE HUB
OF HELL

MARCH OF 1889

THE HENNEPIN County jail was an imposing brick structure with tall, narrow windows. It stood in the heart of Minneapolis at the corner of Fifth Street and Eighth Avenue. Sheriff James Ege and his family lived in the residential portion of the building, separated from the prisoners.

It was the 21st day of March, and despite the penetrating, damp chill in the air, people came from sunrise to sunset to visit two convicted brothers. Only one visitor was allowed to stay into the evening hours—Joe Mannix.

Joseph T. Mannix, known to many simply as Joe, was a reporter for the *St. Paul & Minneapolis Pioneer Press*. He had already written many reports about the trials of the brothers, and at their request he stayed to talk with them that night. The three men had discovered early on that they shared some common ground as Irish Catholics, but far more important than that, Joe was a reporter who did his job with integrity and had gained their trust.

Back in 1888, when Fourth Street in Minneapolis was known for its various newspapers and reporters, Joe Mannix stood apart. Not necessarily because he was more popular, or more sensational, than others, but because he had earned the respect of colleagues and readers alike—his approach was a sharp contrast to the flash-in-the-pan, hyper-sensational technique employed by some reporters. His stellar reputation was later memorialized by A. J. Russell, a reporter for the *Minneapolis Journal*, who wrote a book about his fellow reporters titled *Fourth Street*, published in 1917. Russell wrote that ". . . nearly all of the years since 1877, [Mannix] has spent chronicling the events of Fourth Street and if he has made an enemy in that time, I have not heard of it." He included a direct quote from Mannix: "What I have written may not be literature, but I always tried to tell a straight story and to chronicle things as they were."[1]

In light of all that, it is understandable that Joe Mannix earned the trust of a frightened young prisoner who was desperate for his story to be known. Most likely Peter Barrett began with the family history that had been told to him so many times.

John Barrett was born in County Mayo, Ireland, sometime around 1830, and moved to Scotland a few years before the Great Potato Famine hit the country, presumably with his family, at the age of twelve. He boarded a ship to America at the age of fourteen, traveled to New Orleans, and spent his first year there before moving on to St. Louis, Missouri, in 1845, where he found work aboard the Mississippi River steamboats.

Some years later, the serious-minded, soft-spoken John met a young Irish firecracker of a girl named Ellen Whalen. Opposites do attract! The two courted for a while and then married on Christmas Day of 1855. John's work on the riverboats provided a fairly good living but may have kept the newlyweds apart too much.

Greener pastures beckoned, so in 1857 the couple moved to rural Lyons Township in Mills County, Iowa, and two years later purchased a 300-acre farm there. A local history book titled *1881 Mills County History—Biographical Sketches* describes John Barrett as a good farm manager who had greatly improved the productivity of his land. Although John had arrived in Iowa some twenty years earlier with little more than his new wife, he was described as having reached an "enviable position in life."

It wasn't just the farmland that was productive; over those years he and Ellen became the parents of ten children, eight of whom were then living: Mary B., Catharine (called Kate), John T., Frank, Timothy, Henry, Edward, and Peter, who was the youngest.

Unfortunately, the good times did not last. John remained a rather quiet man, but in contrast the once vivacious Ellen had evolved into a domineering wife. There were even rumors that Ellen was both verbally and physically abusive to John. Shortly after the Mills County history book was published, the couple divorced, sold their farm, and split the proceeds between them.

Ellen left the countryside and moved to a large house in Omaha with most of their children. She took in boarders to help with expenses and eventually purchased some cottages that she rented out each summer. In this way she became a financially independent business owner, which was no small accomplishment for a woman in those days.

John Barrett also left Iowa after the divorce. He moved to California for a time but later settled in Minnesota with two of Peter's brothers. Young men identify with their fathers, so it was really no surprise that young John and Henry followed theirs. According to the 1885 census for the city of Minneapolis, the three Barrett men lived together in Hennepin County at 2830 Fort Avenue and operated a business out of the front room on the main floor of a two-story frame house—a "blind pig."

The place was sparsely furnished with two small tables, several chairs, bar fixtures including an ice chest, and a pool table. Their establishment was known for being rowdy, which was probably to be expected since it was located in a tough neighborhood. The Barretts called their saloon the Hub of Hell, made a simple board sign with that name, and nailed it to the front door. The name caught on, and soon that entire neighborhood became known as the Hub of Hell. (Author A. E. Costello described the Hub of Hell as a "dreaded spot, severely shunned by the timid and approached with misgiving at all times.") According to one newspaper source, the district acquired the name because of the bar, while other sources claim it worked the other way around. Regardless, it would prove to be more than just a foreboding name—it was an omen. [2]

For the most part John got along with his sons John and Henry, but they also had their disagreements; some were minor, others dead serious. During one intense argument inside the bar, Henry threatened his father's life and fired a gun at him, stopped only when his sister Mary and a concerned patron intervened.

Not surprisingly, the Barretts had no license, and selling liquor without a license was illegal. John and Henry were arrested and jailed repeatedly, yet remained undeterred. However, the problem was not merely the Barretts' attitude, nor was it the Hub of Hell or the other illegal saloons. The city license inspector was apparently on the take (more on that ahead).

The constant friction of that atmosphere may have grown tiresome for son John, because he soon moved back to Omaha, where he managed to get into enough trouble on his own. (It seems to have been routine for him to get into trouble, and, in fact, a nineteen-year-old John Barrett is included on a list of prisoners at the Iowa State Prison in Fort Madison, Iowa, on the 1880 Federal Census.) One night in 1885 John got involved in a bar fight. He was thrown out into the street by the bartender, a man named Cook. John retaliated by hurling "a brick through the front glass door," then turned to run just as it shattered. When the bartender ran out after him, John shot at him. Cook was also armed and fired back, hitting him in the leg. The wound got infected, developed gangrene, and young John Barrett died from that wound while a patient at St. Joseph's Hospital in Omaha, Nebraska. [3,4]

Henry was bitter about the situation, vowed revenge on the man who had shot his brother, and traveled to Omaha to visit the bar where John had been shot. He confronted the bartender, loudly announcing that he was there to avenge his brother's death as he aimed his pistol directly at Cook. Fortunately, the gun jammed. Henry was then thrown out into the street just like his brother!

Henry returned to Minneapolis.

In October of 1886 the spiteful, violence-prone Henry—who also went by the nickname "Reddy" (possibly because of his red hair)—proved that he actually had a soft, romantic side. He fell in love and got married. His bride, Minnesota Betts (yes, that truly was her name!), was a girl of about fifteen who was also from the Hub of Hell neighborhood. Her father was Theodore Betts, and their family home was at 3030 Fort Avenue, just down the street from Henry's place. The newspapers would later describe her as a rather frail waif with a fair complexion and dark hair and eyes. Their marriage license, dated October 26, 1886, reads:

> State of Minnesota, County of Hennepin, District Court, Fourth Judicial District. Henry M. Barrett, being duly sworn, deposes and says that he has attained the full age of twenty-one-years; the lady he intends to marry is of lawful age to contract marriage, to-wit: eighteen (crossed out with "fifteen" handwritten instead) years, and is a resident of Hennepin County; that neither party has ever been married, that they are not connected by the ties of consanguinity, and that no legal impediment exists to said contemplated marriage. Subscribed and sworn to before me, this 26th day of October, 1886.

It is signed by the clerk of the district court and a clergyman named Henry Langlois. One of the two witnesses whose signatures also appear on the document was Chloe Betts, the seventeen-year-old sister of Minnie. (We'll learn more about Chloe shortly.) The other witness was Timothy Barrett, Henry's brother.

Minnie Betts Barrett was a young newlywed, but this was quite likely not her first romantic relationship. The year before she had lived next door to her Uncle William and Aunt Rebecca Betts's family in Hutchinson, McLeod County, Minnesota, with a nineteen-year-old man named Kingsley Clark. According to the 1885 Minnesota State Census for McLeod County, on May 1 Minnesota Betts resided with Kingsley. That document recorded her age as sixteen. However, according to the Hennepin County Census, which was taken twenty days later, on May 21, she is shown to be fourteen-years-old and living with her father, Theodore, his wife Liddy, and her siblings Chloe, Samuel, and John.

We can easily imagine various scenarios behind that whole situation, but the basic assumption is that of a possibly not-so-innocent teenaged girl. It may also give a hint to another facet of the attraction between the pretty young Minnesota Betts and Henry Barrett, the hot-blooded proprietor of a rowdy blind pig in the Hub of Hell.[5]

Mary Barrett, Peter's oldest sister, also lived in Minneapolis during that time and had started her own business, a millinery, where she fixed ladies' hair and sold hats. Since a business of that nature would have catered to the upper classes during the Victorian era, Mary met some influential, well-to-do women who became loyal customers and friends—women like Abbie Bryant, the widow of James Bryant, the Register of Deeds for Minneapolis.

We can assume that Mary was a smart young woman and savvy enough to know that insurance was a wise investment, because she had taken out a policy on her place of business. It came in quite handy when a fire destroyed the place. Soon afterward, however, the press got wind of a rumor regarding Mary Barrett's past experience of a house fire in Omaha and fanned-the-flames, so to speak. The rumor claimed that Mary had invested in an insurance policy and then intentionally set the fire to get the insurance payment. The details and news reports were rather sketchy, but involved a Minneapolis woman named Sophia Linstrom who had previously testified in an Omaha court against Mary Barrett and her brother John. The Linstrom woman claimed that the two siblings had plotted to swindle the insurance company and burn the Omaha house, that she knew it was so because she had been a tenant at Ellen Barrett's boarding-house at the time.

The similarities between the two fires and insurance policy pay-outs were deemed suspicious, and the Journal Printing Company ran stories about it in their newspaper. Mary Barrett denied any scandal and claimed there was no evidence. However, since the press in Min-neapolis had already published the story and suggested the possibility of arson and fraud, Mary Barrett decided to sue the Journal Printing Company for libel.

The case went to court, and on January 22, 1887, the *St. Paul Daily Globe* reported about the courtroom proceedings. They described Mary as "dressed handsomely and richly" and noted that she had many friends in the "audience." Mary sued for $15,000 in damages—an ex-orbitant amount for the times. The jury took only minutes to make their decision in the matter. They awarded her the meager sum of $175—but, more importantly, they had sided with Mary Barrett and against the Journal.

Like a peacock feather adorning one of her ladies' hats, Mary was able to walk out of that courtroom with her head held high. She had shown the whole town that she was not a woman to be slandered, nor would she be intimidated by the likes of one of the major newspapers of Minneapolis.

Mary had already received the money from her insurance claim. Rather than rebuilding the hat shop, she purchased a large, brown-colored boardinghouse on the corner of Fort Avenue and 26th Street. Located across the street from the glassworks factory, it was also just blocks away from her father's and Henry's place on Fort Avenue. (This was the same old road that had led to Fort Snelling. The road no longer exists, but at that time it ran adjacent to the Milwaukee & St. Paul railroad tracks, Snelling Avenue, and Minnehaha Avenue, in that order from west to cast).

By the spring of 1887 Peter and Timothy Barrett made plans to visit their family in Minneapolis as soon as they had saved enough money. Peter worked as a garbage hauler, and both brothers worked at odd jobs, doing repairs and painting for their mother in Omaha. As earlier stated, she was a self-employed businesswoman who owned and operated a boardinghouse and cottages. Those properties required routine maintenance, and upkeep on the cottages needed to be completed before the busy summer season began.

Mrs. Barrett promised to reward her sons by paying for their fare to Minneapolis once the work was finished, and she bought each of them a new suit of clothing as a bonus before sending them by train to visit Mary, John, and Henry.

It must have been a rather peaceful view along the route from Omaha to Minneapolis back then. The summertime landscape would have stretched across a vast terrain of tall, slender, sage-colored prairie grasses swaying in the wind. There could have been occasional sightings of bison; of farm scenes with horned cattle, robust workhorses, muddied hogs, barns, unpainted farmhouses, and newly sprouted cropland; and glimpses of quaint country towns with a general store, school, church, and houses with gardens inside white picket fences.

Once they arrived in Minneapolis, Mary may have greeted her brothers at the depot. With big-sisterly affection she provided rooms for Tim and Pete at her boardinghouse. Their father, John, lived with Mary by that time. He may have left the Hub of Hell to give Henry and his bride a little privacy, or possibly the father and son had had a less than congenial parting of ways.

Not long after settling in at Mary's place, Tim and Pete met up with Henry, and that is when, and where, the trouble began.

It was said that Tim flirted openly with Minnie, Henry's new wife, and though supposedly nothing came of it Henry's jealousy burned. It didn't help matters when Tim became romantically involved with Chloe, Minnie's sister. Apparently Chloe was a beauty, with clear green eyes and hair the color of ripened wheat—even young Pete had a brief fling with her! All of that carousing simply added fuel to the smoldering fire of an envious Henry, and he was not about to meekly look the other way.

The brothers had their fights about the women, to be sure, but at the base of it all they were brothers. In spite of a somewhat strained relationship they continued to spend quite a bit of time together playing pool or just hanging out at the Hub of Hell and elsewhere.

Since Tim and Pete were new in town, and as any young person is drawn to city attractions and activities, they spent many evenings downtown. One particular evening in late July, there was the added excitement of a fire at the Big Boston Block, a popular retail establishment that housed the Franklin Bazar on the upper floors. Nearly everything from clothing to building supplies could be purchased there and the large, multi-storied structure dominated the corner of Hennepin Avenue and Third Street.

Pete and Tim watched the exciting, dangerous commotion along with the large crowd that had gathered. Heavy smoke billowed upward as firefighters fought the increasingly intense blaze. The police roped off sections of the streets closest to the fire and kept a watchful eye on the bystanders in an effort to keep them safely out of harm's way.

Pete Barrett.

Source: *Minneapolis Evening Journal*, March 22, 1889,
sketch by Herbert Conner from tintype, Minnesota Historical Society, St. Paul, MN.

Tim Barrett.

Source: *Minneapolis Evening Journal*, March 22, 1889,
sketch by Herbert Conner from tintype, Minnesota Historical Society, St. Paul, MN.

Henry "Reddy" Barrett.

THOMAS TOLLEFSON

THE PEOPLE watching the Boston Block burn were from backgrounds and ancestry lines about as varied as the goods sold by that retail establishment. As they say, America is the melting pot, and the residents of Minneapolis most certainly reflected that.

During the late 1880s one young immigrant named Thomas Tollefson put down roots in Minneapolis. He was born in Norway in 1857, his father's name was Ole, and he had a sister named Serianna. It is not clear when, or how many, family members immigrated to the United States.

There are numerous census records that bear the name Ole as head of household and list a son named Thomas, but none of those families includes a daughter with the name Serianna, which made it nearly impossible to connect-the-dots to make any further factual statements about Thomas Tollefson's family history. Of course, as was the custom in those days, a young woman like Serianna may have been employed by another family as a live-in servant at the time of the census. If that were the case, she may have easily been overlooked by the census taker, especially if she wasn't present at the exact time of the recording. Regardless, Serianna lived in the vicinity and had married a realtor named Ole E. Brecke in November of 1886.[1]

Various sources have documented that Thomas Tollefson was a young man of character who was eager, ambitious, and driven to succeed. And it's likely that because he possessed these qualities and temperament he found secure employment at the Minneapolis Street Railway.

The street railway system was an integral part of city life in those days and provided a very convenient, if not essential, mode of transportation to connect residential areas to local businesses. Fares for the service were inexpensive, which made this a practical option for most people. The streetcar railway originated in the neighboring city of St. Paul back in 1872, but in 1875, when Thomas Lowry joined the Minneapolis Street Railway, the company began to flourish.

Thomas Lowry was an influential, savvy, and highly respected businessman. Nine years earlier he had been a practicing lawyer, but he was also a man of vision who eventually turned his sights to real estate. He invested in vacant land located just outside the city limits because he was certain Minneapolis would expand and make that land a valuable commodity. He became interested in the street railway system when he realized the added benefit of that mode of travel. The streetcars could help draw attention to those newly and yet-to-be developed neighborhoods by providing convenient transportation from there into the city and back.

And so it was that in 1875 Lowry was recruited by the Minneapolis Street Railway owners and joined the company. Lowry had the knowledge and business experience to get things rolling (no pun intended) and became part owner of the Minneapolis Street Railway, along with partner Colonel William S. King (Colonel King was the first to head the company). At that time the business was also aided financially by outside investors, but just two years later Lowry had the financial means to gain controlling interest of the company, and he became the president in 1878 (a position he held until his death in 1909).

Thomas Lowry made the streetcar railway his principle business. He operated it successfully through the boom years of the 1880s and through the transition from horse-drawn cars to electric-operated cars, which was completed by 1891. He led the company through tough times, including the workers' strike in 1889, when 600 employees walked off the job (in protest after Lowry reduced their wages by fifteen percent in order to help cover the costs of the transition to electric streetcars) and later when the company faced economic difficulties from the Panic of 1893.

Thomas Lowry was married to Beatrice Goodrich. While Lowry handled the finances and operations, his brother-in-law Calvin Gibson Goodrich served as the secretary (later as superintendent) of the Minneapolis Street Railway.

According to the city directory, the company was located on Third Avenue and occupied that portion of the block from street number 200 to 206. The streetcar stables were located around the corner on Franklin Avenue and several blocks east. In the days before the transition a blacksmith and a mechanic worked out of the stables, since the streetcars were kept there along with many horses and mules. Each streetcar was pulled by a team of two horses or mules. However, one team couldn't possibly run all day, along with the evening hours, so a driver would switch to a fresh team twice a day. In all, six animals were required daily for each streetcar.

Thomas Tollefson was the driver of streetcar number 132. He was respected by the company and well liked among his peers. The job required on-your-feet labor for sixteen to seventeen hours each day, and drivers were paid about two dollars per day. Each driver carried a cash box made of heavy tin and started out each morning with ten dollars worth of change and ten dollars "worth of tickets." The tickets, also called "checks," were contained in little envelopes that were red-colored; the change consisted of quarters in blue envelopes and dimes in pale-colored envelopes. (More on this to follow.) [2,3]

Thomas worked long hours but still found time to fall in love with a young Swedish woman named Christina Nelson [aka Nillson], also known as Lena. She had immigrated to America about three years earlier and worked at the White Sewing Machine Company, which was located on Nicollet Island. A marriage license from Hennepin County of the State of Minnesota was issued to Thomas O. Tollefson, aged twenty-eight, and Christina Nelson, aged twenty-four, on February 10, 1887.[4]

The couple began their married life in the house that Thomas had bought and paid for with savings from his meager wages. Located at 1905 Seventeenth Avenue, it was only a few city blocks from there to the Franklin Avenue streetcar stable, which made a convenient daily commute for Thomas. Life must have been busy, but it was blessed and happy for these young newlyweds in the summer of 1887 as they experienced all the joys and passions of anticipating a lifetime together.

We don't know whether Thomas had driven other routes previously, but that summer he drove the Cedar Avenue streetcar line, and we can assume that he ran it on time. He was running unusually late, on Tuesday, July 26, not due to any fault on his part, rather he was forced to make changes to his normal route because of the Boston Block fire that evening. However his final stop that night was, as always, at the turntable located at the corner of Cedar Avenue and Lake Street, and that is where his last passenger, George B. Horton, stepped off at approximately 11:30 p.m. Thomas had just turned his streetcar in order to head north on Cedar Avenue, back toward the streetcar stables at the corner of Franklin Avenue, when the unexpected happened . . .

>━┤◆>━O━<◆┤━<

As drivers returned to the streetcar barns that night, some began to wonder about streetcar number 132 and Thomas Tollefson. He was always dependable, and it was odd for him to be so late. They reasoned that the fire had caused some delay, but felt something was wrong.

When driver McKinnon got back and noticed that Tollefson was still out, he quickly recalled their encounter earlier that evening and told the others at the barns about it. McKinnon had been headed back north toward the city from the turntable at Cedar Avenue and Lake Street when his car was unexpectedly derailed. Some wooden planks covered the tracks at that location and he suspected that someone had purposely created the obstruction. Tollefson came along and stopped to help him get the car back on the tracks. At that time, McKinnon warned Tollefson about some men lurking in the shadows near an area along the route where the streetlights were broken. Talking about it stirred up his concern, so he began to walk back down Cedar Avenue toward Lake Street, hoping to meet Thomas en route to the stables . . .

►─◄►─○─◄►─◄

The Boston Block was a department store where various goods were sold. Newspaper ads for the retail establishment ran daily, and so the story of the fire was front-page headline news on Wednesday morning, July 27, 1887.

As was the practice in those days, a major story would often bear a bold-faced title followed by multiple headlines in sentence form. The format was catchy, efficient, and convenient, and a reader could quickly get the gist of the news before reading the complete article. One newspaper headline read:

FIERCE FLOUR CITY FLAMES –
Destroy the Splendid Seven-Story Provision Building
and Do Much Damage to Other Property. –

The Stocks of the Big Boston and Franklin Bazar Suffer Heavily
From Fire and Water. –

Losses to Buildings and Goods, It is Estimated,
Will Reach Half a Million Dollars.[5]

The blaze was described as "one of the ugliest and fiercest fires the city ever knew." It started as a small fire on the seventh floor of the Dorillus-Morrison building, which stood at the corner of Washington and Second Avenue, around 9:00 p.m. on Tuesday, July 26. The fire smoldered for quite a while, but just as the firemen arrived it burst into flames, filling the warm, summer-fresh air with thick, pungent smoke and ash. The fire rapidly moved downward, wooden floor by wooden floor. A large gable fell from the burning rooftop onto the adjoining Morse building, while another flaming portion fell onto the National Hotel building that adjoined the structure on Washington Avenue, and forced about fifty guests to flee the premises. Several firemen fought the monstrous blaze as others tried to keep the curious spectators out of harm's way. By the time the conflagration was extinguished it was almost midnight, and "a fine block was burned out and two others badly damaged."[6]

The Boston Block fire made all of the local papers that day, but so did one other story. A short article with a straight-to-the-point title was placed at the bottom of the front page of nearly every newspaper in the twin cities:

SHOT DEAD,
A Burglar Murders the Driver of a Street Car

**Big Boston Block fire, Minneapolis,
Hennepin County, Minnesota, United States, 1887.**

Source: Photograph collection of Minnesota Historical Society, St. Paul, MN.

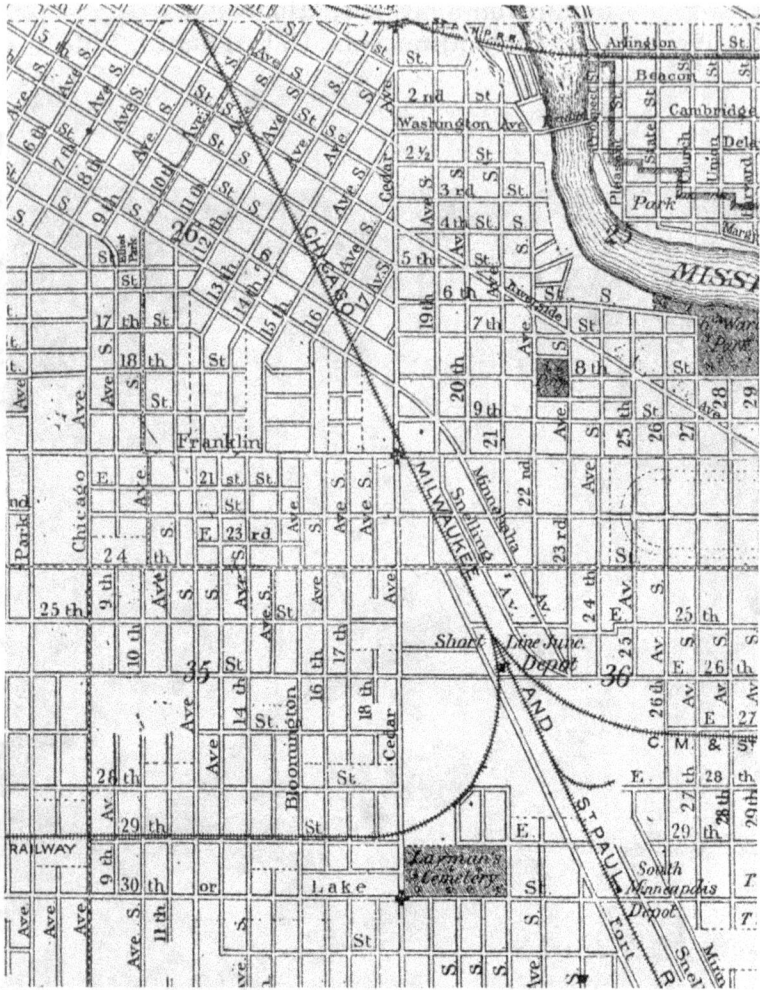

Street map view including the Hub of Hell neighborhood ca 1888. Note the railroad tracks and the turntable markings on Cedar Avenue at Lake Street and at Franklin Avenue (where the streetcar barns were located). Layman's Cemetery is at the corner of Cedar Avenue and Lake Street. Fort Avenue is on the lower right, with 28th Street visible. The Hub of Hell saloon stood at 2830 Fort Avenue. The top left shows the corner of 5th Street and 8th Avenue, where the Hennepin County Jail stood.

Source: Detail from Davison's Atlas Map of Minneapolis, Hennepin Co., Minn., 1888. *The University of Texas at Arlington Libraries Special Collections.*

Thomas Tollefson.

THOMAS TOLLEFSON.

Source: *Minneapolis Evening Journal*, March 22, 1889,
Minnesota Historical Society, St. Paul, MN.

Christina "Lena" Tollefson.

CHRISTINE TOLLEF-
SON.

Source: *St. Paul Daily Globe*, August 31, 1887, p. 3,
Library of Congress, Chronicling America, http://chroniclingamerica.loc.gov
image provided by Minnesota Historical Society, Saint Paul, MN.

Minneapolis Street Railway "bobtail" horsecar.

No. 132, on Cedar Avenue, (Washington and Cedar Line) ca 1886.
Thomas Tollefson drove this streetcar.

3

CORONER—REWARD—FUNERAL

THE NEXT day two men, strangers with a common purpose, were called upon to perform the dreadful task of identifying the body. Streetcar driver John McKinnon and realtor Ole E. Brecke were already somewhat unnerved by the whole tragic event.

McKinnon had found Thomas dead on his streetcar, was present when the officers arrived to investigate, and so was a likely candidate for the job of identification.

Brecke and his wife had been awakened early that morning by authorities about the death, and it is conceivable that he and Seriana went to Thomas's home to be with Lena. All were gripped by shock and grief.

Dr. Towers, who was also a deputy, would conduct the Coroner's Inquest and may have been present when each man entered the room at the Gleason and Byorum morgue where a long table draped in white stood. The undertaker pulled back the sheet covering the body just enough to expose the face for identification.

McKinnon's eyes brimmed, hot and wet.

The deep knot in Ole's stomach loosened as he looked for a spittoon.

A nod and broken "yes" was all either man could muster—it was enough.

>-+-+>-O-<+-+-<

Deputy Coroner Willis Springs performed the post-mortem examination of the body with the aid of his assistant, Dr. D. F. Collins. They discovered that Thomas Tollefson's death was caused by a single bullet that had entered his chest and instantly penetrated his heart. Another bullet wound was found in the front, upper portion of one thigh and had exited just beneath the buttock; there had been very little bleeding from that wound. It was their determination that the gunshot to the leg had most likely occurred postmortem after the heart had stopped pumping blood.

Further investigation of the crime scene and forthcoming witness statements would lead authorities to conclude that Thomas Tollefson was shot because he had refused to yield to the demands of thieves. His life was callously taken for the sake of $20!

>-+-+>-O-<+-+-<

As earlier stated, streetcar drivers routinely worked a long day— anywhere from twelve to sixteen or more hours—in all kinds of weather and were paid from $35 to $54 a month. The other drivers, loyal comrades, were hit hard by the murder of young Thomas. The *St. Paul Daily Globe* reported on Thursday morning, July 28, 1887, that Thomas's fellow drivers had already taken up their own collection to offer as reward money for the arrest of those responsible for Thomas Tollefson's death.

When the Street Railway Employees Association met that night, they decided to request that the Minneapolis Street Railway Company offer reward money as well; the group adopted the following resolution:

Whereas our late brother, Thomas Tollefson, lost his life at the hand of a cowardly assassin, we the members of the Street Railway Employees Association desire to give expression to our deep sorrow and horror at his untimely death, and to testify to our regard for him, both as a brother and a man, besides extending to his afflicted widow our heartfelt sympathy; therefore be it resolved that in the death of Thomas Tollefson we feel that we have been deprived of the companionship of one who has by his manly conduct and upright life been an honor to our order, and who has by his daily conduct exemplified the principles of our order in upholding the true dignity of labor. Desiring further to aid in bringing to justice the cowardly murderer who shot him at his post of duty, the proper officers of this association are hereby instructed to offer a reward of $200 to be given to anyone who will furnish information leading to the arrest and conviction of the assassin.[1]

In response, Calvin Gibson Goodrich, secretary of the Minneapolis Street Railway Company, announced that the company would more than match the amount requested by the association, bringing the total of the reward to $450.

>─┤◆⟩─○─⟨◆├─◄

It was customary in those days to hold visitation at the home of the deceased, so the body may have been taken to the home Thomas and Lena had shared at 1905 17th Avenue. The Minneapolis Street Railway Company graciously and generously paid for all of the funeral expenses, including the casket, which was described as "beautifully draped and fringed . . . with oxidized silver mountings."

The funeral was held at Our Savior's (Norwegian) Lutheran Church, located at the corner of 7th Street and 14th Avenue South. Milton D. Wilson, the owner of a horse stable on South 12th Street, provided carriages for the mourning family to use at no cost. A great number of people attended the funeral, many of whom were streetcar drivers or other employees of the company. All were deeply moved by the senseless loss of the young man with an outstanding reputation. Those who knew him best described Tom as "a man of first-class character in all respects . . . a favorite . . . handsome . . . brave and generous."[2,3]

Thomas's funeral had been held less than forty-eight hours after his death and he was buried near the very place where he had been murdered. Located at the corner of Cedar Avenue and Lake Street, Layman's Cemetery (aka the Old Pioneers Cemetery) was a poignant resting place for the devoted streetcar driver, near the route Thomas had driven so faithfully. Although the funeral had been somewhat lavish, his grave in Lot 17 of Block N was humbly marked with a simple cedar shingle.

Two days later, on July 30, the *St. Paul Daily Globe* gave an updated report about the reward offered for the capture of the murderer(s) of Thomas Tollefson: $500 by the Minneapolis Street Railway Company; $200 by the streetcar drivers and employees; and an impressive $1,000 by the mayor of Minneapolis, the notorious Doc Ames.[4]

><><><>—O—><><><

The grieving young widow was distraught, as any loving wife would be, and the community rallied around her. For example, a baseball game between local newspapermen and lawyers raised $700, and in late August she received a generous donation from the community—nearly $900 worth of "certificates of deposit" with the Farmers and Mechanics Saving Bank and the First National Bank.[5]

Christina Tollefson tearfully responded, "I am very, very much obliged to the people for their kindness, but it does not console me for the loss of my husband, although it makes me feel better to know that I have sympathy."[6]

><><><>—O—><><><

Weeks passed with no leads, but on August 21, less than one month after Thomas Tollefson's death, a newspaper reporter wrote that he had information about a possible clue to the murder. He claimed that an "authoritative source" told him that on the evening of the murder, between 5:00 and 6:00, a "woman, who lives on Third Avenue South rode home in [Tollefson's streetcar]. She [said] three rough-looking men got on the hind platform and Tollefson rang them up for fares" but the men ignored him. "Tollefson stopped his car, went back and demanded [they pay]." They refused. An argument followed that did not end well for them—Thomas grabbed his whip and gave them a lashing. The men, hurt and angry, "swore terribly" at Thomas and threatened to "get even." The woman said she would surely recognize those same men "if she saw them again."[7]

That same source also told the reporter about a man identified as Horman, who lived in the vicinity and was standing about a hundred feet away from the streetcar when Thomas Tollefson was murdered. Horman had heard an argument about fares just before shots were fired. After the shooting he "saw three men" run past him carrying the tin fares box. They passed so closely to the spot where Horman stood in the shadows that he "heard the money rattle in the box" as they ran toward the cemetery.[8]

The reporter then made an interesting commentary. He wrote that "these facts were made known to a tall man with black hair and with black eyes sunken deep in his head, who called himself a detective, but the parties referred to were not subpoenaed before the coroner. In the meantime, Mike Hoy and Mike Quinlan fight. A wide acquaintance and experience with detectives and detective work leads me to remark that as a class they are frauds. Allan Pinkerton was worth the whole of them. He was the first man in this country to conduct the business on a square basis."[9]

This was a bold and publicly made accusation against the detectives working on the case. It leads us to wonder, if a detective was actually told about the eyewitnesses to the confrontation and about the men running from the crime scene, did he investigate? Was the unnamed woman who supposedly witnessed the incident of Thomas and the men ever questioned by authorities? Was Horman interviewed? If not, was the detective inept—or did he have an ulterior motive?

The same newspaper printed another story that immediately preceded this one and sheds light on the workings of some law enforcement officials back then. Titled, "A Lumber Yard Mystery," it tells about the mysterious death of a well-dressed, unidentified man who was found shot in a local lumberyard. It claims that the night before his body was found a couple who lived nearby heard a gunshot followed by a policeman's whistle and two more gunshots. The reporter wrote, "I believe there is a policeman somewhere, perhaps two, who knew how this man met his death and that a murder was carefully concealed by somebody."[10]

Would *the police* have covered up a murder? That's a rather bold—and fearless—accusation of police corruption.

4

CORRUPTION

WE EXPECT officers of the law and elected officials to do their jobs responsibly, reliably, and with integrity and honor, and they in turn deserve our gratitude and respect. That's how it works when laws are fair and no one is above the law, but there have always been some who want to live outside the rules. Corruption has emerged from time to time and from place to place throughout history, and, unfortunately, it had taken root in Minneapolis by the time of the Tollefson murder.

Much has been written about the leadership of Albert Alonzo "Doc" Ames, a doctor turned politician. He served several terms as mayor of Minneapolis, including the years from 1886 through 1888. Several prominent law enforcement officials who were later involved with the Tollefson murder case had strong ties to Mayor Ames. Of course, that doesn't mean they were all corrupt, but there was a personal connection between some of them. For instance, it was Doc Ames who appointed J. W. Hankinson as chief of detectives in 1886, and the very next year the Board of Police Commissioners made Hankinson the chief inspector of detectives.

The Board of Police Commissioners was first organized in 1886 and included Mayor Doc Ames, George L. Baker, Thomas B. Janney, Detective Michael Hoy, and John Baxter. The men served various term lengths of one to three years. By the next year William Guile, Jacob Hein, John M. Hoy, Harry Norton, Dr. E. S. Kelley, and James W. Hankinson had also joined the board. During this second year, the members decided that each man who served on the board would receive an annual salary of $720—a rather attractive sum, considering that at the time police officers only earned between $780 and $2,000 per year, depending on their rank and experience.

Louis Ness, a former cooper, had been appointed to the position of patrolman by Doc Ames in 1883. He was eventually promoted to captain of the Third Precinct in 1886.

Jacob Hein had been on the police force since 1878. Under the leadership of Mayor Ames he was promoted several times, to the rank of sergeant in 1884, lieutenant in 1885, and superintendent in 1887 (to captain in 1890).

In December of 1886 Ames also appointed Charles R. Hill to the position of chief of police.

On another interesting and relevant note, in 1885 Mayor Ames designated the wearing of star-shaped badges, in various styles and colors, by members of the police force. Sergeants and other superiors were to wear "five-pointed gold, silver, or nickel-plated stars not less than two inches in diameter." Each star was engraved with the officer's name. Patrolmen and mounted police also wore stars, but those were simply engraved "Police" or "Mounted Police."[1]

Some police officers were also veterans of the armed forces. Chief Inspector of Detectives Jacob Hein had served under General Sherman during the Civil War. Chief Detective J. W. Hankinson had served in the cavalry during the 1860s conflicts with Native American tribes in the region. Detective Mike Hoy had served during the Civil

War and suffered a gunshot wound that nearly disabled his right arm during the battle of Nashville.[2]

We have no need to question their records of service or their wartime experiences; the point is that these men served in those capacities and were respected, and perhaps admired, because of it. They had been proven capable and obedient to authority.

The newspapers were filled with stories of crime and corruption in the city of Minneapolis, and there was speculation about cops actually working with some of the burglars. In fact, the *St. Paul Daily Globe* for July 29, 1887, included the following:

> Three men . . . riding in a buggy on Lake Street near Minnehaha Avenue about 10 o'clock last night, were stopped by two men, who pointed revolvers at them and told them to hold up their hands. Instead of obeying, [the men in the buggy] whipped up their horses and escaped. This occurred near where Tollefson the streetcar driver, was murdered.[3]

Perhaps most strange and disturbing was the fake news about the "Benevolent Order of Burglars"—a fictitious, satirical article that appeared in the *St. Paul Daily Globe* claiming that the lawbreakers and thugs were organized and unashamed:

> A large number of Minneapolis burglars and highwaymen met at Slugem's hall, corner of Steenth Street and Steenth Avenue south last evening and organized a Mutual Protection and Benefit Association.[4]

The article continues that during the meeting the burglars appointed a chairman named Billie Hitemhard (who had distinguished himself by robbing a farmer in broad daylight near city hall), and included such others as Three-fingered Pete (an expert housebreaker); Sly Sam ("suspected of having robbed the Honorable Hans Mattson's house"); and Bunco Bob, who was credited with delivering the following resolution, which "passed by unanimous vote":

> Whereas it has come to our knowledge that the drivers of the various streetcars are wholly unprotected while out with their cars and carry considerable money in their change boxes. Resolved. That we, beginning from this date, take it upon ourselves to relieve the said drivers of the filthy lucre by any means available, and if necessary to murder the men in cold blood.[5]

Considering the recent robbery and murder of Thomas Tollefson, the article was distasteful and irresponsible, yet the mockery continued, with jabs at the police: "The policemen's white helmets are a great source of comfort—to the burglars." This was supposedly because the color white was so visible in the dark and could be spotted from "four or five blocks away."[6]

The article brazenly mocked the Police Commission:

> [for their] . . . method . . . in handling [suspects during arrest] as it made the work of all burglars and highwaymen much easier, as it was as much as an officers position was worth to arrest a man on suspicion or even ask him where he was going. So long as the commission continued in power . . . there would be no hard times among the fraternity and no member of the organization need go hungry or without plenty to wear.[7]

Following that came advice on how to remove engravings from gold watches, as the mock instructor took one out of his own pocket, held it up high, and asked whether anyone wanted to trade a revolver for it.

Thomas Tollefson was also robbed of a gold watch when he was murdered.

Beyond the distasteful sarcasm the same newspaper gave more

serious attention to the fact that more policemen—"about [seventy-five] or [a hundred] more," according to one officer—were needed to curtail the never-ending string of burglaries and holdups that plagued the city, especially on the outskirts of town. Of course, that may have helped if all of the policemen were honest, but that wasn't the case.[8]

Although it didn't become known until the winter of 1889, Captain Harvey of the Central Police Station in Minneapolis often held stolen goods, such as bolts of silk fabric, at his home. Harvey's excuse was that he kept the evidence, without reporting it, because of jealousy between the detectives and the police, and he was determined to protect *his* ongoing investigation of burglaries. Harvey had gone so far as to partner with a city pawnbroker named Harry DeYoung, who sold the stolen goods. Interestingly, it was DeYoung who introduced Harvey to S. P. Davidson in October 1887. Davidson, a member of the Davidson and Blake gang, was convicted of larceny the following September and sentenced to five years in the Minnesota State Prison in Stillwater. While incarcerated there, Davidson claimed that Harvey actually worked with his gang and would tip them off to police actions in exchange for part of the loot.[9]

Surely the majority of officers and leaders were honorable and trustworthy, but it must have been extremely difficult—and dangerous—for them, since they were never certain whom among their colleagues they could rely on or confide in.

Police battery was also a problem, such as the beating of a seventeen-year-old prisoner named Sweeney by Detective Mike Hoy in May 1887—and it happened at the courthouse, of all places.

Young Sweeney was a burglary suspect who was described as "small and puny looking." While seated on a chair in the courtroom (court was not in session at the time), Detective Hoy abruptly grabbed him, took him to the jury room, and closed the doors. He demanded that Sweeney tell him all he knew about "the burglary." When Sweeney denied knowing anything, Hoy hit him in the jaw "with his fist" so hard it knocked him to the floor. Hoy then kicked him repeatedly.[10]

At that point "Deputy Sheriff Harbitz came in and told Hoy" to stop, to leave Sweeney alone, because the prisoner was under "the Sheriff's care." Hoy stopped but cursed the sheriff and instructed Deputy Harbitz to put the handcuffs back on Sweeney. A jailer named "Johnson . . . was present when the trouble took place. . . . [He] tried to go in and prevent Hoy from hurting Sweeney, but Court Officer John Byrnes and Inspector James Howard, a detective with the police department, would not let him."[11]

Obviously, police brutality was a real thing back then, but of course it didn't start, or stop, at that level. Eventually the truth would come out . . .

Doc Ames was elected to the office of mayor three times prior to the Tollefson crime. During each of those terms he served as a Democrat, but he switched to the Republican Party in the 1890s and was re-elected in 1900. It would seem that he was quite popular among the citizens . . . but was he?

One gutsy, insightful expose titled "The Shame of Minneapolis: The Rescue and Redemption of a City That Was Sold Out" was written several years after the Tollefson murder by Lincoln Steffens, the so-called "muckraking journalist," and published by *McClure's Magazine* in January 1903. From it, we learn that in January 1901 Mayor Ames appointed Norman W. King, a former gambler, to the position of chief detective. Even though this appointment occurred many years after the Tollefson murder, it is significant because Norman W. King was a former partner of Mike Quinlan; the two operated a detective agency in the mid-1880s. They were friends but had a falling-out and parted ways a decade later.[12]

Detective Mike Quinlan was promoted from police officer to detective under Doc Ames's predecessor, Mayor Edward Babb, in June 1884. So we know that Quinlan was *not* one of Ames's men—and that is an important distinction to keep in mind. After Tollefson was murdered, Detective Mike Quinlan went to work on the case. Just a few days later, on July 29, 1887, Quinlan claimed that he had confiscated the stolen streetcar fares box and boasted that he could produce the evidence, as well as identify the men who were guilty of the

Tollefson murder. He boldly claimed, "For $250 I will guarantee the arrest of the men who did the shooting, but I would not walk across the street for a reward. . . . Today I had an interview with C. G. Goodrich, of the streetcar company. He said the company would pay $250 for the capture of the men, but I told him to give me that sum and I would get them. He said he would have to consult others about that. All I want is to have [my] expenses paid as they are incurred."[13]

The *St. Paul Daily Globe* reporter asked Detective Quinlan if there was any information about the murderers that he could print in the paper. Quinlan replied, "I have the team and its owner, as well as the men who drove it from the scene of the murder. . . I have another witness to the murder [who] was standing on the sidewalk, and when the first shot was fired drew back to the trees, while the men passed close by him. He saw one of them take the cash box, and saw him well enough to give an accurate description. The man wore blue pants, a gray flannel shirt, a coat but no vest, and had on a light felt hat. He watched them—there were only two, not three—enter the wagon and drive down Lake Street."[14]

We can assume that this eyewitness was Horman, if we refer to the text a few pages back.

Other news accounts described the possible suspects as "three . . . young men, well-dressed, wearing black stiff hats, one having on a light summer coat."[15]

The man described in the statement "These facts were made known to a tall man with black hair and with black eyes sunken deep in his head, who called himself a detective" was likely Mike Quinlan.[16]

Detective Mike Quinlan had made some very bold statements about the Tollefson crime. But were they accurate? What motivated him to say things that could have been regarded as premature and presumptuous? Was he an opportunist? Did he have an inflated ego? Or was he simply a top-notch detective?

In order to gain some understanding we need to look at his background and personality traits. Mike Quinlan was born in Wisconsin in the mid-1850s and enlisted in the Marines in August 1880, where he achieved the rank of sergeant. When he returned to civilian life he became a police officer. Those experiences demonstrate his commitment to service. He was also married and the father of three children—a family man.

We can assume that he had a favorable reputation based on a news article from June 5, 1884, which reads:

> The promotion of Officer Quinlan to the full rank of detective last evening by the mayor [Babb] . . . [is] a just recognition of an efficient and worth[y] officer. Mike Quinlan has proved himself to be a shrewd and valiant officer, and during the few brief weeks in which he has been detailed for special service he has detected and arrested a large number of the dangerous class which threaten the lives of our city as well as the destruction and loss of property.[17]

When we fast forward to the summer of 1887, we find some interesting character information about him. In a rather Wild West type of scenario, Detectives Quinlan and N. W. King (his partner) had gotten into a brawl with some of their bitter rivals—the "regular city detectives or 'inspectors' at Cardiff and Donaldson's Sporting Emporium and Social Concert Hall on Second Avenue South."[18]

One other brief article mentioned that Quinlan's "[law]suit against the police commission [was] in the courts." The lawsuit may have stemmed from the Police Commission's *false accusations* against Quinlan for assisting with a prison escape (he was acquitted in August 1887). Detective Mike Quinlan, in turn, filed a lawsuit against "Jacob Hein, [Mike] Hoy, George L. Baker, John Baxter and T. B. Janney for $25,000 [in] damages arising from malicious imprisonment" for the incident that occurred in August 1886 (Mayor Ames was in office at that time).[19,20]

Interestingly, Hennepin County Prosecutor Frank Davis filed a personal lawsuit against the Police Commission and the *Minneapolis Tribune* at that time as well.

So it would appear that there was more conflict than camaraderie between private Detective Mike Quinlan and some of those who had been appointed to powerful positions by Mayor Doc Ames.

As further evidence of this ongoing friction, in November 1887 the Police Commission went so far as to issue an order "to receive no prisoners at the lock-up [who had been] arrested by Quinlan and King's men." The ethics of the order was appropriately questioned by the reporter of the newspaper story, and he mentioned his own doubts as to whether "the Police Commission [had] consulted an attorney" in the matter.[21,22]

It would have been impossible for Detective Quinlan to bring in the suspects he referred to that summer, the two men whom he claimed to have knowledge of based on the information given by an *eyewitness* to the Tollefson robbery and murder.

What motivated the Police Commission to impose such a rule against the Quinlan and King Detective Agency? Personal conflict and political overreach could certainly have hindered the solving of the Tollefson murder. Was the timing of the order significant? Who was being protected? What role did corrupt law enforcement officials play, and why? How could justice have been served in such an environment of jealousy and friction?

We'll explore the situation further using information found in numerous newspaper articles and courtroom transcripts—information that will piece together a very complex story of murder, betrayal, and corruption.

Detective Mike Quinlan.

Source: *St. Paul Daily Globe*, August 11, 1887,
Library of Congress, Chronicling America, http://chroniclingamerica.loc.gov
image provided by Minnesota Historical Society, Saint Paul, MN.

Turn the Page: Other News

OF COURSE, various crimes occurred in the city at the time of the conflict between the Police Commission and Detective Mike Quinlan. On Monday, August 15, 1887, the *St. Paul Daily Globe* ran a story pertaining to the problematic "blind pigs." And who should be mentioned in the headlines? None other than Henry Barrett, identified as "the Fort Avenue Dealer" who ran "a saloon at 2830 Fort Avenue, which is just outside the patrol limits."[1]

Henry was called as a witness concerning a court hearing held the previous Friday, a hearing that exposed "how blind pigs were furnished protection under the last administration." While under oath he told the court that he paid the license inspector, sometimes under the guise of a campaign contribution for the Republican candidate (Pillsbury). This accusation drew a heated defense from License Inspector James J. Smith when Henry identified him as the man he had paid, beginning in 1884.

"You see," Henry explained, "I had been running a saloon for about a year and a half under the Ames administration, and when Pillsbury came in the patrol line shut me out. I kept right along and never refused any man who wanted a drink. For the first six months, Smith made it very hot for me, and had me arrested many times, for I was an innocent kid and never dreamed that an officer could be bribed. After I once fixed Smith, I was all right, and never disturbed, and complaints against me were never minded."[2]

Henry stated that there were several times when officer Smith arrested him back then and "dropped hints about fixing it up, but [I] never tumbled."[3]

He recounted one time in particular when Smith had arrested him. Before the court date Henry informed Smith that he planned to just plead guilty. However, Smith told him to simply pay him $50 and the case would be "dismissed." So he set up a time to meet with Smith and paid him. Afterward, Henry watched the papers daily for information about his case; "after two postponements the case was dismissed."[4]

Henry gave Smith protection money on several occasions after that and, by doing so, carried on with his business with no fear of arrest—until the night of a brawl at the Hub of Hell. People started talking when a man named "Maguire . . . lost a watch and some money."[5]

Inspector Smith was angry that Henry had told people about the protection racket, so he went to the Hub of Hell in order to confront him. Henry denied that he had said anything about it but threatened that he would if Smith ever tried to arrest him again.

Smith then told the court about one particular meeting with Henry Barrett, an occasion when another unidentified officer joined them, and Henry admitted to both men that he had never paid Smith protection money.

Henry quickly rebutted that he had only said so at the time because of a prior agreement between himself and Smith. Smith strongly denied this, refuted Henry's claims, and was able to convince the court that he was actually an effective license inspector. Was he?

The report continued:

In this connection, it may be stated that the row at Barrett's place was in all of the papers at the time. It also stirred up all the politicians, and caused much comment [about] the fact that this place was allowed to run openly. Auditor F. S. McDonald alluded to it in an interview in the Journal of March 15, 1886. He was advocating George A. Comp for mayor on the ground that the people were sick of the show-reform administration. He concluded as follows: "The people in the Seventh [District], as I learn from good authority, are tired of sham reform and have no desire to 'vindicate' such an administration. A prominent business man of that ward told me that a saloon [Henry's Hub of Hell] of the worst character has been running near the Milwaukee shops every day in the week with no license, and that men were robbed there often, yet no interference. A few days ago a fellow [Maguire] was robbed there of a watch and $18. . . . A detective was notified and he said to the keeper [Henry], "I will give you three days to return the watch." The saloon-keeper [Henry] replied, "You'll give me three years, won't you?" A prominent citizen present said he would give $100 to have the place closed, and a Milwaukee policeman told the detective he would meet him or the inspector there the next morning with the names of 100 witnesses who would swear to the fact of its open violation of law. The morning came. The detective did not come. Inspector Smith did not come. The Milwaukee policeman was there with his record of witnesses. The saloon is running just the same. The people of the Seventh regard such things as an outrage, and they think another man can be elected. . . . A few days later the Journal contained the following editorial note: "License Inspector Smith wants to know if people are aware of the violations of the ordinance, why don't they prosecute? . . . Well, that's rich. Perhaps if Mr. Smith wanted to he could tell several reasons why a large number of people have had the mantle of reform thrown about them. You are pretty smooth, Mr. Smith, but the public are on to you."[6]

The article concludes that all mentioned events and "facts are given in connection with the 'great conspiracy' and there are more where these came from." That conspiracy referred to the controversial and illegal methods used to acquire campaign money used by the Republican Party for the mayoral election, and to the so-called "show-reform administration" that resulted. It is obvious that corruption was a real issue in Minneapolis at the time.[7]

So, who was in the wrong regarding the situation between Henry Barrett and Inspector James J. Smith? It appears that Henry favored the leadership of Mayor Doc Ames over that of his predecessors, Mayors Babb and Pillsbury. Wouldn't such a sentiment, made public in the newspapers, have somewhat stroked the ego of Mayor Doc Ames?

Barely one month later Henry was back in court, not as a witness but for his own arraignment—charged with selling liquor and beer without a license at the Hub of Hell. The following week, on September 28, a newspaper report titled "Liquor Men Are Scared" appeared. The opening sentence reads, "From all appearances the liquor men who have violated the law and incurred the displeasure of the grand jury are 'in for it.'"[8]

The last paragraph of this article reported that Henry pled guilty to one of the charges and so "the second was allowed to stand." He was sentenced to serve thirty days in jail, fined $50, and ordered to pay for the court and jail costs incurred. If he failed to pay the fine within thirty days, another thirty days would be added.[9]

So Henry was lodged in the Hennepin County jail that fall. It wasn't the first time—he would later admit that he had been jailed between ten and fifteen times over the years. Not surprisingly, he failed to pay the $50 fine on time and was ordered to serve the additional thirty days.

6

AUTUMN OF 1887

SOON IT was November, but there still had been no arrests for Thomas Tollefson's murder. Two more weeks passed, and then came a possible lead.

The *St. Paul Daily Globe* reported that numerous robberies had occurred near Minnehaha Falls. There had been complaints for months about "people being held up [at gunpoint] . . . . [G]enerally ladies . . . were relieved of their jewelry and purses by the big highwayman." The police were frustrated by the lack of any consistent physical description of the thief.[1]

However, just a couple of days before mid-November a woman and her little daughter were accosted by a man who forcefully yanked the girl's gold ring from her tiny hand. The mother reported the incident to the police and described the thief as "rather good-looking, young, fairly well-dressed and weighing about 160 lbs . . . [with] slightly reddish hair, a long, blonde mustache, and . . . exceptionally large boots." She even described the gun he used. It was a "large, nickel-plated . . . 38-caliber" with a "long barrel."[2]

Chief Detective James W. Hankinson did some investigating and, with the assistance of "M. Hoy, the old detective," concluded that the robber was Henry Barrett's brother Tim.[3]

At that point Detective Hankinson and Captain Ness "of the South Minneapolis Station . . . went directly to Barrett's house, near the corner of Twenty-seventh Street and Twenty-ninth Avenue South. Here [Tim] Barrett was found" with Minnie Barrett and her sister Chloe Betts, who was identified in the newspapers as being Tim's very attractive "sweetheart." Tim supposedly jumped up, "made a move as if to pull a gun," and was arrested by the officers, who promptly delivered him "to the First Precinct Station."[4]

Of course, the newspaper reporter wasn't actually present at the time, so the story he wrote was based solely on information the police had given him.

Remember that Henry was still in the Hennepin County Jail at the time. It's worth noting that the physical description of the "big highwayman" could have fit Henry, who was considered very tall, whereas Tim was of more average height. We also recall that James W. Hankinson and Louis Ness were Doc Ames's men, as was Mike Hoy, the detective who had roughed up Sweeney, the young prisoner, six months earlier.

The officers questioned Tim at the police station. He denied any wrongdoing, so the officers called in Detective Mike Hoy, who reportedly worked Tim over for about an hour, until "Barrett broke down" and confessed. Tim said he would show the officers where the missing ring was, so "Capt. Hankinson, Capt. Ness and Patrolman McNulty went . . . [back] to the house with Barrett. When they reached the place . . . the Betts girl created quite a scene by flinging herself onto Barrett's bosom and sobbing wildly. Barrett, who was handcuffed, began to fondle the girl's hands, and by so doing aroused the suspicions of McNulty, who took hold of the girl's hand and found . . . the ring" that had been stolen. Tim was then compelled to surrender the remaining plunder from the robberies and showed the officers "his room."[5]

The article listed several items that were found there, including "a big fur coat, . . . boxes of cigars, two or three watches, a revolver," and numerous small items. Tim "claimed that the fur coat" was Henry's, and the officer started to believe him until he saw the expression on Minnie's face as she denied it. So the officers confiscated all of the items to take back to the station.[6]

We know that at this point Henry Barrett was serving a sentence in the Hennepin County Jail for illegal liquor sales at the Hub of Hell, and that on November 16, 1887, his brother Timothy Barrett was arrested for the crime of highway robbery and admitted to the same jail.

Two days later, on Friday, November 18, the *St. Paul Daily Globe* ran a story titled, "Still a Question—As to Whether Tim Barrett Was Connected With the Tollefson Murder," about an ongoing "effort to connect Tim Barrett with the murder" of Thomas Tollefson.[7]

The same article reported that Henry Barrett had just paid his $50 fine and was released from jail. (Henry later claimed that he had most of the money but borrowed a small portion, "$3.75," from Deputy Sheriff Johnson.[8])

Furthermore, (with a jab at a competitor's reporter), "an evening paper . . . intimated that [Henry] is also suspected of being connected with the Tollefson murder, but there seems to be no foundation for such a conjecture. The statement that the county authorities allowed his release for the purpose of thwarting the city police seems equally silly and absurd."[9]

Was it?

Of the various newspaper stories about crimes, such as the highway robbery of which Timothy Barrett was accused, perhaps none were more serious than the stories that strongly hinted at the prospect of some dishonest cops who were actually working with the criminals. Those alliances occurred anywhere from the outskirts of town to the backstreets and downtown shops all the way to city hall.

Though not fully exposed until several years later, various written accounts prove that there was rampant, persistent corruption in Minneapolis during the late 1880s. The Minneapolis Police Department was controlled by the Board of Police Commissioners that was formed in 1886 by the Minneapolis City Council in "an attempt to thwart the corrupt Mayor Doc Ames who had replaced the police force with crooks." However, Ames and some of his men were actually members of the Board of Police Commissioners, a group that the press often wrote about in a demeaning manner. (The board was finally abolished in 1890.) There is a strong probability that justice was not always served.[10]

One week after Timothy Barrett's arrest, on Wednesday, November 23, the *St. Paul Daily Globe* ran yet another story concerning the Tollefson murder with a possible link to the Barrett brothers, titled "Up to Date—The Police have a Probable Murderer, and Still They Haven't—." By then Peter was also wanted for the crime. He was "out of town," but the authorities tracked him to Nebraska and "arrested [him] at Omaha" on Monday, November 21. However, the police refused to give any details about the arrest to the press, which led to some rather "sensational newspaper accounts."[11]

As the situation began to unfold in November 1887, the reporters had not yet heard the most sensational news: that Henry Barrett had turned informant and implicated his own brothers, Timothy and Peter, in the murder of Thomas Tollefson. He became a protected Witness for the State, was secretly moved thirty miles away from Minneapolis to Waconia, Minnesota, along with his wife Minnie, and sister-in-law Chloe, where they lived under the surveillance of police officer Levi Gorman.

The four moved into the Lake House, located on the corner of Vine and Main Streets. It was a popular summer tourist destination in those days, and though it stood some distance from the shore there was an unobstructed view all the way to the south side of Lake Waconia. Henry and Minnie checked in as "Mr. and Mrs. Henry Smith" and Chloe under the name "Miss Johnson."

John Behrenfeld had built the Lake House back in the early 1860s, but local businessman Andrew Schutz owned it during the time when Henry, Minnie, and Chloe stayed there. (Schutz also had political ambitions, according to a history book of the area published by the Waconia Heritage Association.) Photographs from that era show a large, two-story structure with white siding, dark painted shutters, and a second-story balcony that extended the entire width of the building across the front, providing a shady sitting area on the porch beneath it. Advertised as a "first-class hotel . . . [a] summer resort . . . [that accommodated] fifty guests," it even had its own livery and fleet of boats. Winter was the off-season, of course, so there was plenty of privacy.[12]

Hennepin County paid officer Gorman $100 each month for his services and also paid for the living expenses of Henry's family. According to one newspaper account, the arrangement was considered an extraordinary expense, and at least one complaint was filed. Regardless, the cost was considered necessary in order to secure Henry's testimony, because without him, the "state's case [was] worthless."[13]

Another interesting aspect of this entire arrangement was the romance that soon developed between Chloe Betts and Levi Gorman. In fact, their affectionate behavior eventually caused problems for all four of them, which will be explained later.

>—◦—◦—◦—◦—<

Ellen Barrett, the boys' mother, was determined to get the best possible legal help for her sons. She hired the seasoned attorney William (Bill) Erwin to defend Timothy and Peter.

Erwin had been doing business in the city of Saint Paul since the 1870s. The city directory for 1888 lists his residence at 481 Iglehart, and his law offices were located at "9 and 10 Mannheimer block." Bill Erwin was nicknamed "The Pine Tree of the Northwest" due to his height and professional reputation as successful, strong, and prominent, somewhat like a towering pine tree. His assistants were attorneys William Donahue and John T. Byrnes, and they were determined to win yet another case.[14, 15]

County Prosecutor Frank Davis had a positive reputation as well and was an experienced, capable attorney. His assistants were attorneys Robert Jamison and John W. Arctander. (In fact, after Davis's term ended, he returned to private practice, and Jamison became the county prosecutor.)

That autumn, during the waning days of his position with the county, Frank Davis lost the Wickman case (a charge of grand larceny). The defense had presented stronger evidence than he could, and Davis simply "gave it up." It must have been a harsh blow to the ego of the proud prosecutor, but the Barrett case could provide him a chance to leave office on a high note. The case would also receive a lot of publicity. The Barrett trials would be a high profile murder case that, if the brothers were convicted, could possibly result in a *double execution*—a first for Minneapolis.

Robert Jamison could potentially begin his role as Hennepin County Prosecutor with a prestigious courtroom victory . . . if *only* they would win.[16]

>-+-<>-O-<>-+-<

The Barrett brothers' first court appearance took place on the morning of November 28, 1887. Police Lieutenant Day, from the North Minneapolis Station, brought Peter Barrett to the courtroom shortly after 9:00 a.m.

Slim and of average height, Peter's red hair was cut short with long bangs across the forehead of his clean-shaven face. He wore checkered pants with a black patch over one knee, and the shoes on his feet were tattered with holes. His eyes darted nervously from person to person in the room. With weather-chapped hands he fidgeted, twisted, the scruffy fur hat that he held on his lap. At times he would lay the hat over one leg in order to wipe the sweat from his face with a dirty blue cotton bandana that he kept stuffed in his pocket.

"He is little else but a boy," a reporter wrote, adding, "He looked little like a murderer."[17]

Attorney William H. Donahue arrived a half hour later. He hadn't yet met his client but looked at Peter and commented sarcastically to

Assistant City Attorney Rand, "There is the terrible desperado we have been reading so much about . . . Dangerous looking man, is he not?"[18]

Pete briefly glanced back at Donahue with a half-smile, then stared at the floor.

Rand replied, "I would like to meet about seventeen men like that on a cold night; it would be any amount of fun."[19]

At that point Mike Hoy arrived with Timothy Barrett, who was slender but taller than his younger brother. A handsome man, he wore a moustache. Hoy led Tim to the chair beside Lieutenant Day and then sat on the other side of him.

The brothers' gray-haired father, John Barrett, entered the court-room with hesitation and fixed his eyes on his feet. He had no greeting for his sons, not even a glance, and refused a chair offered to him. Somberly, restlessly, he paced the room as they all waited for the judge to arrive.

By 10:00 a.m. Judge Bailey entered his courtroom. He called Peter to the bench first and he approached timidly, staring at the floor while the "clerk read the charge against him."[20]

Tim was then called. Although pale and trembling, he looked directly at the clerk as the charge was read.

Attorney Donahue spoke up before either of his clients was asked to make a plea. He requested separate court examinations for the brothers and stated that he was ready to proceed.

However, Prosecutor Jamison claimed that he was *not* ready and asked the court to grant more time—"at least ten days"—so he could secure witnesses. He stated that many were out of town and claimed that he had not yet completely investigated "some facts connected with the case" but that the police would have more information to give him if he were only granted more time to prepare.[21]

Judge Bailey considered both attorneys' views, but since he could not set bail he advised that the examinations should be completed as soon as possible. He would not grant more time if it were simply used to "hunt up new evidence" but that because witnesses needed to be contacted he would allow for a delay.[22]

Donahue was not pleased with the judge's decision.

Although their first court appearance was before Judge Bailey, Judge William Lochren would preside over both of the Barrett brothers' trials. Newspaper reporters described Judge Lochren as having a "slow, measured voice" and wrote that he was "the embodiment of real woolsack dignity."[23, 24]

William Lochren had immigrated to America from Ireland, arrived with his family as a young boy, and lived in Vermont before moving to Minnesota. While a young man he served with the 1st Minnesota Infantry during the Civil War. He studied law after that, was admitted to the Minnesota bar, practiced as an attorney for several years, and became a judge for the U.S. Fourth Judicial District Court of Minnesota in 1881. (He continued to serve until 1893 and had a favorable reputation, according to *History of Minneapolis, Gateway to the Northwest*, published in 1923—nine years after his death in 1914.)[25]

He also had a sense of Old-West-style humor. As habits go, he was a tobacco-loving pipe smoker. A reporter once wrote about how Lochren's pipe had gotten him into trouble back in the days when he was still a practicing attorney: "One afternoon proceedings were unusually dull and [Lochren] thought he would like a smoke, [so he] took a chair, [sat] down back of the jury box, out of sight of the judge on the bench, and lit his pipe." Shortly afterward a smoky haze rose above the space, and the presiding judge noticed, but couldn't tell who was causing it. A bit of commotion ensued, and when Lochren stood up to see what was the matter the judge spied him and reprimanded him with a fine of "two dollars for smoking in court." Right then and there Lochren took a five-dollar bill from his pocket and handed it to the clerk. In turn, the clerk gave Lochren his change. "As [Lochren] resumed his seat, he turned to an acquaintance and said with a chuckle, 'I guess I am even with him. This [three dollars] is good and that [five-dollar] bill was not.'"[26]

Judge William Lochren was a highly esteemed judge. Both the State's Attorney, Frank Davis, and the attorney for the defense,

William Erwin, a "brilliant" and "eminent criminal lawyer," were experienced, respected, and qualified. As reporter Joe Mannix wrote
in the St. Paul and Pioneer Press, "Perhaps Mr. Erwin . . . is himself
as much an object of interest as anybody connected with the case. If
County Attorney Davis gets the death sentence passed on these men
[Barrett brothers] it will be the first instance of the kind where Erwin
was for the defense. Consequently, it will be something of a feather in
the cap of the accomplished state's attorney if he can convict . . . be
assured that he will make the big effort of his life."[27]

Ellen Barrett, mother of the Barretts.

Source: *St. Paul & Minneapolis Pioneer Press*, March 23, 1889,
Minnesota Historical Society, St. Paul, MN.

Tim Barrett in jail.

Source: *St. Paul Daily Globe*, March 17, 1889,
Library of Congress, Chronicling America, http://chroniclingamerica.loc.gov
image provided by Minnesota Historical Society, Saint Paul, MN.

THE TRIALS BEGIN ... TIMOTHY

ON DECEMBER 10 Tim and Pete appeared before Judge Lochren and were indicted for murder in the first degree. Both brothers entered a plea of not guilty.[1]

About ten days later Tim's trial began. The *St. Paul Pioneer Press* reporter Joe Mannix described the scene inside the Hennepin County Courthouse. He wrote, "No murder in Minneapolis during the past ten years has attracted more general interest than that for which the Barrett boys are arraigned. . . . The courtroom was crowded. The space inside the railing was completely occupied by lawyers, reporters and those more directly interested in the trial. Judge Rea occupied a position beside Judge Lochren until business in his own court required his presence."[2]

Mannix continued, "The small group at the left of the attorneys' table was the center of interest. Behind Mr. Donahue sat Mr. Erwin. To Mr. Donahue's left sat an old gentleman, . . . evidently upward of sixty years of age. He listened to every word and watched every movement with the keenest interest. Close to Mr. Erwin's chair sat Mrs. Mary Coleman, sister of the accused. Her face was closely veiled and at times she showed some emotion. To Mrs. Coleman's right was her brother, Tim Barrett, who is not the murderous-looking man some have pictured him. He is of the average height, about twenty-five years of age, has sandy hair and a small moustache of the same hue. He is a bright-eyed young fellow with a look that does not particularly indicate viciousness. To Tim's right sat a trio of the family—Peter, the youngest boy, arrested near Omaha, Mrs. Barrett, the mother of the accused, and Frank Barrett, a brother, whose presence in the city was unknown to the authorities until he appeared as an interested spectator yesterday morning. Mrs. Barrett, who like her husband is small in stature, looks like a woman who has gone through a great deal of trouble."[3]

He added, "Among the spectators were all the streetcar drivers who could get away from their work." It was obvious that Thomas Tollefson's fellow drivers went out of their way to show support and concern for their murdered friend.[4]

Mannix also wrote, "Close to County Attorney Davis and his assistant, Robert Jamison, were a large number of the state's witnesses. Among these were Superintendent Hein, Chief Inspector Hankinson, Inspectors Howard, Kinney and Fairbairn, Police Commissioner Hoy and other officials."[5]

It was a Monday morning, December 19, 1887, and the court began by selecting jurors. This was a very slow process. To make matters worse, Bill Erwin was not feeling well and appeared tired, but he managed the somewhat tedious task diligently and gracefully. Of the thirty-nine men questioned in hopes of filling the twelve juror seats, by noon only six had been selected, and by 4:00 p.m. that afternoon one more had been chosen. The names of the first seven jurors were Leonidas Armstrong, John H. Fisher, George Wilson, Mr. Paulie, H. H. Conary, S. S. Boynton, and M. C. Burr. Five more were needed, but by then everyone involved was exhausted. The judge ordered a "new panel of fifty men" from which to select on the following day.[6]

As to why there had been so much difficulty with the jury selection process, Joe Mannix explained, "The greater number of those who were called were dispensed with because they were biased. They had read the papers and formed an opinion as to the guilt or innocence of the culprits." However, there was more to it: "The question of nationality entered into the case. The prosecution seemed disposed to object to Irishmen . . . thinking that their sympathy for men of their own nationality would possibly interfere with their dealing justly with the Barretts, who are of Irish extraction. The defense was just as particular about excluding Scandinavians from the jury. The dead car driver was [Norwegian]."[7]

By the end of the following day four more jurors had been selected: George Houghton, O. J. Roberts, George Overmire, and W. A. Miller—but they still needed one more.

On Wednesday afternoon, December 21, they finally chose William Powles to fill the last position on the all-male jury. The jury members came from various backgrounds and occupations, and included a butcher and a realtor.

With the jury finally in place, the trial was opened immediately with a statement from Attorney Robert Jamison, the assistant to Hennepin County Prosecutor Frank Davis. He addressed the court, saying, "The case is one which weighs heavily on the prosecuting officers, from the fact that upon its outcome depends human life. It would be especially severe upon us if we had any doubt as to the guilt of Tim Barrett, the prisoner . . . But when we review the long chain of evidence, which is bound together by the strongest links, then we enter the case with the consciousness of right. I say that the blood of Thomas Tollefson, the murdered streetcar driver, is upon the head of Tim Barrett."[8]

The first witness called to the stand was John McKinnon, the fellow streetcar driver who was one of the first to find Thomas Tollefson dead. He lived in Minneapolis and had driven the Cedar Avenue line on the night of Thomas Tollefson's murder. (We'll assume they drove the Cedar Avenue line on different schedules.) He had known Thomas for two years. His testimony on that first day of the trial was brief, since it was primarily for identification.

Deputy Coroner Willis Spring, who, along with Dr. D. F. Collins, had performed the "post mortem" exam of Thomas Tollefson's body, was the second witness called. He explained their findings and described the wounds, and Dr. Collins testified to the same. Attorney Erwin displayed his obvious knowledge of medical terminology by his detailed questioning of both doctors.

Ole E. Brecke was called to the witness stand after the doctors. The brother-in-law of Thomas Tollefson, he had identified the body at the morgue but had no knowledge about the crime.

The last witness called on that first day was a young neighbor named Lottie Welch who lived on Fort Avenue near Henry's place during that summer of 1887. She recalled the evening of the murder because she happened to be visiting with Chloe Betts and Minnie Barrett on their front porch (a six-foot-wide platform) and saw all three brothers leave together. She said, "[They left to go] uptown at 7:30 or 8 o'clock. They said they were going to see what the fire was."[9,10]

While she testified, Mrs. Ellen Barrett moved her chair closer to attorney Bill Erwin and whispered to him. (A reporter later wrote that Ellen had visited Lottie twice before the trial to ask her what she knew.) Erwin questioned Lottie intently, but she never wavered or contradicted herself.

The courtroom was filled with spectators the next morning, including more police officers than before. Judge Lochren and the attorneys were all in place and ready to begin, but there was a problem. All of the jurors were present except for Mr. Miller, and the Court could not proceed without him. They waited. It was well after 9:00 a.m. when Miller finally arrived. Judge Lochren asked why he was late. Miller must have had a worthy excuse, but with no explanation to those waiting Lochren simply convened with the strike of his gavel.

John McKinnon, a witness for the State, was recalled to the witness stand. He testified that he saw Thomas the night of July 26 before 11:00 p.m. on Cedar Avenue between "22nd and 24th Street"; at that time he helped John "lift [his] car back on the track." (The car had jumped the track due to some wooden planks that had been laid across it.) John said, "[The] turntable of this line [was] located at the intersection of Cedar Avenue and Lake Street, near the corner of [Layman's] Cemetery." He explained that the two streetcars were traveling in opposite directions, "At that time, my car was [heading] towards the city and [Thomas's] car was going towards the turntable, located on Lake Street." [11]

The Boston Block fire had caused delays for the streetcar drivers in the area, so it was late by the time McKinnon finished his own route and arrived back at the streetcar barns, but Thomas Tollefson had still not returned. McKinnon thought back to the problem on the tracks, as well as to the suspicious-looking men he had noticed lurking in the shadows there, and was worried. "I told Patrolman Hans Burli and we both started walking down Cedar Avenue, hoping to meet Thomas on his way back to the streetcar barns, but in fact, I dreaded worse."

All eyes were on him in the quieted courtroom as John stopped for a moment, looked down, folded his hands, and sighed. "I saw [Thomas] again about midnight—dead." [12]

The next witness who was called to the stand by attorney Frank Davis caused quite a stir among the six members of the Barrett family who were present that day. Mrs. Ellen Barrett and her daughter Mary both began to weep as Henry Barrett stepped forward to take the oath.

One reporter noted that if Henry had looked his brother Timothy in the eye, he "would have caught a terrible gaze. If there ever was murder in those eyes of Tim's, it was when Henry coolly sat down to give his [testimony]." [13]

8

ᕼENRY'S ᔖESTIMONY

ᖴROM THE moment Henry stepped into the Hennepin County Courthouse that December morning, he caught the attention of the "courthouse officials and employees" and caused such a commotion among others gathered there that one reporter described the scene as a "stampede for the main court room." Now Henry boldly approached the witness stand, shoulders squared. He was tall and lanky; his stride even and swift as he glanced toward his family, then quickly averted his gaze away from the glares of Tim and Pete. After being sworn in, he focused on the attorneys before him with a steadfast calm betrayed only by the occasional twitch of his mustache.[1]

Before he could utter a single word, attorney Erwin voiced concern to the court that whatever Henry said would be "a system of falsehoods, as he is not in possession of the facts. . . . This man has been informed as to what he shall testify and has been induced to testify that Tim implicated him in this crime. [Henry] expects to secure immunity."[2]

Judge Lochren quickly overruled the objection, and prosecutor Frank Davis began to question his most favored witness.[3]

Henry testified flatly, "I was at home on the afternoon of July 26, and had supper there in the evening. I left the house about 8:30 with Tim and Pete. . . . When we left . . . my wife, Lottie Welch, and Miss [Chloe] Betts . . . were on the porch. I carried part of a billiard cue in my hand as I left the house. It was about three feet long. Tim and Pete each had a revolver. Tim had a 38-caliber Smith & Wesson. . . . It was loaded. Pete carried a smaller, commoner one, and it was loaded. We were not going anywhere in particular. We went to the Big Boston [Block] fire. There was plenty of light."[4]

At that point Frank Davis asked the emotionless Henry to tell the Court what he had done that night. Judge Lochren remarked that he did not need to answer if doing so would incriminate him.

Henry "seemed to understand" and continued,

> We followed the Hastings and Dakota railroad tracks down to Cedar Avenue. . . . We went up Cedar Avenue toward the city. We crossed the tracks. We went toward the street car and stopped it. I . . . went up town. I don't exactly remember what we did up town. We went to the fire, and afterward to Lally Brothers saloon. Before this we had separated for about an hour. We then went out to Cedar Avenue again. We rode part of the way and got off at Franklin Avenue. We walked to Cedar Avenue. Our purpose was to stop a car and get some money. We had talked a little together and we had agreed if we met anybody to hold them up. I don't know just which one of us originated the idea. We placed some obstruction on the track, and a car drawn by a pair of mules was thrown off the track. We went about thirty or forty feet from the car. When the car was thrown off we agreed that we should let this car go. I suggested this. I had nothing in my hand at the time. I had dropped the piece of billiard cue over a picket fence about thirty feet from the

Hastings & Dakota tracks. When the first car was thrown off, the mules were stopped and the driver jumped off. The car drove on. After this we went toward the turntable, where there is a clump of trees, near Layman's cemetery. One light wagon we passed going south. The wagon passed us about twenty feet from Lake Street. I thought at the time the wagon contained Mr. Foster, a grocer.[5]

At that moment the attorney stopped Henry in order to call on Mr. Foster to stand up. He did so, and Henry identified him, then resumed his testimony.

When we got near the turntable we found a car there. I think Tim said, 'We will take this man's box anyway.' Tim started ahead and I [was] behind. We went to the front of the car. Tim said to the driver, 'You'll have to give up your box.' Peter was leaning against the platform of the car. . . . Tim, as he spoke, held a revolver close to the driver's belly, and Peter did the same. The driver grabbed the box and put it under his left arm. He caught both revolvers and turned them away from his body. Tim and Pete told him to let go or he would get hurt. He answered, 'Not much.' Then Pete shot the driver, who began to scream. Pete and I turned to run down Lake Street. We stopped near the entrance to the cemetery. Tim came after me with the driver's box under his arm. As he came up to me he said: 'I killed him. I killed him. I shot him through the head.' As Pete and I ran, I heard the driver and Tim say some words to each other. When Tim joined us we went in at the gate of the cemetery. We went a short distance and turned to the right, a little further, then to the right again, climbed a fence; went through an open field to Twenty-first Avenue, and then went home. We agreed to get out of the cemetery on Lake Street and cross the prairie. It was about 12:30 when the driver was killed. We got home at 1 o'clock.

We stood in the hall. I do not remember who had the driver's box. I went upstairs and saw my wife. She came out of her bedroom into the hall. I talked to my wife a minute or two. Tim and Pete had remained in the hall downstairs. Tim had the box. He opened it, took out the money left the checks in the box, and these, the checks and the box, were taken downstairs. The cellar is nothing but a hole dug in the ground. It is reached by a hole in the floor. I took the box down. Pete had a light in his hand to show the way. We dug a hole with an old shovel and in it put the box. Tim held a revolver in his hand while in the cellar. It went off. After we went upstairs we remained in the saloon for a time. I went upstairs to bed. I got up at 9 o'clock. I saw Pete and Tim when I got up. We did nothing with the box that day. On the next day, July 28, we dug the box up, pounded it with an axe. I saw the tickets emptied out and some of them were thrown under the building. I think I did this. We concluded it would be a good idea to put them under the house. Some of the tickets and the box, which had been cut up, were put into a tobacco sack and we took them upstairs, and put them into a small room. We cut the box into small pieces. Tim and I took the box out to Mud Lake and threw it in. We hired a boat so we could get it out into the center of the lake. We also threw the checks and tickets into the lake. We hired the boat from a girl who had a house about half way down on the east side of the lake.[6]

Attorney Davis again stopped Henry in order to call on the boat girl, Sene Larsen, to stand up. She was described by one reporter as a "neat-looking Scandinavian girl," and Henry identified her as the girl from whom they had rented the boat.[7]

"Pete did not go to the lake with us," Henry continued. "We brought back some water lilies. We gave them to children and to Mrs. Lennon."[8]

Frank Davis showed Henry some streetcar tickets. He claimed

they were "the same kind as they threw under the beams of the house. I think there was $6 in money in the box. The box was like that one you hold. I think it was No. 37."[9]

The attorney then held up the revolver that Henry had said Tim used to shoot Thomas Tollefson. "What marks this revolver to your mind as the one Tim used in killing the street car driver?"[10]

"Those initials upon the handle," Henry replied. He also pointed out a niche in the barrel of the gun, but when Davis asked him to tell the Court what that mark was, Henry refused to answer.[11]

Judge Lochren advised Henry to answer the question, unless he claimed it would incriminate him.

Attorney Erwin piped up, "He has no privilege; he has waived it. This is mere bagatelle and drama, after he has gone through with this whole business."[12]

Henry finally answered, "Tim made it."[13]

"What did Tim say when he marked it?" asked the attorney.

Henry was quite reluctant to answer, but the judge ordered him to.

"I believe he said something about this being a mark to indicate that this was the first man he had killed."[14]

This ended Davis's direct examination of his main witness.

Some reported that Erwin appeared to be caught off guard by Henry's statements implicating Tim and Peter in the crime. By that time it was noon, and Erwin requested an adjournment so that he could "consult his client," which Judge Lochren obliged.[15]

Henry quickly stepped down from the witness stand, and officers immediately escorted him out of the courtroom.

Henry's testimony had greatly disturbed the Barrett family. Ellen Barrett's wrinkled hands cupped her face as she sobbed. John Barrett sat still as a rock, the deep creases of his face chiseled into a frown.

When court resumed that afternoon, Bill Erwin used the rest of the day to cross-examine Henry Barrett. For the most part Henry remained calm, but at times he bristled and responded rudely to Erwin.

During this round of questioning Henry told about his experience of living under protected custody as the State's primary witness:

I don't believe I could tell in whose custody I was. I don't know that any officers had charge of me. I believe there was an officer on the train with me. He got off the train with me. I think it was a Mr. Gorman, a deputy sheriff. Officer Ward was also on the train. I was at Waconia, on the Minneapolis & St. Louis railway. I was at the Lake House. My wife and my wife's sister were with me. I was not concealed. I went under the name of Henry Smith. My wife went under the name of Mrs. Smith. My sister [in-law] went under the name of Miss Johnson. Mr. Gorman went by the name of Johnson. I made no special statement there. I was in jail before I went to Waconia. I went out four weeks ago Monday. I spent time in the west side of the Hennepin County Jail. I was not in jail for several days just before going to Waconia. I had lived at 2429 Twenty-eighth Avenue South. I spent fifty-two days in the Hennepin county jail. After being convicted I was taken directly to the jail. I was not seized by the throat when en route to the jail. Could not tell when I first said anything about the Tollefson murder. I did not say anything about my connection with the murder while in jail. I first talked to Mr. Jamison about the murder. I met Mr. Jamison at my house the night after I was released. I sent for him. Mr. Johnson, turnkey of the jail, was also there. I was allowed the same privileges as other prisoners in the jail. *I went out occasionally* (emphasis added). I got some liquor when I went out, on one occasion. Don't remember being criticized by a jail officer for abusing my privileges. I did not say to a jail officer that if he had in his mind what I had in mine he would get drunk. I had been in jail four or five days when I said that.[16]

Henry talked about his confession to Jamison:

I told Johnson I knew about the murder. I might have been suffering from remorse of conscience for the deed. I did not intimate who did the deed. Thomas Pitts and I went down to my brother Tim's house. I asked Pitts to go down with me. He was a prisoner and in for petit larceny. I never had any communication with Thomas Pitts about what I was going down there for. I never told Thomas Pitts that I was suspected of that murder. I did not tell Pitts that I wanted to get admissions from my brother that he was connected with that murder. Pitts and I were outside the jail and we went across the street, got several drinks and went out just for a walk. I had no opportunity to talk to Tim about it. I talked with my wife. I was not told by an officer or by anybody else that I was suspected of the murder. My telling Mr. Jamison about the murder was fully voluntary. I believe I asked if I would be protected if I told about the murder. Mr. Jamison promised immunity. I had previously led Mr. Jamison to believe that the Barrett family had nothing to do with the murder, but that I knew who it was. I knew that there was a large reward offered for the apprehension of the murderers of Tollefsen. I gave Mr. Jamison to understand that I did not want any part of the reward, or any part of it. I never asked anybody for the reward. I understood I could not get it even if I wanted it. I had not signed a written statement. I first signed a written statement a day or two after I first saw Jamison. Mr. Davis drew up the statement. I signed it at Mr. Davis' office. I never signed any other statement. Tim was arrested before I made any statement. I had not been told before making a statement to Mr. Jamison by some person other than Mr. Jamison that I was suspected of the murder. I was not told before this that Tim was suspected.[17]

Henry also said that he had married Minnesota Betts in Minneapolis on October 26, 1886. The newlywed couple lived with his father, John Barrett, at 2830 Fort Avenue. He admitted that he did not see his mother, Ellen Barrett, much until the summer or early fall of 1887;

he was not close with her or other family members. In fact, Erwin's questions exposed Henry's deep hatred of his mother and the rest of the family.

At times Erwin proceeded in such a slow and methodic manner that even Judge Lochren became impatient with him. "Mr. Erwin, it seems to me that this cross-examination should proceed faster."[18]

"Your Honor, it is because I could not see my clients. I had an arrangement with the Sheriff whereby I was to see the Barretts at the jail. When I presented myself, the jailer would not let me see my clients. I finally got a chance to see them this noon, up in a dingy room in the jail, with a terrible noise and pandemonium about there, which is a disgrace to any civilized community. I have been working under very great disadvantages."[19]

The cross-examination continued and finally wrapped up about 5:00 p.m. Henry was dismissed and as he was escorted from the courtroom again, Tim clenched his jaw and glared.

Henry had shown precision and consistency in his statements, but was he sincere, or simply polished? As one reporter saw it, "Henry Barrett's ability as a witness is probably owing" to several occasions on the witness stand and his own "numerous trials" for running a blind pig, adding that "the license inspector regarded [Henry] as a hard man to convict."[20]

>-+◊-O-◊+-<

Henry, Minnie, and Chloe remained under the attentive and watchful eye of Levi Gorman and stayed at Clifton house, a private boarding house, when they first returned to Minneapolis for the trial. But the four weren't there for long—and Bill Erwin had discovered why. During questioning he goaded Henry, "Did you not get [thrown] out of the Clifton house because Detective Gorman was found in bed with your wife's sister? . . . Did not the hotel proprietor fire the whole batch of you and say he would not have any of those people stop there any longer?"[21]

Henry denied it.

"Well, it is a fact just the same," Erwin replied.[22]

Henry would only admit that all four had left the Clifton house and moved into rooms at the Arlington Hotel. We know that the city provided for their lodging, and we can assume they remained under the surveillance of the police, just as Deputy Gorman had done at the Lake House in Waconia.

They weren't the only ones kept under watch—Judge Lochren sequestered the jury. Although he ordered that they be provided with the "best possible accommodations," he strictly advised the jurors "not to discuss the case or read the newspaper accounts of the trial."[23]

The trial was the big news of the day, and tensions were rising—especially in the Barrett family. The *St. Paul Pioneer Press* reporter Joe Mannix reported some of the remarks made about Henry: Peter, referring to Henry's entire testimony, exclaimed, "It is a lie," and Ellen Barrett stated coldly, "That fellow [meaning her son, Henry] wants to get the boys out of the way so he can get the property, but he cannot do it."[24]

Older brother Frank Barrett appeared to be "an honest, hardworking man." He lived in Omaha, yet attended nearly every courtroom session. He kept to himself for the most part; he did not sit with the family or speak out, but his eyes were often tear-filled as the gravity of the testimony weighed against his brothers. At the end of each day's session he would tell Tim and Pete good-bye as they left the courtroom on their way back to jail. Distressed over Henry's testimony, his words reflected that of a broken family: "It is terrible. But it is no surprise to us. We expected he would tell this kind of a story." Frank's growing bitterness toward Henry was obvious, and some were concerned that he might even try to attack him.[25]

The same newspaper article included the possibility of another interesting twist to the scenario of the Tollefson murder. This may well have simply been hearsay, but the reporter wrote that the defense "would try and prove that Henry Barrett fired the fatal shot." An unidentified "material witness for the defense said that Henry was [actually] the man who did the shooting, and that this would be proven before the trial was over. This witness claimed that Tim held the revolver, and that while standing making threats, Henry came up from behind, elevated Tim's revolver and fired into Tollefson's chest."[26]

The reporters combined public sentiment with their own take on the whole brother against brother scenario and soon labeled Henry a "Traitor Brother." Of course, the Barrett family thought so, believing that Henry was terribly envious. Did his jealousy drive him to the point of betrayal, knowing that the penalty could mean the deaths of his brothers? Such a hatred among brothers would not only have been repulsive, it would have been insane.

Let's suppose that Henry was just trying to do the right thing, knowing it would likely sever any remaining ties with his already estranged family. Such might have been the case if he had demonstrated the behavior of a model citizen with high morals, but his reputation was quite the contrary. Henry was a known law-breaker; after all, he had been in jail just one month earlier. And he was prone to violence. Could something, or someone, have changed him for the better in such a short time?

Henry admitted during his testimony that he knew he would not receive any reward money, so we know it wasn't about that. He also admitted his own guilt in the crime and reported that the prosecution had promised him immunity for acting as an informer. Henry was present at the crime scene and had firsthand knowledge of the murder, but he also was a married man—with a baby on the way. The hope of what might lie ahead for Minnie and himself could have been dashed to pieces if he faced conviction for the crime.

Hennepin County Prosecutor Frank Davis.

The Heavy Burden

ON CHRISTMAS DAY the news reportage revolved around attorney Bill Erwin's theory about the crime. He believed that Henry had done it with the help of one other man and that Tim and Pete had not been involved. Of course, the prosecution was quick to dismiss the possibility based on the witness accounts that three men were present at the crime. The speculation only generated more interest in the murder.

People were curious and wanted to see and hear for themselves. The courtroom was so crowded each day with spectators for Tim's trial that not everyone could fit. That first week Sheriff Swenson built a makeshift bar on the stairway and had a deputy tend it. Apparently that helped make everyone a bit more comfortable and a bit less thirsty—although it certainly was no deterrent to those who continued to gather at the courthouse.

By the second week the trial had drawn such a large number of onlookers that there was concern about the structural integrity of the courthouse. Apparently it had endured some additions over the years that were not quite sturdy enough to handle the burgeoning weight of the daily crowd, and the old floors began to sag under the stress of the load. An expert was called in, who examined the foundation and told the sheriff that the courthouse was actually sinking!

The sheriff relayed the startling findings to Judge Lochren, who promptly announced that all courtroom spectators should move to a safer place—but no one seemed alarmed, or willing to give up their spot. The judge kept urging them and finally said to the sheriff, with a sly grin, "If they don't go, Mr. Sheriff, just take them into the next building (the jail)."[1,2]

><+>-O-<+<

The trial continued with Mrs. Sarah Lennon, who lived next door to the Barretts' house on Fort Avenue. She testified they were her friends and that she had known Tim and Pete since mid-June of 1887. On the night of July 26 she visited Minnie and Chloe at their house and saw the three brothers leave. She had watched them walk across the prairie on their way to town. The next time she saw them was two days later, as they walked "up Fort Avenue from the direction of the glassworks" factory, carrying water lilies. According to her testimony, Tim told her they had found the flowers "at the lake", while Henry told her they "got them at the river."[3]

It was an interesting discrepancy as to where the water lilies had come from. Why would the two men have said that the flowers had come from such different places? Was this a minor inconsistency or an unexpected glitch for the prosecution? Something must have been up, because at that very point in her testimony Frank Davis quickly requested that Sarah Lennon be excused. His explanation for this abrupt halt to her testimony was that "her children needed her attention."[4]

However, Erwin refused to grant his consent, so Sarah stayed and her testimony continued. "The relations between the Barrett boys, as far as I could see . . . were friendly. I remember the circumstance of a horse being stolen in the Barrett family."[5]

She was unrattled when Erwin cross-examined her testimony.

The next witness Frank Davis called forward was George A. Chamberlain, who worked at the Hennepin County Savings Bank. Chamberlain took the oath, and Davis immediately picked up a revolver from among other items held as evidence in the case. He intended to have Chamberlain identify it as the gun stolen from him shortly before the Tollefson murder.

"Hold on," Erwin interrupted. "I object to the introduction of that evidence. It is incompetent, irrelevant and improper. It is introduced to prejudice the interests of my client, by tending to show the commission of a felony prior to the commission of the murder. It is attacking the character of the defendant. They want to prove that the defendant secured the pistol over two weeks before the homicide."[6]

Judge Lochren sustained Erwin's objection. Chamberlain's irrelevant testimony was stopped before it ever began.

Mr. Foster was a witness who owned a grocery store on Cedar Avenue. He recalled driving his "spring wagon" around midnight on the 26th of July and said that he passed about ten feet away from three men standing beside the cemetery fence about midway between the turntable and the Cedar Avenue entrance to Layman's Cemetery. He could not see them distinctly but could tell that two of the men were average sized, while the third was taller. He also passed Thomas Tollefson's streetcar, headed in the same direction and en route to the turntable. Foster noticed wooden planks oddly strewn over the streetcar tracks on Cedar Avenue and worriedly sped past to get through the area without incident.[7]

The next witness called was a young boy named Ollie Van Valkenburg. Described as a "bright twelve-year-old," Ollie lived with his family on Cedar Avenue between 28th and 29th Avenues. He testified that he and his older brother found a cue stick in their yard beside the picket fence the day after the murder. (Henry Barrett had already testified to having had a cue stick with him that night, before dropping it over a fence.)[8]

Frank Davis called forward Inspector James Howard, who was followed by Chief Inspector Hankinson. Both men testified separately about the inspection of the Barrett house cellar. Davis and his assistant, Robert Jamison, took turns questioning the witnesses, whose testimonies corroborated one another. The prosecution also presented the streetcar checks held in evidence, and both men identified them as the ones found in the cellar during the search.

Defense attorney Will Donahue then began to question Hankinson about the reward money, implying that it may have been what motivated him. However, when Frank Davis piped up about the rules prohibiting officers from accepting reward money according to a police handbook and offered to show the court, Donahue quickly dropped that line of questioning.

By then it was late Saturday afternoon, and more importantly, it was Christmas Eve. Judge Lochren adjourned the court until 9:00 a.m. the following Monday.

Members of the jury hoped to spend some time with their families and loved ones on Christmas Day, but the judge would not allow it. If permitted to leave the secured environment of the hotel where they were sequestered, the jurors could have been influenced about the case in some way.

"I was just thinking how I would pass my Christmas," young Peter commented to one reporter.[9]

Christmas seemed to be on the mind of accused and juror alike, but none would have a merry one.

10

WITNESSES

ASSISTANT COUNTY Attorney Jamison worked hard to develop the case against the Barrett brothers. Before the trial he had traveled to Waconia (where Henry, Minnie, and Chloe were kept) to interview the witnesses and even up to Northfield to gather more information. Timothy Barrett had been arrested in Northfield, Minnesota, on September 12, 1887, by Chief of Police Gershom Truax, who, apparently, considered him a suspect in the Tollefson murder because he carried a 38-caliber revolver—and the prosecution summoned Truax to testify.

Chief Truax, a "stalwart gentleman with an immense fur overcoat," approached the witness stand when court reconvened on Monday, December 26. Under state's examination by Frank Davis, Chief Truax identified the gun shown to him as exhibit T. B. as the one in Tim's possession when he had arrested him. Davis then questioned Truax further and, although Erwin objected, Judge Lochren overruled each time.[1,2]

During the cross-examination later that week, Bill Erwin asked Chief Truax how common it was for him to confiscate a weapon of that caliber. Basically, he tried to cast a shadow of doubt as to the ability of Truax to make an absolutely positive identification of the exact gun held in evidence, because this type of gun was so common at that time.

Attorney Davis objected to Erwin's questions, Judge Lochren sided with Davis each time, and the Court sustained those objections.[3]

But Erwin couldn't resist one final jab: "If a murder is committed, do you arrest the first man with a 38-caliber revolver?"[4]

Judge Lochren spoke up: "Is not that going pretty far?"[5]

"I withdraw the [question] Your Honor. That is the point I wanted to [make]," Erwin replied with a slight grin.[6]

Others called to testify were D. W. Sharp, Lieutenant Daniel Day from the 4th Precinct, and Mrs. Louisa Cashman.

D. W. Sharp was the Superintendent of the Minneapolis Street Railway Company and had been for several years. His testimony, first off, confirmed that Thomas Tollefson had been employed as a street-car driver. Sharp also gave a description of the tickets and envelopes of change and confirmed that drivers began each morning with a fares box that held $10 in change and $10 worth of tickets.[7]

Lieutenant Day testified about helping to drag Mud Lake in November. He and other officers spent an entire day searching for evidence of the broken up fares box, but found nothing even though Henry Barrett had assured them they would. They had only spent that one day looking, because that night the lake froze over and it was impossible to continue the search.

Louisa Cashman was a neighbor of Henry and Minnie Barrett who lived in a house behind theirs. She testified that on the day after the murder, she noticed the three Barrett boys nervously peering through the back windows of their house, watching while she talked to a police officer.

After these three had testified, the courtroom hushed to a whisper when a well-dressed Minnie Barrett came forward to be sworn in. She answered the attorney's questions slowly, as though giving much thought to her statements. Her overall manner was interpreted to be both timid and embarrassed as she softly spoke:

> I was at home on July 26. I saw the boys between 8:30 and 9 o'clock in the evening. The boys, my sister, myself, and Lottie Welch were there. I went to bed at 11 o'clock. I saw Henry again that night. I heard Pete and Henry downstairs. I heard some tin rattling. It sounded like money pouring from a tin box. The sounds came from the hall. I heard no strange voices. I heard the boys going down stairs, and afterward heard a pistol shot. It seemed to come from under the house. I got up about 8 o'clock next morning. Pete, Tim, Henry, my sister, and myself were at breakfast. I do not know where Pete and Tim slept that night. The boys had bed clothes in the billiard room, and were in the habit of sleeping on billiard tables. . . . I was in bed when the boys came home; I could not understand anything the men were saying when they were in the hall; I was lying on the bed, not paying much attention to the talk in the hallway. I might have been mistaken, but I think it was the Barrett boys. I boarded at Waconia. I boarded at the public expense; it was the wish of others that I went under an assumed name at Waconia. . . . [T]he pistol shot alarmed me a little, I thought it was downstairs. It did not startle me enough to make me go downstairs and see what it was. I did not wake Chloe up. I am not able to identify that pistol. [The pistol Tim is said to have had was shown the witness.] Am not used to handling pistols . . . have been with my husband since we returned from Waconia. I don't know whether I have been more of a prisoner than a guest since I went to Waconia. . . . When Henry came upstairs after the pistol shot on the night of the 26th of July he did not speak about it, neither did I refer to it. I don't remember exactly when they brought water lilies to the house.[8]

Minnie also testified that around that same time she saw Tim Barrett wearing a "stiff hat" and noticed him with a gun like the one shown to her as evidence, although she admitted she couldn't positively identify it as having belonged to him.

Her testimony did not last a very long time, but while she was on the stand a reporter noted that Henry appeared to be nervous and kept fidgeting with his mustache. Was he nervous because of the discrepancies in her testimony versus his own? For example, Henry had said that his brothers remained downstairs with the fares box that night while he went upstairs and called Minnie out into the hall to talk. However, Minnie said she had heard talking in the hall, which sounded like the Barrett boys, but did not pay much attention. She had heard a pistol shot from below and after that Henry came upstairs and they talked, but not about the gunshot. (Apparently the sound of a fired gun did not alarm or concern her.)

Although the prosecution had planned to recall the boat girl of Mud Lake, Sene Larsen was ill with diphtheria and unable to return to court. However, they did not believe further testimony from her would bring any new revelation or even positively identify Timothy Barrett as the man who had accompanied Henry that day. Therefore, the Court decided not to delay the trial by waiting for her to get better.

So the prosecution began to wrap up their examination of the witnesses.

They recalled D. W. Sharp, who showed a diagram of the turntable at Lake Street and Cedar Avenue. He then described how it worked and the procedure involved in order for the driver to turn a streetcar.

Inspector L. W. Kinney testified regarding the Boston Block fire on the night Thomas Tollefson had been murdered.

George A. Chamberlain was briefly questioned one last time about the night he had supposedly lost his revolver to an assailant, presumably Tim Barrett, in the weeks prior to Thomas's murder. Frank Davis admonished, "I do not expect that Mr. Chamberlain can look into [Tim Barrett's] face and say that he is the man; but I do expect that he can give such a general description as would warrant me in saying that this is the man."[9]

Bill Erwin objected to that suggestion, and this time Judge Lochren sided with him. Regardless, Frank Davis had effectively imposed a presumptuous suspicion into the listening ear of each juror and confidently "announced that the State would rest."[10]

The sudden move came as a bit of a surprise, but the defense was ready.

Defense attorney William "Bill" Erwin.

Source: *St. Paul Daily Globe*, March 17, 1889,
Library of Congress, Chronicling America http://chroniclingamerica.loc.gov
image provided by Minnesota Historical Society, St. Paul, MN.

William H. Donahue attorney for the defense.

Source: *Minneapolis Evening Journal*, March 22, 1889,
found at Minnesota Historical Society, St. Paul, MN.

DEFENSE

IT WAS already 3:15 p.m. when Attorney Will Donahue addressed the jury:

> I doubt if the criminal annals of Minnesota has a case like this. We are almost ready to allow the case to rest on the evidence now in, without putting in a defense. *The law of the state requires that the testimony of an accomplice has to be corroborated* (emphasis added). We will show that this is all a terrible conspiracy by this unnatural fiend Henry. I cannot designate him by any other name than dog. He is the counterfeit on humanity. We will show you that the defendant is as innocent of this crime as you and I are. We will show you that Henry Barrett has for a long time entertained the intensest animosity toward the whole family. He knew that [his] mother loved those two boys, and he wanted to get them out of the way so he could get the property. I don't

think any lawyer ever appeared in a criminal case where he received worse treatment than I have at the hands of the police of the city of Minneapolis. They gave Peter Barrett infamous whiskey when they arrested him at Omaha, and got him to lie. After he was brought to Minneapolis I went from station to station, but could not get a chance to talk with the man accused of the most terrible of crimes. We will show you that the boys left home on July 26; that they took a street car; went to Lally Brothers saloon; that Henry Barrett had a croquet mallet handle; that he had it at Lally Brothers and that after purchasing a glass of beer Tim and Pete parted, leaving Henry behind. We shall put this cold-blooded and diabolical murder on the head of this wretch and two others. We shall put on the stand a man who heard Henry Barrett and two others, not Pete or Tim, talking at Minnehaha Falls about robbing a street car. That Pete and Tim Barrett boarded a Riverside street car; that they slept at their sister Mary's house on the night of July 26; that Henry Barrett went to Mud Lake the Thursday after the crime in company with a man who is not here. The laws of the state require much greater corroboration than has been given in this case.[1]

Although it was late afternoon by the time Donahue had finished, the very first witness that Erwin called to the stand was the defendant himself, Tim Barrett.

"The accused stepped up promptly and was sworn in. He held his hand up high. . . . There was a very nervous winking of the eye lids and quite a restless attitude [while] on the stand. [Timothy] frequently turned toward the jury. He denied Henry's story," wrote one reporter.[2]

Timothy told the court that he was twenty-two years old, the brother of Peter and Henry, and lived with his sister Mary at her boardinghouse on Fort Avenue across from the glassworks factory. Then he started to recall the night of July 26 and that he and Pete had been at Henry's place for about a half hour before the three brothers headed uptown at 8:00 p.m.

"It was just getting dark," Tim said. "I had no arms, no revolvers with me." Henry had what Tim called a rake handle. "We went right across the prairie . . . [walked along] the Hastings & Dakota tracks to Cedar Avenue. [One] block north of the railroad tracks [we] boarded a [street]car, went up town and got off about a block above the Big Boston [Block] . . . . Henry had the [rake handle] when we got up town. . . . [W]e had no talk about robbing a street car. Pete and I did not stand up with Henry and purpose to stop a street car; I did not see Henry put his [rake handle] over the picket fence."[3]

It took the brothers about a half hour, and Tim said it was about 8:30 p.m. when they walked into Lally Brothers saloon. (However, during his testimony the following day he reported that they had walked in at 9:00 p.m.).

"Henry set up the beer. We were there about five minutes." He added, "Men came up to Henry, shook hands with him. I never saw them before. . . . [Y]es, I can describe them: one of them was a short, thick-set man with a black mustache; the other looked something like Pete." (However, the following day Tim claimed he had seen those same men before at Henry's.)[4]

Tim and Pete started to leave at that point, but Henry called them back and offered them another glass of beer. The two drank the beer and left. "We went to Nicollet Avenue to buy some clothing." The brothers stopped at a secondhand store on the right side of Washington Avenue but left because they didn't find anything they liked. They visited another store on the same street and eventually went further uptown. When they turned to go back, they noticed the fire at the Boston Block and the ropes that had been put up around the perimeter to keep people from getting too close. Tim noted, "I saw a sign fall at the Jumbo Saloon across the road."[5]

After watching the fire for a while the brothers went back to Lally Brothers saloon to meet up with Henry, but he was already gone. "We went to another saloon and got a glass of beer," Tim said. "We then took a Riverside [street]car." He recalled that there were several people on board, including two glassworks factory workers named Frank and George, whom he had seen at his sister's place before, and they exchanged greetings. "We took this car about three blocks from the Washington Avenue viaduct . . . clean to the street car barn at Twenty-seventh Avenue, I don't know what street, the baseball grounds are on the west side of where we got off [as did Frank and George]. . . . [T]hen we went on Lake Street to Twenty-sixth Street. I am not acquainted with the streets." He said that Frank and George had gone on to Billy Thurston's barber shop for a shave. Tim and Pete stopped in there, too, for a few minutes but were anxious to get back to check on Mary. "We went down Twenty-sixth Avenue to my sister, Mrs. [Mary Barrett] Coleman."[6,7]

It was about 10:30 p.m. when they got to Mary's house. His father, sister Mary, and George Coleman were there. That night Peter slept with their father. Tim slept with their brother-in-law, George Coleman, in a bedroom toward the back of the house.

"It was a common thing to go there to sleep. I used to go there to eat frequently. I used to go to my sister's more than to Henry's. My sister was sick that night. I went to bed about 10:45. I got up about 7 o'clock in the morning," Tim testified.[8]

He went to Henry's a half hour later, and Peter came at noon. He returned to Mary's place later that same day.

"I saw Henry about 2 o'clock. He was at my sister's with a man whom he called Murphy, with a black mustache," Tim recalled. "Henry had some water lilies. . . . [T]he other man had a bunch of water lilies, he left them out on the porch."

Tim and Henry then left Mary's house, carrying some of the water lilies as they walked back down Fort Avenue to Henry's place. When they arrived, Tim claimed, "I put the flowers I had on the center table."[9]

This wasn't the last time Tim saw Murphy. He testified that he had seen him go into the back room with Henry at the Hub of Hell in August. "I [saw] them counting a lot of small change, silver," he stated.[10]

Bill Erwin questioned Tim regarding the statements Henry had

made about the murder of Thomas Tollefson, statements that implicated him in the crime, and Tim claimed that they were all lies. Erwin
asked pointedly, "Did you run up to Peter and Henry and call out, 'I
killed him, I killed him, I shot him through the head'?" [11]

"No sir, no part of it is true at all," Tim replied as he looked toward
the jurors. [12]

Erwin wanted more time to review the details of Henry's lengthy
statement before he proceeded, so he asked the judge for the favor
of an early adjournment. However, Judge Lochren was not about to
oblige as it was a full hour before 5:00 p.m., the usual time to adjourn, and would be an inconvenience of sorts. The "Pinetree of the
Northwest" steadfastly reminded the judge of the noisy and disruptive
atmosphere in the jail and the difficulties he regularly encountered
whenever he attempted to consult with his clients. In contrast, Erwin's
request seemed rather modest, and Lochren finally agreed to adjourn.

Dr. Heflin testified on the morning of December 28, 1887. A graduate of Iowa State University, he had practiced as a physician and
surgeon since March 1883, moved to Minneapolis in May of that year,
and become certified to practice medicine in the state of Minnesota in
December 1884. The doctor had lived at 929 Marshall Street NE, on
the east side of the river, "for the past six to eight months." His practice
was located across from the depot, at 401 South Washington where his
office was conveniently located on the second floor, above a drug store.

He was in the habit of going to his office at 7:00 p.m. and on the
night of July 26, 1887, he arrived shortly after that. Some time later he
received a phone call, went back out to hitch up his horse and buggy,
and while doing so "talked with some . . . friends a little while" before
starting back to his office. While going in that direction he noticed
the commotion of the Boston Block fire a block south of Washington
Avenue. It was growing dark by that time; he thought it was "about
9:00 p.m." After watching the excitement for a bit, he headed down to

see his patient, Mary Barrett, whose house was quite a distance from there by horse and buggy.

Dr. Heflin likely took the most direct route. If we reference the old Davis's Minneapolis dime store map from that era, he may have traveled fifteen city blocks southeasterly down Washington Avenue, turned south on Cedar Avenue for eleven blocks more, turned east on 24th Street for one block, and then turned south onto Fort Avenue. He still had to go approximately two more city blocks through relatively undeveloped prairie until he reached Mary Barrett's home at the corner of Fort Avenue and 26th Street, near the railroad tracks. By the time he arrived it was sometime between 10:00 p.m. and 11:00 p.m.

"I rapped at the door," Heflin recalled. "An old gentleman came to the door. I asked him if Mary Barrett was sick there and he said, 'yes.'. . . . I asked where she was and he said, 'upstairs.' The old man led the way upstairs to her room. [T]here were two or three persons there . . . three young men, I think, an old man and the girl. Two young men were in the hall outside of Mary's room and she told me, 'Those are my brothers.'"[13,14,15]

He recalled beckoning the larger brother—Tim was larger than Pete—into the room that night. "I told him I wanted it quiet and that is about all I told him. I spoke to him afterwards." Dr. Heflin pointed toward Tim as he sat in the courtroom, identifying him as the young man he talked to that night.

He then examined Mary and diagnosed her ailment as "cholera morbus; pain in the stomach."[16]

As Mr. Erwin questioned him further about that night, the doctor stated that he had remained at Mary Barrett's house until about 12:30 a.m. and was certain that he left between midnight and 1:00 a.m. Before leaving, he went to the room where two of the men had gone to get some sleep. He awakened the larger brother, Tim, gave him instructions about the medicine he had left for Mary, and told him to call if she got worse.

When Bill Erwin asked the doctor whether he was sure the man he spoke to was Tim Barrett, he replied, "Well, he looks like the man that I saw there. I don't think that I am mistaken. I have never seen him since, until yesterday, but I don't think I am mistaken about that." He also mentioned that he recognized the voice as belonging to the same man he had spoken to shortly after he had arrived. Dr. Heflin stated that when he saw Tim at Mary's he thought the man "was a little drunk" and he recalled that he had a mustache.

Upon cross-examination attorney Frank Davis behaved in a rather cocky, unprofessional manner as he prodded the doctor, asking repeatedly whether he was sure the man was Tim Barrett and if he would swear to it.

Heflin would not mince words or be manipulated. "I ain't sure of anything," he said. "I am pretty sure it was the young fellow sitting there," he said, pointing to Tim. [17]

Davis continued, "Well, you will even modify that, won't you, Doctor? . . . You can't swear to this man being the same one you saw down there at Mary's that night?" [18]

"I will swear I think it is," replied Dr. Heflin. [19]

"But that is as strong as you will put it." [20]

"That is as strong as I can put it." [21]

"You may be mistaken about it, may you not, doctor?" [22]

"May be," Heflin admitted. [23]

"There is a large possibility, almost a probability of that, is there?" [24]

"No, sir. I would not be afraid . . ." [25]

Davis interrupted, ". . . to bet ten cents?" [26]

"I ask to have that struck from the records," interjected Bill Erwin. [27]

Davis quipped, "Strike her out." [28]

Dr. Heflin straightened his posture and stated clearly, "I should say that this is the young man that was there that evening." [29]

Frank Davis continued, "Is there any distinguishing feature about him in any way that impresses your recollection that he is the man?" [30]

The doctor replied, "Well, his actions and talk." [31]

The doctor told how he had treated Mary with opiates for her pain and remained with her for about an hour. After that he had gone to the door of the upstairs room, the bedroom where the young men had gone, to advise them about their sister's condition and directed Timothy to call him if she got worse. He saw the men in the bed at that time; one was already asleep, so he talked to the other man. This was the same man he had talked to after he had arrived and gone up to Mary's bedside. Dr. Heflin identified that man as Timothy Barrett.

The courtroom transcript shows continued interrogation of this witness in an effort to cast doubt on his recollection of other events that evening, such as what time he had eaten supper, whom else he may have visited that night, what time, etc. The fact remains that Dr. Heflin was an unbiased witness with no reason to lie about whether or not he saw the Barrett brothers that night.

Davis's final question to Dr. Heflin concerned time. At what time had he left the Barrett house that evening? The doctor replied, "[It was] between twelve and one."[32]

It is perfectly reasonable to believe that Mary Barrett was there, as were her father and her two brothers. The other young man was George Coleman, a glassworks factory employee who boarded there at the time (he and Mary were later married). The murder of Thomas Tollefson occurred during the time when Dr. Heflin was there with all of them. The brothers had already gone to bed by the time the doctor left, since he had to go in and awaken Tim to talk to him.

Henry had testified he came home late that night, woke Minnie, and that she stepped out into the hallway to talk with him. He admitted he was at the scene of the crime, but who else could have been with Henry?

Others had witnessed three men in the shadows shortly before the crime and observed men running from the scene. Who might these two other men have been? Could they have been the men who met up with Henry at Lally Brothers saloon that night? The two who came up to Henry were seen by Tim and Pete. According to their descriptions, one man had a mustache and the other wore "a star." And just what did that mean in those days? Who, back then, wore a star? A lawman.

During one round of questioning Tim told the court about his arrest on November 16, 1887. He was at Henry's house at the time. The police did not disclose why they arrested him until they had brought him to the station. They said he was the suspect in a murder case and locked him up in the Hennepin County jail. On November 18 attorney Robert Jamison, the assistant to Hennepin County Prosecutor Frank Davis, came to see Tim at the jail. Jamison informed Tim that his brother Henry had accused him of murder and advised him to tell whatever he knew. Jamison assured him that if he did so he would be safe, but Tim denied knowing anything about it. Tim said it appeared that he and Jamison were alone during the conversation, but that Jamison spoke very loudly.

Defense Attorney Bill Erwin later learned that other lawmen had actually been present during that jailhouse meeting without Tim's knowledge or consent. The men had positioned themselves out of Tim's sight, yet in such a way that they could hear what was said as long as the voices were loud enough. Erwin then identified the concealed men as Detective Howard, Mr. Stanley, and Superintendent of Police Jacob Hein.

Unfortunately for Tim Barrett, he became easily confused when questioned. The fact that he had a drinking problem may have led to memory lapses even though he was such a young man; however, there had also been serious doubts about his mental capacity dating back to his childhood. Regardless of the underlying cause, the effect was obvious, and Frank Davis worked it to his advantage. Davis often seemed to badger the defendant on issues of little significance. Tim struggled to recall petty information, such as when or where he had eaten breakfast on any certain day during the preceding months. He also had difficulty recalling exactly what he had said in court on previous days. The prosecutor easily trapped Tim, who was like a fly caught in a spider's web—pitifully snared and slowly devoured. Tim Barrett had weaknesses that led to inconsistencies in his testimony, and Davis did his job by drawing attention to it. Why should anyone believe such a bumbling witness?

Besides, he already had a criminal record dating back to 1882; Tim admitted it. In the October 9, 1884, edition of the *Malvern*

Leader, an Iowa newspaper, a one-sentence report stated that Tim had been convicted of horse stealing and sentenced to "three years in the penitentiary"—although less than three years later he was back living in Omaha. After his November arrest at Henry's house he showed the police some stolen goods but claimed that the items were Henry's, not his. (Even if this were true, Tim had knowledge of the goods, which was criminal—but then, so did Minnie Barrett, and she was never questioned.)[33]

Tim Barrett was not very clever, and he was surely no angel. He had openly flirted with Minnie, his own brother's wife. But was he a murderer? Could Frank Davis convince the jury that Tim Barrett had shot and killed Thomas Tollefson? Or would they believe that Henry simply had it in for the rest of the Barrett family and was out for revenge?

For example, Henry was once so angry at their mother (because he believed she had cheated him out of $1,000) that he threatened to go to Omaha and *kill* her. Upon hearing that, Tim told Henry "he should be ashamed of himself." Apparently the argument took place at Henry's and had started when Henry angrily accused Peter, claiming he "had seduced his sister-in-law, Chloe Betts, and that he was going to tell his mother about it." Furthermore, Henry thought Peter should be cut off from his inheritance because of his behavior toward Chloe—and if not "he would kill him or put up a job."[34]

Tim added, "I heard that Henry swore vengeance on me."[35]

MURPHY AND HART

IM TESTIFIED that two men, named Murphy and Hart, were at Henry's saloon the night of July 26, 1887, but left soon after he and Pete got there. Later, when all three Barrett brothers stepped into Lally Brothers saloon on Washington Avenue for a beer, those same two men came up to Henry and shook his hand. Was that handshake merely a cordial greeting (they had already met earlier that night), or was it symbolic of a deal? (Bill Erwin would later question Henry about Murphy and Hart, as well as another man named Steele, who also had a conversation with Henry at Lally Brothers that night.) Tim and Pete left to go shopping for clothes, but Henry stayed there with Murphy and Hart.

Tim described Murphy as tall and heavy-built, with dark red hair and a thick black mustache. He wore what Tim called a "slouch hat." Hart was about Pete's height but slimmer, clean-shaven, and he wore a "straw hat."

The next day, on July 27, Murphy came along with Henry to visit his ill, bedridden sister, Mary, and they brought her a fistful of water lilies. The fact that the flowers were water lilies was significant. The chopped-up fares box was supposedly thrown into Mud Lake, and water lilies grew there.

As the case evolved, another "prominent attorney" (unconnected with the case) who had been following the court proceedings made a prediction that was recorded in a newspaper column. He believed that Henry Barrett and another man had committed the murder of Thomas Tollefson; that Henry had met up with the man at Lally Brothers saloon, and Peter and Timothy had left the two men there.[1]

Research of 1880s newspapers from the area offered intriguing glimpses of different individuals named Murphy and Hart. Could any of the following have been *the* Murphy and Hart who met Henry on the night of Thomas Tollefson's murder?

The June 13, 1885, issue of the *St. Paul Daily Globe* reported that a man named Mike Murphy, identified as the "acknowledged leader" of the notorious Rice Street Gang, was in jail for larceny. He was mentioned numerous times throughout the 1880s and had a lengthy history of being in trouble with the law for anything from drunken fights to burglary to robbery. The Rice Street Gang was a group of about a dozen young men who basically terrorized the neighborhood that lay just beyond the "bridge." Most came from comfortable homes, but their parents just could not control them. (Mike Murphy's family was respected, his parents were well off financially, and his two sisters were teachers.) A couple of the young men worked for the railroad, another even served as a fireman, while the others were unemployed. So although some of the gang members actually worked, when the boys were together they got drunk and made trouble.[2,3]

The *St. Paul Daily Globe* regularly listed the names of people who had appeared in district court on various charges; on December 10, 1887, the list included Richard Murphy and James Murphy, both of whom had been indicted for grand larceny in the first degree and were to be tried four days later.

The March 12, 1889, edition of the *Omaha Bee* reported the arrest of Frank Murphy. He, along with four others, had tried to rob the Citizens Bank in South Sioux City, Iowa, the previous month. Frank Murphy was also charged with committing a separate crime of burglary.[4]

Any one of those men could have been *the Murphy* who met up with Henry in the Lally Brothers saloon.

During questioning at Tim's trial, William Erwin referred to a man named Murphy who was locked up at "the penitentiary at Stillwater, sent up from Faribault."[5]

It is obvious that a known criminal named Murphy truly did exist, so it may be assumed that the man identified as Hart also did exist. The Minneapolis City Directory for 1887 lists numerous Harts and Murphys. Were they overlooked? Did the authorities search for them?

When questioned by Erwin, Henry denied seeing or having a drink with Hart at Lally Brothers saloon on the night of the crime. He said, "I didn't see Hart that night" and then quickly added, "I do not know the man. Wouldn't know him if I saw him now."[6]

Henry's well-polished testimony got a bit clumsy and suspicious at that point. It was almost as though he were trying to protect someone *other* than himself.

Also, during Tim's testimony a small yet significant statement was made concerning one of the men who had met up with Henry at Lally Brothers on the night of the murder—*he wore a gold star.*

As mentioned previously, gold stars were worn by the police. A local newspaper article from that era gives reference to a police officer named Hart. Could an officer of the law have been, either directly or indirectly, involved with the robbery and murder of Thomas Tollefson? To even consider such a thing there must be strong evidence of dishonest officials in Minneapolis during that time—and there is. The city supposedly had strict laws, but they could be broken with little consequence. Crooked officers were willing to look the other way for a price, as already shown. Such circumstances were more like incentives than deterrents for criminals, and the city was filled with them.

Henry Barrett and his father, John, ran their Fort Avenue saloon, the Hub of Hell, without a license. Pete and Tim both testified they were with Henry at Lally Brothers saloon when a man who wore a star approached Henry and that the two men had a private conversation. Several weeks later, in September of 1887, Henry was arrested for selling liquor and beer without a license. Are those events related?

Henry pled guilty to one charge, and "the second was allowed to stand." He was sentenced to thirty days in the Hennepin County jail and given a $50 fine, in addition to costs. If, after the thirty days, he refused to pay the fine, he was ordered to serve another thirty days, or up until he did pay it. Henry refused to pay. He was in the midst of serving the additional thirty days with just over two weeks left to go, and he'd had a lot of time to think as he sat in jail.[7]

Tim and Pete had been thorns in his side, and his anger burned.

Minnie was expecting a baby, and he hadn't worked for several weeks.

He, like everyone else in the city, knew there was quite a large reward for whoever could help bring in Tollefson's murderers. The extra money would have been welcome.

Jailer Riley had watched Henry pace in his cell numerous times. He seemed troubled, deep in thought, and Riley finally asked, "Is anything wrong, Henry?"

"I want to see the county attorney."

When Hennepin County Assistant Prosecutor Robert Jamison arrived at the jail, he entered Henry's cell and the two were left alone. Henry asked what could be done for someone who had information on the Tollefson murder.

Jamison replied, "Plenty."

Shortly after that initial meeting Henry paid his fine in full, left the jail, and immediately went to Jamison's office, but he was not there. Henry then went on home to Minnie for the night. Within twenty-four hours Henry gave Jamison his confession and, in turn, became the primary witness for the State regarding the murder of Thomas Tollefson. From that moment on Henry was protected by the State.

13

VARIOUS WITNESSES

POLICE SERGEANT Thomas Coscran was called forward to witness for the State about the November day when he and four other officers dragged Mud Lake in search of evidence of the tin fares box.

Coscran testified that the officers had split up into two boats. They used a "scoop with a wire netting and raked . . . [for] a couple of hours." He described the bottom of the lake as muddy and weedy. They found no signs of the box and it was too cold to stay, so they left. They never returned because the lake had frozen over by the next day.[1]

Bill Erwin asked the witness several questions regarding the fact that no pieces of tin were found and whether anyone had accused Henry Barrett of lying about it. When County Attorney Davis objected to those questions, the judge sustained the motion.[2]

On December 28, 1887, Mary Barrett-Coleman was called to the stand as a witness for the defense by attorney Bill Erwin. He asked about her husband, George Coleman. She replied that he was "sick in bed" with pneumonia, had been for "over a week," and could not appear in court.[3]

In consideration of the vital information George could give concerning Tim, Erwin asked the judge whether he would be willing to go to the Barrett-Coleman residence in order to "take his testimony."[4]

Judge Lochren replied, "I don't think we could go; I don't see how we could." This was an extraordinary request to make of the judge, and he certainly had the authority to deny it. (However, as we will see, when Frank Davis made a similar request for one of his bedridden witnesses Judge Lochren willingly obliged.)[5]

Judge Lochren's refusal was highly unfortunate for the defense, since George Coleman would have backed Tim about the night of July 26. It had already been stated that George was at Mary's home that night, slept in the same bed as Timothy, and was there at the time Dr. Heflin gave Timothy instructions about Mary's care.

However, Mary continued to testify about that night. Both Timothy and Peter were at her house when the doctor arrived around 11:00 p.m. Her brothers had gone into the city earlier that evening, and she noticed that Timothy was drunk, so she told him to go to bed.[6]

Erwin continued to question Mary regarding Timothy's demeanor. She said, "Oh, well, when I have seen him drunk why he is noisy; sometimes puts a good deal of life in him." In contrast, speaking of her brother when sober, "Oh, he is simple and not very smart."[7]

Erwin then directed his questions to the area of Timothy's intellect and used such terms as "simple minded . . . bordering on idiocy." Davis objected, and Judge Lochren warned Erwin against leading the witness.[8]

But Mary persisted, "He was simple minded. We always considered him so in the family. . . . [W]e talked sometimes about trying to get him in the insane asylum."[9,10]

(Mary likely referred to the Iowa Institution for Feeble Minded Children located in Glenwood, Mills County, Iowa. Established in 1875, the institute provided "care and training" for mentally challenged children between the ages of five and eighteen years of age who were residents of Iowa.)[11]

During the following day, December 29, the last witness called was a witness for the State. Although it was his third try, Frank Davis finally managed to get G. A. Chamberlain on the stand.

Chamberlain told the court about the night of July 23, 1887, when two armed men had ordered him to put his hands up. However, he was also armed and pointed his gun at the head of the closest thief instead. Chamberlain's revolver appeared to be in better condition than that of either thief, and one of them tried to steal it. A scuffle ensued. Chamberlain finally let him have the gun, gave him a shove, and the man fell backward into a ditch.

Chamberlain ran to the nearby streetcar barns to summon help. Two men hurried along with him back to the spot. Both thieves were already gone but had left behind a felt hat and two shoddy handguns. Those three items were then displayed as evidence to the Court, and Chamberlain identified them. He claimed that the other gun held in evidence, with the initials TB carved on the handle, was actually his stolen revolver.

The *St. Paul Dispatch* reported about the manner in which attorney Bill Erwin cross-examined Chamberlain. Erwin, the reporter wrote, "[T]ackled the witness and led him a merry dance. He held the revolver in his hand and asked Mr. Chamberlain by what marks he identified it."[12]

"By the rust marks," replied the witness."[13]

The attorney asked where the rust marks were, for a detailed description of the marks, and how many there were. Chamberlain was unable to answer any of those questions. So Erwin asked him to describe the handle—what it was made of, the barrel, the weight of the gun, or any other means of specific identification.

Chamberlain simply replied, "I don't know."[14]

The reporter for the *St. Paul Dispatch* stated that this line of questioning continued "until 5 o'clock, and the witness had shown how much he didn't know about revolvers. The attorney did everything but dissect the pistol."[15]

The owner of a gun should have been able to answer at least some of those questions in order to identify his own weapon, especially with so much at stake. If Chamberlain could not identify his own gun, how could he positively identify the ones held in evidence? Was it not a bit of a stretch on the part of the prosecution to attempt to connect Chamberlain's experience to Thomas Tollefson's murder?

On January 1, the *St. Paul Pioneer Press* wrote that the Barrett brothers' elderly father, John, testified at Tim's trial. His words were few and softly spoken in his heavy Irish accent, but the message conveyed was clear. He stated that Henry had lied all through his testimony—*especially concerning the story of Tim and Pete trying to rob Chamberlain.*[16]

In other words, Davis made the connection because it fit Henry's story. Perhaps it seemed a bit contrived, because it was.

A. H. Griffin testified that he had been in the "gun business for the past six years." He was knowledgeable of, and "familiar with pistols, guns, and bullets." Attorney Davis showed a bullet in evidence and asked him about it. Griffin replied, "The bullet is a Smith & Wesson, number 38." The attorney then showed him the revolver, exhibit T. B., and Griffin told the court, "That revolver is a Smith & Wesson, 38-caliber and single action; the bullet is made for this revolver and could be discharged from it."[17]

(Of course, the investigation was limited by the times. To match the fatal bullet to a gun capable of having fired it was about all one could do. If today's forensic capabilities had been available, the investigators could have compared the bullet taken from Tollefson's body with a bullet fired from the gun held as evidence. Even so, this would not have identifed the actual shooter.)

Mrs. Dora Foster, another witness for the State, lived only one block from the turntable. On the night of July 26, 1887, she heard one shot between 11:30 p.m. and midnight, followed by a "holler [and then] heard another shot, [but] heard nothing after the second shot."[18]

Other credible witnesses also claimed they heard only two shots in all and a scream only after the first shot. Among them were A. C. Silverthorn, a special policeman for the Milwaukee Railroad; a clergyman named Samuel Fisher, who was a resident of the area near the turntable; and Gabriel Erichson, who lived in the house closest to the turntable.

Clergyman Samuel Fisher "lived in the vicinity of the murder at the time it occurred." He was awake around midnight and testified, "[I] heard a pistol shot then a terrible scream and then another pistol shot; I heard only two shots; my windows were open and I could hear distinctly."[19]

Gabriel Erichson lived "nearest to the turntable, a distance of but a few feet." That night, at about midnight, he was sitting at his "front window, which looks out onto Cedar Avenue." The window was open as he read the Bible to his wife. He, too, heard one shot followed by "terrible screams" and then another shot. He said, "There were but two shots in all."[20]

One other potential witness for the defense abruptly left town just before Tim's trial began. Why did he leave? Was he afraid? Identified simply as Rollins, he and his father operated a barbershop under the same roof as the Hub of Hell, and the men knew Henry Barrett well.

Louis Riel Jr. was a former detective who had "fired the coat, star and brass buttons of his detective life and was no longer in the ring" (the reason why might have proved interesting). He testified that he had been at Minnehaha Falls on the day of the murder, purchased a cigar, and sat down at one end of the pavilion of shops to light it when he overheard a conversation between Henry (aka Reddy) Barrett and two other men as they stood on the sidewalk nearby. He didn't pay much attention until he overheard talk about robbing a streetcar.

The men said that if "necessary they would kill the driver in order to obtain the cash box. One said, 'Well, if it's murder, then I'm out of it,' but Henry replied, 'We will have to do something to get some money.'"[21,22,23]

At that point, the men noticed Riel watching them. All three turned to face him and Henry drew a pistol from its holster just enough to show Riel before slowly putting it back. The message was clear. "I got up and moved on," said Riel.[24]

After he heard about the streetcar driver's murder, he told police

Lieutenant Walton of the Third Precinct about his encounter in such detail that he even described the clothing Henry wore as "a sack coat and light pants."[25]

But Walton simply advised, "Get a bottle of whiskey . . . get the men drunk and find out more."[26]

Apparently plying suspects with whiskey and interrogating them while they were intoxicated was common police procedure in those days. Riel did not follow Walton's advice. Instead, he met with private detective Norman W. King, the partner of detective Michael Quinlan (who had made statements to a reporter about the murder suspects in August 1887). The two met—not just once, but twice—about the incident.

As Riel stepped down from the witness stand, attorney Davis called out and asked whether he was known as the Young Cyclone Detective of the Northwest. This was asked not only to embarrass Riel but to insult the defense for putting confidence in his testimony. Erwin frowned, and Judge Lochren shook his head disapprovingly. For the county prosecuting attorney to mockingly call Louis Riel the Young Cyclone Detective was extremely inappropriate, not to mention very unprofessional!

The name Young Cyclone Detective referred to some prank letters that had been sent to Police Chief Hein weeks before the trial began. The letters contained threats but were poorly written. No one took them seriously, and it was generally thought they had been written by an imaginative young boy who was fascinated with, and influenced by, dime store mystery books. Each letter was signed by "Wild Frank, the Scout" and told about the "Young Cyclone Detective."[27]

After Davis's outburst, Bill Erwin called Detective Norman W. King to the witness stand. Unfortunately, he was absent, and Erwin requested a few minutes to allow his team to locate King; his testimony could corroborate the statements made by Louis Riel. Judge Lochren conferred with Erwin and Davis about this but decided that King's testimony was unnecessary.

Judge Lochren told the jury, "This case has taken a long time, which I need not say to you. The evidence is all in . . ."[28]

CLOSING ARGUMENTS

ON MONDAY morning, the 2nd of January, County Attorney Frank Davis gave his closing argument—and a lengthy one it was. He began at 9:00 a.m. and there were the usual breaks, of course, but it was nearly 5:00 p.m. by the time he finished that afternoon. Reporters described his speech as "masterly," "powerful," and "convincing"— although they also admitted that it often appeared as though Davis spoke to impress the crowd rather than to sway the jury.[1]

A large portion of his argument was devoted to slamming the testimony of nearly every witness who testified on behalf of the defense, including Peter Barrett, Mary Barrett-Coleman, Dr. Heflin, and former Detective Louis Riel.

He attacked the character of Dr. Heflin by speaking about his previous fine by a neighboring court for "peddling obscene literature" and criticized him for not having written records of his house call to Mary Barrett-Coleman to show the Court.[2]

He mocked the testimony of Louis Riel. "Where [did] this [incident] happen? In the pavilion, near this man smoking his afternoon cigar . . . .You know that criminals always seek a public place where there are plenty of people present when they conspire together. But these poor conspirators did not know that Old Sleuth was sitting by and noting every movement."[3]

Davis continued, "There was once a man named Tollefson who had a wife. Does not that call for your sympathy?"[4]

When Davis brought up the details of the murder, Thomas Tollefson's widow sobbed. Many in the courtroom turned sympathetic glances toward the place where Lena and her mother sat behind the Barretts.

Tim Barrett even turned around in his chair and faced the widow briefly. He showed no hint of emotion (oddly, neither did his sister Mary or either of his parents), but then, he had shown little to no emotion throughout the entire trial, even though his life was at stake. Was that the demeanor of a cold-blooded, insensitive murderer, or of an uncomprehending man?

As for the testimony of brother against brothers, Davis explained, "Henry Barrett's testimony was the free confession of a heart so burdened with the consciousness of its sin that it must disclose it . . . so that the guilty should be punished."[5]

He continued, "There has been no evidence in this case, material to the defense, that has not been given by some person whose character is smirched with crime. . . . When this Barrett case, the most celebrated in the annals of Hennepin County, shall pass into history, the blood and thunder story of Louis Riel shall shine out as the most magnificent defense; and wherever the Barrett case shall be known, shall go the story of Louis Riel, the young cyclone of the Northwest. . . . I do not stand here as the apologist of Henry Barrett. Let the vials of wrath be poured on his head, if you will, but let us see if they can break down his story. Truth is truth, no matter what its source. No murder was ever yet traced home to its perpetrators where the evidence was purely circumstantial unless one of the parties gave it away. Before God, I have done my duty."[6]

Davis's dramatic appeal ended, and court was adjourned for that day. We can well imagine a range of courtroom reactions to Davis's finale, from a sigh to a stifled outburst.

The next morning defense attorney Erwin was ready to address the jury and would not be outdone by his adversary Frank Davis— either in substance or in length of argument. His strong voice never reached a crescendo pitch, but he used carefully chosen, sometimes forceful words. Some of the statements he made concerned the integrity of the detectives who were involved in the case, and also of Assistant Prosecutor Robert Jamison. There had been a rash of "foot pad robberies" throughout the locality that remained unsolved. "Why were not these famous detectives seeking out the perpetrators . . . were they waiting for a reward to be offered?" asked Erwin. "I will find the red-handed murderer of Thomas Tollefson for you—he it was who, with the aid of these so-called detectives, for the sake of getting this reward have together hoodwinked Robert Jamison, the assistant county attorney. We will only be able to get justice in this fair city of yours when these so-called guardians of the peace are removed, and honest men put in their places, men who will not commit murder for reward. . . . I only hope that . . . when you . . . consider the evidence in this case you will also consider the undue zeal which certain detectives have taken." Erwin admitted, "The principal work of criminal lawyers is to protect innocent parties from [corrupt] detectives. . . . Half of the men who are convicted are convicted on the perjured testimony of these detectives."[7]

And regarding Henry, he stated, "This man of blood, this Reddy Barrett, are we to believe him under oath? There is no foundation for believing his story. . . . It is absolutely unsupported. By its own weight it must fall—a monument of lies, uttered by a man without a semblance of manhood, whose very form is a libel on God's attributes. What will we think of these detectives who rushed in and bolstered up Reddy's story to the prosecution when they knew it was not true; who but this man could you expect to tell a story like this?"[8]

He commented on the fact that the very name of Henry Barrett's place, the Hub of Hell, had been intact years before either Tim or Pete had come to visit. Henry had earned his own rough reputation without any help from his brothers, and Erwin reminded the jury of the various testimonies that proved it. Ellen Barrett held a lien on the Fort Avenue property, and at some point after Henry's arrest in September she had taken it over and closed the Hub of Hell, and he and Minnie had been forced to move out. In Erwin's opinion that only made Henry more bitter and bent on revenge.

Erwin also reminded the jury of a small, yet important, blunder Henry had made during his testimony. It occurred when Erwin told Henry to simply tell his story about the night of the murder. Other witnesses had willingly and effortlessly shared their personal recollections. But Henry seemed uncomfortable in doing so and replied, "I would rather you would ask me the questions." Erwin suggested to the jury that Henry had rehearsed specific questions but was afraid he would make mistakes if he simply told the story from memory. An example of this was the error Henry had made when he stated that on the night of the crime there was "plenty of light."[9]

In reality, it had been a dark and rainy night, so Frank Davis had quickly blurted out in the midst of his witness's testimony, "You mean there was plenty of light at the Boston fire."[10]

Regarding the immunity the State promised to Henry for becoming their informant, Erwin questioned whether it was actually legal for them to do so, and whether the immunity had been secured by the governor. "He has not been indicted and may go free, self-convicted as he is," said Erwin. "The court will tell you that Reddy must be corroborated before he can be believed. Was he corroborated?"[11]

Erwin recalled the testimonies of various witnesses and explained how they did not corroborate Henry's story. In fact, the only witness to do so was Minnie—and her testimony was largely based on what Henry had told her. Minnie admitted that she *never actually saw* Tim and Pete with Henry when he came home late on the night of the murder. She was in bed at the time but went out into the hall to see and speak to Henry.

Bill Erwin claimed, "Tim's statement to Robert Jamison was overhauled . . . [and] pointed out statements which . . . Henry must have made to the county officers and afterward changed to [coincide] with subsequent information." [12]

In fact, when Robert Jamison took the stand on December 30, Bill Erwin drilled him about the tactics he used to question Tim Barrett at the jail. Jamison wanted to get "evidence to corroborate Henry's story" but did not inform Tim that anything he said could be used against him. Jamison admitted that he only asked Tim questions that could incriminate him, nothing that would help to exonerate him. [13]

At one point during Jamison's testimony that day, Erwin had asked, "Did it ever occur to you that it is a part of the duty of county attorneys to protect the rights of prisoners while in confinement?" Jamison said it had not. "Did you ever inform his attorney [of] what you had done, and furnish him with a copy of [Tim's] admissions?" Jamison had not. Strangely, Jamison had even gone so far as to have a stenographer present during questioning, without Tim's knowledge. [14]

Erwin had acquired a list of the questions that Jamison had asked Tim. He read it aloud to the jurors. (Frank Davis objected, but Judge Lochren allowed it.) And, according to one reporter, it was obvious to everyone in the courtroom who heard it that Jamison had gone so far during his questioning as to have "threatened to jog Timothy's memory if he did not tell about the Tollefson murder"; he had even boldly "called [Tim] a liar a number of times." [15]

The defense pointed out the crass way in which his clients had been treated by the detectives—the bribes of money, whiskey, and freedom—if they would admit their guilt. Yet neither had budged or weakened. "I will not stop now to criticize the methods of the authorities. I will not dilate upon the fact that these boys were subjected to treatment the most outrageous. Not only have they been tried here, confronted by the facts, but they received an inquisitional trial, without the color of the law. Yet they have never shaken." [16]

Erwin concluded by pointing out the witnesses who had contradicted Henry's story: John McKinnon, George B. Horton, Mr. Foster, Louis Riel, and Lieutenant Walton.

Timothy Barrett's trial ended. It had been another long day, and when the jury left the courtroom to make their decision it was nearly 5:30 p.m.

Those involved must have been somewhat relieved at that point, even though they surely wondered what the jurors would decide. Judge Lochren went home. Bill Erwin felt ill and went back home to St. Paul. Frank Davis attended the opera that night. The deputies all went their separate ways throughout the city.

However, just hours later word came that the jury had reached a verdict, and there was quite a scramble to return to the courtroom. By 8:45 p.m. Judge Lochren, along with Attorneys Frank Davis, Robert Jamison, and Will Donahue, had returned.

The courtroom was quiet except for the ticking clock, a rhythm soon joined by the muffled sound of approaching footsteps growing ever louder, ever clearer, until a handcuffed Tim Barrett appeared in the doorway between Deputy James Ege and Jailer Johnson. Tim took his seat beside Attorney Will Donahue. His faced showed no emotion, even as the jurors filed in.[17]

Jury foreman Leonidas Armstrong handed Clerk Terrill a folded piece of paper. The clerk brought it to Judge Lochren, who unfolded it, silently read it, and gave it back to the clerk. Terrill read aloud, "We the jury, find the defendant guilty of murder in the first degree." The clerk added, "So say you all of you?"[18]

Frank Davis instructed, "Poll the jury."[19]

They did so, calling each juror by name. The verdict was unanimous.

Defense Attorney Will Donahue stood. "We would like to have a stay of sixty days." He explained, "Mr. Erwin has gone home and asked me to make this request in the event of this verdict."[20]

"That is scarcely customary," Judge Lochren replied, adding, "There is no rush about passing judgement. What time do you want?"[21]

A short discussion followed, but Judge Lochren agreed to wait only until the next morning.

On January 4 the *St. Paul Daily Globe* ran the following front-page headlines:

IN THE FIRST DEGREE
Twelve Good Men and True Pronounce
Timothy Barrett Guilty of Murder.

Timothy Receives the Verdict Coolly —
He is a Ruffian or an Imbecile.

His Mother Wrings Her Hands and
Tears Her Hair in Great Agony.[22]

As court convened the next morning, Bill Erwin refused to accept defeat for his client. He made one more request, asking Judge Lochren to delay sentencing rather than impose it immediately following the verdict, as was his habit. He reminded Lochren that it was the custom of other judges to wait. Erwin also called attention to a stipulation in section 166 of the penal code that regarded the sentence for first-degree murder and allowed the option of life imprisonment rather than death. "You must be enlightened by counsel on both sides as to whether there are any exceptional circumstances in this case. We want to have time to go over the record and prepare such arguments that should be presented to the court. In consideration of the peculiar power vested in the court, we ask a stay of at least one week to go over the record."[23]

Frank Davis had no objection to Erwin's request but preferred to have Judge Lochren pass sentence immediately.

Erwin must have been considerably pleased when Judge Lochren granted his request to delay sentencing for one week.

Lochren explained, "In so momentous a case, an opportunity should be given to carefully review the record and the law." He also indicated that in his opinion the legislature should have had explicit sentencing guidelines for murder cases.[24]

❧ ⦿ ❧

The week passed, and on Thursday, January 12, 1888, it was time for Judge Lochren to pronounce sentence. By 9:00 a.m. the courtroom was filled with curious spectators and reporters. Timothy Barrett sat behind his attorneys. John Barrett, who had attended every day of his son's trial, sat at Tim's left. Judge Lochren entered the courtroom, and the session began.

Bill Erwin seized the moment to make one more strong (albeit a bit insulting) appeal on behalf of his client. Speaking for nearly a half hour, he claimed that Tim Barrett was "a quasi-imbecile," a "man of immature mind." Erwin added, "The children who testified on the stand had a better grasp of things. . . . That this man is a perfect imbecile is apparent."[25, 26]

The claim was well timed. Less than twenty-four hours earlier Will Donahue had discussed Tim's mentality with a reporter and told him, "He does not realize his danger . . . [or] comprehend that he has been convicted of murder and that the penalty is death." Donahue had tried to explain the seriousness of it, but Tim shrugged it off, convinced that he would be okay.[27]

Erwin admitted to Judge Lochren that Tim should receive punishment but suggested that it be in the form of imprisonment for life.[28]

(Was this a turning point for the attorney? At that point did he actually believe Tim was guilty, or was this just a ploy to convince the judge to go easy on his client? There are no records to indicate that Erwin ever believed the brothers were guilty of the crime; in fact, further on we will see how he tirelessly defended them and remained convinced of their innocence.)

Prosecutor Frank Davis disagreed. In a short, to-the-point address to the court, he ridiculed the insanity notion. He had not observed any signs that Tim Barrett was insane. Tim did not exhibit what he described as a "vacant stare of imbecility . . . ." Davis said, "If that man escapes the law on that ground the law becomes a farce."[29]

Erwin replied, "We do not ask for mercy, and you could not grant it. The law does not give the [C]ourt the power or right to do so."[30]

Judge Lochren stated that the matter of Timothy's mental capacity was not an issue and that simply because he was not bright did not imply that he was "irresponsible, or that he did not know" right from wrong when "the crime was committed."[31]

"Let the defendant stand forward," said Judge Lochren.[32]

Tim approached the clerk's desk and silently stood before him.

Clerk Davenport asked, "Have you anything to say why sentence should not be pronounced?"[33]

Tim hesitated, trembling as he looked up at Judge Lochren. "Yes, sir I have," he said loudly. "I am not guilty at all. I know nothing about it, at all. My brother, when he told about me, lied."[34,35]

Judge Lochren "leaned forward and looked" straight at Tim. "As the result of a long and careful trial you have been found guilty. . . . I fully concur in the verdict. There is much. . . evidence. . . which indicates that your course for some time has been in the paths of crime, culminating in this murder of an entire stranger, a poor, laboring man quietly pursuing his peaceful vocation, having no motive other than to possess. . . the paltry. . . few dollars. . . in his possession. This crime. . . which necessarily shocked the entire community, seems to have nothing in it in the nature of extenuation or mitigation. There can be no extenuating circumstances in a crime so foul as this was. It is one which can only be expiated by the highest penalty of the law. Experience shows that nothing else is sufficient to prevent the recurrence of offenses of this kind and give proper security to human life." He then advised Tim to spend his remaining time in repentance and preparation to meet almighty God.[36,37]

The courtroom hushed as those present began to absorb the gravity of the coming sentence.

Judge Lochren continued, "It is considered and adjudged that you, Timothy Barrett, as a punishment for the crime of murder in the first degree of which you have been convicted, be taken hence to the common jail of this county of Hennepin and that thereafter, and after the lapse of four calendar months from this day, and at a time to be fixed by the Governor of the State of Minnesota and designated by his warrant, you be taken to the place of execution and there hanged by the neck until you are dead, and may God in His infinite goodness have mercy on your soul."[38]

Stone-faced, Tim quietly returned to his seat. He whispered to Bill Erwin, even smiled faintly at his father. He had just been sentenced to death. Did Tim Barrett fully comprehend that?

Three deputies named Luckor, Eaton, and Bader escorted him out of the courtroom, back to his jail cell. According to one of these deputies Tim blurted out, ". . . [H]ang and be damned. . . . Ha, ha. 'Hung by the neck until dead!' Ain't that good? I came near telling the judge that I would rather hang than be sentenced to Stillwater for life."[39]

Why would there have been such a sudden change from his demeanor in the courtroom? Was the reportage about Tim's cocky attitude deliberately inaccurate?

Tragedy—Preparation—Peter's Trial

JANUARY 12, 1888, was a life-changing day for Timothy Barrett. It was also a life-changing, tragic day for many others. It was not a typical Minnesota winter day; in fact, that morning had dawned with extremely mild, almost spring-like temperatures. Activities carried on as usual, of course: children went off to school, and farmers and other outdoor laborers went about their activities, all pleasantly unhindered by the cold, snow, and ice of the usual January weather. But the reprieve did not last for long. Within hours, a bitter cold front blew in from Montana across the Dakotas into Minnesota, and spread as far south as Texas. It brought heavy snowfall as temperatures drastically plunged to thirty-seven degrees below zero.

Concerned teachers dismissed school early, intending to send the children home while they could get there safely, but the storm suddenly grew in intensity. Several schoolchildren tragically froze to death, lost in the blinding flurry of white. Those who worked outside nearly suffocated in the relentless snow, and cattle died by the hundreds of thousands throughout the Plains states. Although sources vary on the exact count, more than 200 people lost their lives before the storm—known as the Schoolhouse or Schoolchildren's Blizzard, and considered one of the worst in Minnesota history—ended the next day.[1]

Other headlines that month brought pleasant news: a humorous fishing story about Mark Twain, told by his San Francisco buddies; the formal details of elegant White House state dinners hosted by President Grover Cleveland; and intriguing stories about new technological inventions, like Thomas Edison's phonograph and Alexander Graham Bell's graphophone.[2]

Those were the current topics of interest to the people of Minneapolis that winter, but none had captivated their attention or dominated conversations more than the Thomas Tollefson murder and the trials of the Barrett brothers.

Peter's trial was scheduled to begin by the end of the month, and Bill Erwin was one busy attorney. He was in the midst of planning an appeal for Tim when he discovered a new key witness for Peter's trial. Erwin claimed that if he had known about this man previously, he would have had him testify during Tim's trial. Erwin had learned about him from John Barrett. During a private conversation with Henry in January, John was told that there was "one witness that the State could not buy and that the defense had not subpoenaed" who would be of "utmost importance to the defense." John Barrett identified the man to Erwin, who planned to introduce him at the most opportune moment during Peter's upcoming trial.[3]

On Monday morning, the 30th day of January, Peter Barrett entered the courtroom to begin the process of selecting the jury for his trial. He was upbeat and optimistic as he spoke kindly to the observing newspaper reporters.

One reporter later described Peter as a young, "beardless boy" with "an innocent face and a look that is rather stupid" but added, "[He] is bright, possessing vastly more intelligence than most people dream of . . . and . . . has wonderful nerve. He is as confident of being acquitted as he is that the sun shines."[4]

Both Frank Davis and Bill Erwin expected the jury selection to take about six days. There was a pool of 200 men to choose from that Monday, and "a special venue for 170 more [had] been issued." However, the process went quickly, and by February 2 Peter's trial began.

The prosecution opened with testimony from streetcar driver John McKinnon. His testimony was unchanged from that of Tim's trial, with one exception. During Peter's trial he told the court about identifying the body of Thomas Tollefson at Gleason & Byorum's, the undertakers.

After McKinnon testified, the coroner was called to the witness stand. Willis Spring was a physician and surgeon with nearly twenty years of experience and had served as the deputy coroner of Hennepin County for seven years. He and his assistant, Dr. Collins, had performed the postmortem exam of Thomas Tollefson's body on July 27, 1887, and he discussed his findings:

Tollefson weighed "about 160 pounds . . . [and stood] five feet ten inches." Spring then described the position of the wounds: "In the right thigh a puncture wound one inch inside of a line drawn from the interior spine of the ilium. . . . [T]he skin about it was burned to the size of a dollar . . . being similar to what would be produced by gun powder; we found at the back of the leg, nearly to the center of the leg, a wound one inch below the fold of the buttock, possibly an inch above the wound in the front part of the leg."[5]

Concerning the leg wound, he could not "swear as to whether or not there was one or two wounds; it is highly improbable that there [were] two wounds on the leg." Dr. Spring concluded, "[In my] judgment both wounds were made by the same pistol bullet."[6]

He continued, "On making further examination on the body, I found on the right side of the chest, about three inches to the right of the medium line, and about three inches above the nipple . . . another puncture wound. This passed through both lungs and the aorta into the interior part of the body, it had cut the second rib at its junction with the cartilage; it passed through the shoulder blade and lodged beneath the skin, and we cut it out. I kept it in my possession till I gave it to County Attorney Davis."

At this point Davis displayed the bullet, Spring identified it, and it was set aside as evidence. "These were all the wounds found," said Spring. "Death had been produced by hemorrhage, arising from the wound in the chest produced by [this] bullet; death would result almost as quickly from this wound as it would from a heart wound."[7]

Interestingly, Dr. Spring added, "[We] discovered no powder marks upon Tollefson's left hand; the wound on the chest was on the right side; we found no evidence of hemorrhage in any of the thigh wounds to speak of."[8]

Since there was so little bleeding from either of the leg wounds, had they been from the *first shot* fired, as Henry Barrett testified? Neither of the leg wounds showed evidence of hemorrhage during the postmortem exam, which makes sense if they had occurred after the heart had stopped pumping blood. In that case it would seem as though the chest wound must have occurred first, since, as the coroner stated, it produced almost instant death from sudden, severe internal bleeding. Also, due to the severity of the chest wound, Thomas Tollefson would have had mere seconds to live, just long enough to scream out briefly with both lungs punctured. If, as Henry testified, the gunshot to the leg was first, and *minutes* passed before the second and fatal shot, wouldn't Thomas have screamed out in pain or called for help during those minutes? Henry had stated during Tim's trial, "As Pete and I ran, I heard the driver and Tim say some words to each other"—implies a different scenario from that displayed by the actual wounds.

Other witnesses called forward on that first day of Peter's trial were Tollefson's brother-in-law Ole Brecke and surgeon D. F. Collins, who had assisted Dr. Spring. Undertaker Ole Byorum had received the body from the coroner after the examination. He remarked that in his opinion "Thomas Tollefson was quite a stoutly built man."[9]

After these men had testified, Henry Barrett was sworn in.

John Barrett, father of the Barretts.

"THE OLD MAN."

A Word About the Late Paternal Ancestor of the Illustrious Boys—Not a Bad Man.

Source: *St. Paul & Minneapolis Pioneer Press*, March 22, 1889, Minnesota Historical Society, St. Paul, MN.

16

ᴴENRY ᴛESTIFIES ᴬGAIN

ᴴENRY BARRETT testified against his brothers, making nearly identical statements at both trials, but there was a marked difference in his demeanor during the trial of Peter. One reporter wrote, "[H]e is still a good witness, but there is something dragging at his heart strings. He answers the questions plainly, and he never contradicts himself, but he does not reply as positively as on the former trial."[1]

Henry remained the primary witness for the State and was still under protective custody. By the time of Peter's trial he and Minnie had been moved to an area of North Minneapolis where they were unrecognized by the locals.

Back during Tim's trial, on December 28, attorney Bill Erwin had stated his opinion that Henry held a deep "hatred towards the entire [Barrett] family," which motivated him to make up a story to implicate his brothers in the Tollefson murder—a crime Henry had admittedly been involved with. So Erwin began by questioning Henry about the time he'd spent in the Hennepin County Jail that autumn and of his "privileges" while there—primarily that Henry was permitted to "go out and come back again." In fact, on one such occasion he and fellow prisoner Thomas Pitts had gone to Henry's house to see Minnie. Timothy was also there, but Henry claimed that the brothers did not talk to each other. Attorney Erwin questioned Henry about that day and insinuated that he had intended to set a trap for Tim and implicate him in the Tollefson murder crime.[2, 3, 4]

Of course, Henry denied it, saying that he had only wanted to be with his wife. He also claimed he had no more privileges than any other prisoner and that he had only gone outside "a couple of times" to help do work for the jail turnkey—even though on one of those occasions Henry got his hands on some liquor and got drunk. The jailer confronted him and criticized his behavior, but Henry explained that he simply had a lot on his conscience. Shortly after that incident, Henry asked to speak to the prosecutor.[5]

That was a rather strange jail sentence. Since Henry was able to wander back home, even to get drunk, what else might he have been able to do? Where else might he have gone? Whom else might he have talked to? Who might have conspired with him to accuse his brothers of the Tollefson murder crime? Henry had served the original thirty-day sentence but could not afford to pay his $50 fine so was given an additional thirty days in jail. He had only days to go of what had become a sixty-day sentence when he suddenly paid his fine and was released.

At that time, he told "turnkey" Johnson that he wanted to speak to Assistant Prosecutor Robert Jamison. He left the jail as a free man and walked to the courthouse to see whether he could meet with Jamison, but he was unavailable. Henry went home. Jamison showed up at his house that same night, but it was late and Henry was too tired to talk. They agreed to meet the following morning at Jamison's office. This meeting was followed by another that included County Prosecutor Frank Davis and Chief Detective Hankinson, and Henry told them his story. He claimed he had no desire to receive any reward money for turning in his brothers; he simply wanted to do the right thing—as long as he would receive immunity and protection.[6]

That sounds rather noble. Was Henry noble? What do well-documented examples show us about Henry's character? For starters, he sold liquor illegally and had served several jail terms because of it. His saloon, the Hub of Hell, also had the reputation of being a dangerous, violent place. Henry had a terrible temper and was prone to violence. He had shot at his business partner—*his own father.* He planned, and tried, to shoot the man who had shot his brother John. He forged his brother Timothy's name on a bill of sale for furniture for himself and Minnie. Henry once kicked a man severely in the jaw, was arrested, convicted, and fined $75.[7]

And then there was the incident of threatening city editor Jones of the local *Star News* newspaper, which was reported in the *St. Paul Daily Globe* on January 2, 1888: "It was probably a surprise party of liberal proportions to the Star News people about 5 o'clock when . . . Barrett and Gorman entered with the appearance of lofty indignation and inquired for the editor . . . City Editor Jones who is so small that his feet don't touch the floor when he sits at his desk, indicated mildly that he was in charge. . . . Gorman, who is about seven feet tall, glared down at the little man . . . and growled out, 'I want you to retract what your newspaper said about my being found in bed with Chloe Betts . . .' [Henry] Barrett rushed forward and, pounding on the desk, yelled, 'Yes, and I'm going to smash your head for what you have said about me.'"[8]

Of course, the newspaper reporters would not simply take Reddy's threats silently. "Just think of it! Here's a self-confessed murderer allowed to wander around the streets and threaten reporters for printing the evidence he gave on the witness stand. I admire his nerve," quipped the representative of the *Star News.* The retraction demanded by Gorman and Henry was never printed.[9]

Apparently the relationship between Henry Barrett and Levi Gorman had become more than just that of the guarded and his guardian. It was said that Henry had become rather fond of Levi and that the two often talked during the weeks of protected confinement (oh, to have been a fly on those walls).

Henry also had a fiercely jealous side that was easily exposed when Erwin's questions took an interesting turn—he asked about Peter and Chloe: "In July, did you not advise . . . Peter as to the manner and form with which he should approach your wife's sister, Chloe, in order that she might grant him favors?" He continued, "After you had advised Peter . . . [did you] discover him and her in bed together [and] make a great fuss . . . and . . . state to your brother Timothy that Peter had seduced your wife's sister and that you would tell your mother . . . and if that didn't stop her [from] giving her property to Peter you would kill Pete, or put a job on him and at the same time ask Timothy to remain and live with you?"[10, 11]

Henry firmly denied it, saying that he had never had any trouble with Peter.

Attorney Erwin persisted, "After you had made this statement in substance and effect to Timothy, didn't Timothy say that he would prevent you and would tell Peter and did he not leave your house the next day and go to stay at Mary's? . . . Did not Timothy state to you that he would expose this attempt on your part . . . and did you not swear vengeance on Tim?"[12]

But perhaps more potentially damaging were the questions regarding streetcar checks, like those from the fares box that had been stolen from Thomas Tollefson. Erwin asked Henry, "Did you not on two different occasions after the murder of Tollefson, at your house, before you were arrested in September . . . the last of August or September, give to your father a package containing six street car copper checks, similar to those shown on the stand here, done up in papers similar to those shown you on the stand here; packages unbroken? . . . Did you not keep street car checks, similar to those shown to you in evidence here, in the middle drawer behind your bar after the murder of Tollefson, at different times, up until the time you were arrested for selling liquor without a license?"[13]

Henry denied having knowledge about the streetcar tickets and claimed that after his father, John Barrett, had left for California on

July 25, 1887, Timothy and Peter operated the bar and he had nothing to do with it.

If that were true, why was Henry arrested in September for selling liquor without a license? He also must have had the date wrong concerning his father's trip to California. John Barrett was at Mary's place and had let Dr. Heflin in to see her on the night of the murder, July 26, and he had slept there that night.

Henry testified that he, Tim, and Pete left the house/saloon at 2830 Fort Avenue together on the evening of July 26, 1887, to go to town. He claimed he often used a cane and owned two or three. The brothers walked across the prairie to 28th Street and followed it west, a block or two, to the H & D Railroad tracks.

During Timothy's trial he had said that they boarded a streetcar but he couldn't remember the number of the streetcar or any details about other people on board. They rode into the city, got off, and all three entered the Lally Brothers saloon. Pete and Tim left almost immediately. Henry claimed that he had never been in Lally Brothers before that night, nor since. However, he stayed, drank beer, and spent time walking around and talking to people until his brothers returned about an hour later and they all left together.

"Didn't you have a talk with a man named Steele in Lally Brothers that night when Peter and Timothy weren't there?" Erwin asked.[14]

"If I did I don't know nothing of it," Henry replied.[15]

Erwin questioned Henry further and asked whether he had met a "copper" while at Lally Brothers saloon. He asked whether the true reason Henry had stayed was to meet with that policeman "for the purpose of confirmation, corroboration?"[16]

Henry insisted that this was not so. He didn't even know whether a policeman had been there that night.

During Peter's trial Henry testified that the three brothers had left his house on the night of the murder at about 8:00 p.m.—armed. He said that Pete and Tim had each carried a revolver. Peter had a "32 caliber self-cocker" with a "red pearl or ivory handle," Tim carried a

"38 Smith and Wesson," and both guns were loaded. He himself had no gun, only a broken billiard cue he used as a cane. After walking along the H & D tracks they came out on Cedar Avenue shortly before 9:00 p.m.; "it was dark; we stopped there a while; streetcars passed us. . . . [W]e were four or six feet from the track." The brothers stood side by side as a streetcar approached on its way from the turntable at Lake Street. "We had a conversation about stopping the car, robbing the driver; went out for that purpose; I guess we all had something to say; none of us said anything to the driver, or to anyone while standing there; nothing was done at that time."[17]

The brothers had then walked up Cedar Avenue until a streetcar came up to them; they boarded and rode into the city. Once there, they went into the Lally Brothers saloon. Pete and Tim left Henry there, he waited until they returned and they all left together. They walked down various streets and witnessed the fire at the Boston Block. Eventually the three boarded a streetcar near Washington and "went home, or out to Franklin Avenue . . . down Cedar Avenue to 26th Street, and stopped there and put some planks across the [streetcar] track." Henry said that they "got the planks from a pile on the east side of the street; they were eight feet long; we placed about two or three upon the track . . . and says to each other that we had come this far and had not met anybody."[18]

Erwin asked Henry to be more specific as to who had said what during this incident, but Henry replied, "I do not know as I am able to answer who said anything; it was said that we should place these planks across the track and stop the car and rob the driver, and whoever else was in the car of what money they had; there had been a conversation about robbing somebody."[19]

After more questions about this, Henry said, "Well, I think it was Tim that first spoke of going down Cedar Avenue, and if we met anybody to hold them up and take what money they had. . . . [W]e were all present at the time."[20]

He continued to explain that the streetcar came by, struck the planks, and "was thrown off the track." The driver was alone on the car, which was pulled by a pair of mules. The brothers had "stood in the shade of bushes . . . thirty or forty feet" from the derailed streetcar, but done nothing and the streetcar soon resumed its route. "I said if we cannot do better than twenty dollars, I guess we might do nothing; we went on towards the turntable."[21]

They stopped at the corner of Cedar Avenue and Lake Street, at Layman's Cemetery. Mr. Foster, a grocer with a store on Cedar Avenue, happened to pass by them, driving his "spring wagon." Henry said that the brothers had stood on a "foot-path between a row of trees, and a picket fence that enclosed the cemetery." A streetcar approached that had a passenger who got off, and the car proceeded on to the turntable. Henry recalled that Tim then spoke up: "I guess we will have to relieve this fellow of his [fares] box."[22]

So the brothers followed the car, and by the time the driver had turned it around they were standing at the front of it.

> I think Tim told him he would have to relieve him of his box; they [Tim and Pete] shoved their revolvers against his body; he did not say anything at that time, reached down and grasped hold of the revolvers in each hand; Peter told him to let go . . . [that] he did not want to kill him; he told him if he let go of the revolvers he could go ahead and keep his box; the driver said 'not much.' The next thing that happened [was that] Pete shot; the driver was standing on the front of the platform of the car; my brothers stood at that time against the front platform of the car; Tim stood on the side towards the team; Pete stood at Tim's left hand; the driver [with his right hand] took hold of Pete's pistol and held it down somewhere about his leg and [simultaneously] took hold of Tim's and held it above his head with the other [left] hand; I stood right behind the boys, probably three feet, when Pete shot; after Pete shot, the next thing that was done, Pete and I turned and ran down Lake Street; Tim remained in the same place he had been; after Pete and I went

away, we could [hear] him (the driver) howl and holler; the next thing we heard was a shot; then Tim came running and caught up with us, and had the cash box; he had it in his hand, I guess; I think Tim said, 'I have killed him, shot him through the head,' something of that kind; at the time Tim caught up with Pete and me, we were somewhere near the south entrance to Layman's Cemetery; we went into the cemetery and stayed there a little while, and came out on Lake Street again, about [forty] or [fifty] feet east of the entrance, on Lake Street." [23]

Henry continued his testimony and indicated the location on the map displayed in the courtroom.

We went right down Lake Street to 21st Avenue, over to our house; it was about one o'clock when we arrived home; we went upstairs; I went up alone first and Tim and Pete stopped in the hall below; my wife came out of the room; I spoke to her, I told her to go back into the room again and close the door; the boys then came up into the hall where I was; the money was taken out of the box and we took the box downstairs and buried it in the cellar; I guess the money was poured out on the table in the hall; Tim poured it out; the money was all silver, I think; there was streetcar tickets in the box besides; they were in packages; there was a cigar in the box besides. There was money in two or three different kinds of packages and tickets in one kind; the tickets was in kind of a colored paper, some kind of a red; the money was in blue ones and paper that had no color. [24]

Attorney Erwin then showed the court and the witness samples of the ticket and change packages issued to the streetcar drivers and asked Henry whether they were similar to the packages he had seen that night.

He replied that they were and pointed out which ones held change and which ones held tickets.

> I dug a hole in the cellar to put the tickets in; Peter held [a] lamp and box for me. . . . Tim came down into the cellar while we were there. . . . [W]e came up out of the cellar immediately after Tim accidentally discharged his revolver down there; we stayed in the saloon and talked a while; I went upstairs; I think they laid down on the pool table there at that time; I got up about 9 the next morning; Tim and Pete were there. . . . I heard a noise down in the cellar and concluded that they had dug up the box, or something of that kind; I went down in the cellar, and they had the box dug up and the tickets put in a pile; they were pounding the box with an old axe; they said they were going to chop it up a little and throw it between the floor and ground of the building; think it was Tim who said that. There was a space between the floor and the ground; you could see out under the house from the cellar. I said to them that it would be a poor idea to throw the pieces of the box and tickets there, and they said they would throw the tickets there anyway, and picked up one package of six tickets, tore it open, took them out in his hand and threw them under the joist; I tore a package open and took them and threw some of them in there and they struck the joist and fell back into the cellar; I think I picked one up and laid it down on the corner of the cellar; we then concluded it was a poor place to put them so put the rest in a tobacco sack and Tim put them in his pocket; we then burned up the envelopes or packages in the cellar, wrapped the pieces of the box, which we had cut up, in newspaper and started down Fort Avenue with this package for Mud Lake; it was in the forenoon; hired a boat from a young girl and distributed the tickets and pieces of box around the lake; paid twenty-five cents for use of the boat;

got a large number of water lilies and brought them home
with us; Tim and I went to the Lake; Pete stayed at the saloon; the tickets, or checks were just like those," he said as
he pointed toward exhibits Y and W.[25]

Erwin asked, "Was Tim regarded by the family as weaker minded
than the rest of the family? . . . Was not Timothy the weaker minded
boy?"[26]

But the State objected to that line of questioning, the Court sustained, and Henry never answered.

Erwin asked Henry where he currently lived. He replied, "740
Third Street North." He said that he was not under guard but admitted that Levi Gorman was living there, too, "to look after me."[27]

Erwin told Henry he had been under guard "ever since . . . [he'd
told his] story." Which led to the subject of Henry's statement.[28]

"I never was taken before a magistrate," Henry replied. "I made
one statement in writing; I think it was the 17th of November; was
made to Mr. Davis, the County Attorney; he wrote it down as I told
my story."[29]

Erwin requested to see Henry's "written statement . . . for the purpose of cross examination."[30]

But Frank Davis refused. "It is a matter that pertains to my office
and was taken down for my convenience. I decline to produce it unless instructed by the Court."[31]

The Court denied Erwin's request "on the ground that communications to a public officer disclosing the conditions of a crime are
privileged and cannot be inquired into."[32]

17

THE CRIME VERSUS TESTIMONY

U NDER CROSS-EXAMINATION Erwin recalled that Henry
had testified, "Tollefson, when he was accosted by the robbers,
grabbed his box and put it under his left arm." Erwin remarked, "This
fact he had failed to detail in his direct examination. . . . If the subject
of this murder is a matter of such great importance to you that you
would surrender your brothers to the law, how could you forget to tell
so material a part of that story?"[1,2]

"It is not true that this story about grabbing the box is false [nor]
did it escape my memory at any time; I did not tell it because I did not
go into the details, that is all," Henry explained.[3]

"Can you explain to the jury how, if Peter stood upon the right,
in this way, how he could discharge his revolver on the right hand side of
the man . . . which would pass in on the right side, and come out here?"[4]

Henry had testified that Tim had stood next to the team and that
Pete was to Tim's left. Facing Thomas, Pete would have been at Thomas's
right.

"Peter did pull his revolver, and tried to get it out of Tollefson's hands, I think; he did say let go of our revolvers, and we will let you go, we don't want to kill you; he said that very thing," Henry said, as he demonstrated the position to the jury. Using the fares box exhibited in the courtroom, he "placed the box under his left arm and explain[ed] how and where each man stood and how the revolvers were held and how the driver held [the] box."[5]

But Erwin questioned the feasibility of the actions demonstrated by Henry. "A man standing to the right," Erwin asked, "How could a man standing in this position, shooting with his right hand, cut off the aorta produce instant collapse of his system, how could [Thomas] grab that box without falling?"[6]

Coroner Spring had testified that the fatal bullet had entered from the right. If Tim had shot Thomas from the position given by Henry, the bullet would have logically entered from the left. Also, Thomas was found upright, in a seated position, not fallen over.

The State objected, calling the line of questioning "incompetent, immaterial and calling for an opinion and argumentative." The Court sustained.[7]

But Erwin pushed through, accusing Henry of changing his testimony to fit the story of another witness for the State and also suggested that he had been coached after his initial testimony. "[You've had] something placed in your ears to be told out through your mouth."[8]

Of course the State objected, the Court sustained, and Henry certainly denied it—but let's consider the probabilities of the scenario, according to his testimony. Earlier, Coroner Willis Spring had stated that there were no powder burns on Thomas's left hand. Henry said that Thomas had grabbed the barrel of Tim's gun with his left hand and held it above his [Thomas's] head while he held the fares box under that same arm. That would have been awkward. Thomas stood nearly six feet tall, but Tim Barrett was shorter. The streetcar platform was about two feet above the ground, so as Thomas stood there the top of his head would have been eight feet above ground. If Thomas had grabbed the barrel of Tim's gun and held it above his own head, that would have been quite a stretch for Tim's arm.

While standing in that position, according to Henry, Thomas then used his right hand to grab the pistol in Peter's hand and pressed it down toward his own leg. Regarding the leg wound, Willis Spring testified that there was an entry wound and exit wound. The entry wound was on the front of the upper thigh and had left a powder burn the size of a dollar on the skin around it. The exit wound was located on the back of the thigh about "an inch above the wound in the front" as though the gun were fired at a slightly upward angle. Henry also had testified that this was the first gunshot wound, but, if it was, and if it had occurred in the midst of the struggle, why didn't it bleed? Willis Spring testified that he had "found no evidence of hemorrhage in any of the thigh wounds." Why didn't Thomas repeatedly scream out?

Was Henry, an admitted participant of the crime, just mixed up about the order of the gunshots? He had been so solid and unwavering regarding minor details during his testimony. Would he have erred during such important ones?

Let's further consider the description Henry gave of Tim's struggle with Thomas. If Tim had fired the fatal shot, and Thomas had held the barrel of Tim's gun, why was there no indication of powder burns on Thomas's hand? Thomas may have let go of the gun, but if the struggle were just between two men at that point, would he have done so? (Henry claimed that he and Peter had already run off.)

Also, the fatal shot had entered at the front, right, pectoral area and passed through the right lung, pierced the aorta and the left lung before lodging beneath the skin of the left shoulder blade. The bullet had clearly moved from right to left inside Thomas's body. However, based on Henry's testimony, Tim had held the gun in his right hand as Thomas had grabbed it with his left. Wouldn't that bullet have entered his body on the left side and moved to the right? Maybe there had been a fierce struggle and Thomas had twisted his body around, but if so, wouldn't Thomas have bent forward and toppled over, or, at the least, fallen in the direction of the weakened, wounded right leg? However,

Ole Byorum, the undertaker, had said, "Thomas Tollefson was quite a stoutly built man." If such a sturdy young man had struggled with a gunman, why was Thomas's body found in such an untroubled state? He had been found seated upright on the front platform, and the only obvious sign of disturbance was that of his hat—it had slipped down and covered his face. There was no other indication of struggle.

On the other hand, if the chest wound had come first, the force and shock might have knocked Thomas back against the streetcar. The severed aorta would have caused massive internal bleeding and may have rendered his legs useless as he gently slipped into the seated position in which he was found. Death would have come almost instantly, with no time for Thomas to call for help.[9]

Henry stated that Tim had told him "I shot him through the head." Thomas Tollefson had no head wound. The fatal shot was fired through his chest. Wouldn't a gunman know where he had shot someone at such close range?

There is another point of contention when we consider the perspective of the victim. Sure, the times were rather Old West, as various chapters in this book clearly demonstrate, but the idea that Thomas Tollefson would have put up such a struggle against three men—two of whom were armed—seems questionable. Why would a recently and happily married man, with so much to live for, have risked his life, his very future for the sake of $20 in streetcar fares? Truth may be stranger than fiction, but the pieces of the puzzling story told by Henry just don't quite fit.

Jealousy and rage make dangerous partners. One day during Pete's trial Bill Erwin showed the Court how easily Henry could be coaxed into an angry posture. "Did you not, Henry, on the 28th of January, at the Gault House, meet your father, and . . . say to him that while you were in jail, incarcerated for selling liquor unlawfully, Tim, your brother, had had criminal intimacy with your wife and your wife's sister, Chloe Betts? Did you not then say to him, in answer to his question as to why you had put up such a horrible game upon your brothers, that it did not matter since all the property had gone to them, and then, did you not tell your father that there was one witness which the state could not buy that would, if brought forward, be of the greatest importance to the defense?"[10]

"Like a flash Henry half arose in his seat, and glaring at Erwin like a lion at bay, shouted: 'I want it understood that I will bear no questions such as this, nor will I have my wife and her sister brought into this trial.'"[11]

Erwin addressed Judge Lochren: "I should like to have an answer, Your Honor."[12]

"You must answer the question," Judge Lochren told Henry.[13]

"I did not tell my father anything of the kind," Henry seethed.[14]

"You lie!" From the back of the courtroom, oldest brother Frank Barrett jumped up from his seat, fists clenched.[15]

The courtroom fell into a momentary state of confusion as the spectators murmured and stared at Frank. For the most part he had sat quietly, listening, but hearing Henry's response that day he grew livid. He had left his Omaha home in December to attend the trials of both Tim and Pete, and at the end of each session would "bid his brothers 'goodbye'" as they left in the company of the deputies. A reporter had spoken to Frank previously and wrote, "He is not very communicative, as might be expected, but this does not come apparently from any desire to be cautious. He hangs his head, and after he reflects on the nature of the charge against his brothers his eyes become dimmed with tears. He was terribly worked up over his brother's [Henry's] testimony, and when later asked about it would say, 'It's terrible. But it is no surprise to us. We expected he would tell this kind of a story.'"[16]

Judge Lochren was not about to let sibling rivalry hijack the trial. He reined his courtroom back to order with a slam of his gavel—and a harsh warning aimed directly at Frank Barrett: "If there is any repetition of any such thing as this, the perpetrator will be punished with a degree of severity which will certainly be effective."[17]

That wouldn't be the last time Frank voiced his opinion. He often, and openly, cursed his brother Henry, Frank Davis, and Robert Jamison. In one rather humorous exchange that occurred during attorney

John Byrnes's testimony, Robert Jamison glanced over his shoulder toward Frank Barrett and hissed, "'I'm not a wart . . .'" To which Frank Barrett responded that, if not, he was certainly a "___ ___ ___ ___." The press did not disclose the entire comment, but we can imagine what those four little unflattering words might have been.[18]

Calm prevailed once again in Lochren's court, so attorney Erwin resumed his question to Henry about the meeting with his father at the Gault House.

"My father came to me. . . . [H]e wanted me to help . . . Pete." Henry paused. "I had destroyed all Tim's hopes, and he wanted me at least to be merciful to Pete. He said that he could not believe that I would have been the one to divulge as I had the secrets of the crime, and that more would he have looked for it from the others. He told me that there was a law in the state of Nebraska, as well as in Minnesota, and that even should I go free here, after the state had finished with me, I would be abandoned by the prosecutors, and that he and the rest of the family would see that I was held and punished for another crime. He asked me if I would see Mr. Erwin and I said that I would; as far as I knew I had no objections to an interview with Mr. Erwin."[19]

Erwin changed the direction of his questioning to ask Henry why he had used a fictitious name while at Waconia, implying that he had done so out of fear. Henry denied it. "No sir. I did not hide my name because I was afraid it would be proved I was one of the murderers."[20]

Erwin persisted.

Henry was in the midst of answering when Erwin interrupted him with another question. Henry apparently had reached his limit. "If you will keep your mouth shut a moment, Mr. Erwin, I will answer your question. I did not suppose there was any secrecy in keeping me there, as it was only done to save me from unpleasant interviews. Tim had a pretty good chance of knowing what my testimony would be, and there was also considerable [information] published in the various papers. I had talked with reporters in regard to the case before the trial. But this matter was withheld until my testimony had been given."[21]

"Was Tim given any opportunity of knowing what you would swear to before you went on the stand?"[22]

"He was. I had an interview with him at the Central Police Station. Tim and I were in the cell. There were officers outside. [Neither] the county attorney nor his assistant were . . . present."[23]

"Were you not sent in for the purpose of getting Tim to tell something?"[24]

"Well, I don't wish to tell for what purpose I went in to see Tim."[25]

Erwin addressed the Court: "[H]e does not come here to simply ease his conscience, but he comes here to get revenge on his brothers, and for that purpose he entered Tim's cell, with detectives on the outside to hear what Tim would say, so that his [Henry's] story might be corroborated. I claim it as my right to know why this man went into his brother's cell."[26]

Frank Davis objected, discussion followed, and Judge Lochren decided that the question was irrelevant to Peter's trial, although it may have been relevant for Timothy's. Erwin once again demanded to see Henry's written confession—and once again he was denied. All the while Henry sat listening, arms folded across his chest, brows furrowed as though troubled in thought.

Erwin turned back toward Henry with a piercing look. "Just before you were released from the county jail in November, where did you get the money to pay your fine?"

"I had most of it. All but $3.75. Deputy Johnson loaned me that."

A small detail, but was it minor?

None of Henry Barrett's family members supported him in his claims against his brothers. Not his father—he testified under oath that Henry had lied. Not his mother. Not Mary. Not Frank. They knew Henry well and regarded him as spiteful and vengeful. His testimony was the ultimate family betrayal.

Regardless of their disappointment and anger, Henry, aka Reddy, deeply loved his wife, Minnie. She was his comfort, and they were about to begin their own family.

Henry "Reddy" Barrett and his wife, Minnie.

REDDY BARRETT AND HIS WIFE.

Source: *St. Paul & Minneapolis Pioneer Press*,
Minnesota Historical Society, St. Paul, MN.

MINNIE

URING THE Victorian era, expectant mothers would cus-tomarily take to bed during the final stage of their pregnancies to prepare for the birth. The stress of the trials fell heavily on Minnie—who was, by all accounts, a rather frail young woman. Under these circumstances of emotional turmoil, she gave birth to their first child, a son, on January 30, 1888—the same day that jury selection began for Peter's trial. They named the baby Henry Barrett Jr. Sadly, the little newborn lived for only a short time, and the bereaved mother remained bedridden as the trial for Peter ensued. It was no wonder that the grief-stricken Henry seemed different during his testimony.[1]

Regardless of her physical and emotional state, Minnie Barrett was still an important witness for the State. Since she was unable to come into the courtroom to testify, Judge Lochren made an excep-tion, and he and the court officials went to her. On Tuesday, Febru-ary 7, all twelve jurors; Frank Davis; Bill Erwin; and the defendant, Peter Barrett (along with the police who guarded him), all crowded into her tiny upstairs bedroom. The room, described as small and plainly furnished, was nonetheless neat and clean. There was not enough room for them all to sit down, so the men—including Judge Lochren—stood, encircling Minnie's bed while Henry and Chloe sat close beside her throughout her testimony.[2]

Pale and thin, Minnie was propped up with pillows. She answered each question with a faint, somewhat trembling voice. County Attorney Davis quickly read her previous statement from Tim's trial aloud. Judge Lochren politely made an effort to hurry things along for her sake, and the whole matter took only a short time.

One particular question presented by Davis during that time referred to Tim and a hat. According to Minnie, Tim had worn a "slouch hat" up until a few days before the murder, but on the day of the murder he began to wear a "new stiff hat." This tended to corroborate statements made by Mr. Chamberlain about the incident on July 23, 1887, when thieves had stolen his revolver and left behind a felt hat.[3]

Erwin objected to that line of questioning "as immaterial, irrelevant, and incompetent," but the judge overruled.[4]

Minnie also claimed that she had seen Pete with a pistol the day of the murder. She stated that on the night of July 26 she went to bed "about 11 o'clock" and slept beside her sister Chloe until she heard Henry come upstairs. She then got up and stepped out into the hallway to see him. They spoke briefly. He told her to go back to bed, and she did. Shortly afterward, she heard others coming up the stairs talking with what "sounded like the voices of Henry, Pete, and Tim [and then a] noise as if money [were] rattling against tin; heard them go downstairs and then heard a noise as of a pistol shot." Finally, she recalled, "Henry came up . . . [and I] heard no strange voices."[5]

Oddly, throughout all of the commotion she never spoke to Chloe. Minnie continued to lie beside her sister, she didn't know for how long, until Henry called for her to come to their own bed. Once there together, the couple talked awhile, but she did not "recollect how late" it was. Nor did she say what they talked about. The next morning they ate breakfast downstairs at 9:00 a.m. and Tim and Pete were also there, but she did "not remember whether the boys [Tim and Pete] were there the next day, in the afternoon."[6]

Attorney Erwin seized an opportunity to challenge Minnie's last statement by referring to Louisa Cashman's earlier comment about Tim and Pete peering out the back windows of the Fort Avenue house that afternoon as she talked with a policeman in her backyard. He asked Minnie, "If you had been there [that] afternoon . . . and the boys had been there uneasy, looking out from one window to another . . . you would have been very apt to remember it, would you not?"[7, 8]

However, Davis objected to this question as "incompetent, irrelevant and immaterial and not cross examination." Judge Lochren sustained.[9]

Minnie's testimony ended, and the trial resumed back at the courthouse.

MORE WITNESSES

OLLIE VAN VALKENBURG lived on Cedar Avenue near the H & D railroad tracks. He testified that "a few days after the driver was shot" he had found "a piece of billiard cue just inside of the picket fence" near his house. "It was lying about fifty feet from the H & D track; it was the butt end of the cue, and about three feet long. . . . [I]t was lying there in the grass."[1]

Sene Larsen, the young "boat girl," who lived with her parents in a house at the back of Mud Lake came forward to testify. She had been sick with diphtheria and unable to testify during Tim's trial, but she had recovered by this time. Sene did not know the name of her street but said that she frequently rented out boats with paddles for twenty-five cents. Mud Lake was murky, somewhat swamp-like, however, beautiful, white water lilies grew there each summer. She testified, "I do not know Henry Barrett or Timothy Barrett . . . do not remember of their coming to my house in July."[2]

Chloe Betts testified that on the night of July 26, 1887, she had fallen asleep beside her sister, Minnie, but she was awakened by the sound of Henry talking outside the bedroom door. Minnie got up and went out into the hall to see him. Chloe said, "I heard nobody else in the hall." She fell back to sleep and did not know how long Minnie stayed in the hall.[3]

Chloe recalled that a bit later she awoke to the sound of a pistol shot. Although it had been loud enough to awaken her, she said, "[It was] not so loud and sharp that it directed my attention very closely." She heard nothing "unusual" after that.[4]

At 9:30 a.m. the next morning she ate breakfast downstairs with Henry, Minnie, Peter, and Tim, and they all ate dinner together there that afternoon. She noticed that there were "bed clothes downstairs" (sheets, blankets, etc.) and for the first and only time, there were water lilies at the house.[5]

A. H. Griffin, the owner of a gun business and considered an expert on firearms, testified concerning the bullet removed from Tollefson's back. His testimony was the same as it had been during Tim's trial.

Julius C. Heyn, the newly discovered, key witness for the defense, came forward to testify during Peter's trial on Wednesday afternoon, February 8. Not only had he been the first person to arrive at the scene of the crime—he was the only eyewitness. In fact, as his testimony would demonstrate, Julius had the character marks of a true hero. He did not shrink back from the hazardous situation in fear but selflessly ran toward danger in order to help.

The defense had made a very grave error by not recognizing or calling Julius to the witness stand during Tim's trial, but, as previously stated, and for whatever unknown reason, they were not aware of him. Why not? We can only speculate. There had been little time to prepare their case for Tim's trial; Bill Erwin had been ill during most of Tim's trial, and since he wasn't at his best he may have simply overlooked Julius. Whatever the reason, the defense was now fully aware of him and determined to present his testimony to the court.

Julius Heyn had immigrated to the United States from Germany as a teenager, and his native tongue still flavored his speech with a strong accent. Tall, thin, thirty-three years old with a "boyish face, a prominent nose, and light hair," he was the husband of Gertrude and father to their only child, a daughter named Julia. The family had moved from New York to Minneapolis, where Julius was employed as Assistant Superintendent of the Metropolitan Life Insurance Company. By the time of Peter's trial, Minneapolis had been the Heyn family's home for a little over one year.[6]

Julius testified that he had left work on the evening of July 26, 1887, at 11:15 p.m. and boarded the streetcar of John McKinnon in the area near the Milwaukee depot. He exited the streetcar at the turntable on Cedar Avenue near Lake Street about ten or fifteen minutes before midnight and walked to his home at 3009 Cedar Avenue, just 130 feet from the turntable.[7]

Julius entered his house and began to prepare for bed. He had "partly undressed" and gone to relieve himself in the water closet out back when he heard a "scream, which came from the [area of] the turntable." He quickly stepped back out of the privy and, from his backyard, could see a streetcar positioned on the turntable. A pistol fired, and he saw the flash from it. Flustered, he fumbled with the buttons of his pants as he ran through his own yard, into the front yard of his brother Adolf next door, and headed toward the turntable. Before he reached the street, he briefly "stopped to button [his] pants." By then he was so close that he could see "three more [pistol] flashes . . . and heard [the shots] . . . fired in rapid succession.[8]

In the darkness, Julius saw the outlines of two men as they ran away from the turntable up Cedar Avenue and entered Layman's Cemetery on the corner.

The streetcar had completed its turn. Julius said, "I think the time between the first shot . . . and last three shots . . . might [have been] a minute." He added that the two men ran from the "front . . . right-hand side of the car from the same point where the pistol shot was fired."[9]

Julius ran down Cedar Avenue toward the streetcar, but it was harnessed to a very frightened pair of mules and began moving faster. He managed to jump onto the back of the streetcar. "I looked through the door, but did not see the streetcar driver. I assumed he had jumped off in front to follow the assailants, so I jumped off and ran alongside the car toward the cemetery to help." It was a rainy night, and the road was muddied and slick. "I slipped and fell."[10]

"I do not exactly recollect where the two men went, whether they jumped over the fence [to the] right side of the gate, or ran [through] the gate . . . on Cedar Avenue going into the cemetery," he said, and pointed to the gate as it appeared on a map displayed in the court. "What I could see of the men, I thought they were well-built men, and one taller than the other. The man running ahead was the tallest of the two. They had on dark clothes. I could not describe them [further]."[11]

Julius turned his attention back to the rolling, driverless streetcar and decided to stop the car first, then search for the driver to find out what the trouble was. Thinking it might stop at the H & D tracks a short distance ahead, he ran and caught up to it a second time beyond the cemetery, just before the H & D tracks on Cedar Avenue. He hoisted himself aboard and made his way toward the front of the empty, still moving car.

"[I] opened the front door, there finding the driver dead in the box . . . in a sitting position . . . with his cap [slid down] over his face . . . supported by the railing of the car. . . . I then tried to stop the car. One [of the reins had] fallen down and the other [was] up. About the corner of 28th Street and Cedar Avenue I got [the streetcar] stopped."[12]

Charles F. Peters, a nearby neighbor, had stepped outside to check out all the commotion. He also jumped aboard the streetcar, and the two men finally gained control of it and proceeded to drive it up Cedar Avenue, where they eventually met John McKinnon and a policeman.[13]

Julius repeated, "I saw two men distinctly running in front of the car some distance ahead before I got to it; I am sure there were four shots, I saw all four of the flashes; I was summoned to the Coroner's Inquest."[14]

At the end of Julius's statement, Prosecutor Frank Davis took the floor and asked, "When first did you talk to anybody connected with this defense, or interested in them? . . . Had you talked with officers who were prosecuting this case or connected with it? . . . Were you not talked to about this case, before the trial of Timothy Barrett, by [prosecutor] Mr. Jamison?"[15]

Each question was objected to by Bill Erwin and sustained by the Court.

However, when Julius was asked whether he had talked with any officers who were prosecuting this case, he responded, "Yes, sir"—and Frank Davis requested that the answer be stricken from the court documents.[16]

Why would the prosecution not have wanted that information documented? If the prosecution were interested in knowing facts—as they certainly should have been—in order to secure justice for any given crime, wouldn't they have wanted to question the one and only eyewitness to that crime? Julius Heyn's experience that night should have been considered vital information to the law enforcers—unless it didn't fit the prosecutor's narrative, and unless they were just hoping that the defense team would never contact Julius, realizing that his story could blow the cover off their own.

Under cross-examination by Defense Attorney Bill Erwin, Julius repeated much of his previous statement to the Court. He did add one more small, but rather important, detail—he had "testified before the coroner's jury that he thought" he had heard the streetcar driver scream out "murder." He also stated that at the time of the inquest "the facts were all very fresh in my mind. . . . I made my statement under oath and after I had testified, what I said was read over to me and I signed it." He added, "[T]he last three shots were in rapid succession and fired from the same pistol in the same position."[17]

We now know that, according to the only eyewitness, Thomas Tollefson cried out 'murder' before the first shot was ever fired. After that first shot there was no scream—no sound from Tollefson—even though there was a delay of several seconds (perhaps that delay accounted for the time it took the assailants to grab the fares box from Tollefson). Was the first shot fatal? The last three shots were rapidly fired by one shooter, from one gun. There were two assailants, not three, not one.

The defense then questioned Julius Heyn as to whether he had told various others (E. P. Bowditch, G. W. Fassett, anyone else who may have been near the scene that night, or Sophia and Adam Disper) that he had heard only two shots fired. "Did you tell officer Henry Krumweide about what you had heard and seen the night of the murder?"[18]

Julius replied that no, he had not, and added that neither had he made such statements to three other men, whom he identified as Charlie Peters, Frank Stone, and S. T. Littleton.[19]

Bill Erwin continued with repetitious questions regarding the statement Julius had signed at the coroner's inquest. These questions addressed the number of shots fired, the number of men who had run from the scene, and their descriptions. Most of these questions met the objection of the prosecutor, until the Court finally asked Erwin to simply read from the statement Julius had signed, which he then did: ". . . Think there were as many as two men anyway; think they wore black clothes; think they started to run when I got within [fifteen] or [twenty] feet from the door [of the streetcar]." Erwin asked Julius, "In addition to that, did you not state the direction in which they ran?"

But this question was also objected to by the State as "incompetent, irrelevant and immaterial"—which the Court sustained.[20]

Over the course of this examination other bits of information provided included the "planks across the [streetcar] track between 24th and 25th Streets" that Julius and another man had removed after the crime.[21]

Erwin asked Julius whether his eyesight was good, and he replied that it was. Referring to the number of pistol flashes and the number of shots fired, he asked Julius, "If you might have been deceived by an echo, you would not have been deceived in your eyesight, would you, on the flashes?"[22]

He also asked how many people Julius had told about his experience that night.

Julius replied, "I am not sure. I told a great many people."[23]

Julius talked about Mrs. Disper, indicating that he knew her and that he "saw her in the neighborhood . . . where" the streetcar finally stopped on Franklin Avenue." He said, "[She] took me over to her house and got some shoes and stockings for me."[24]

He admitted that he had talked about what happened but that he didn't recall whether he had talked about the number of shots fired because they were interrupted mid-conversation when the "patrol wagon came out." He claimed he had no personal conversation about the crime with Adam Disper or Officer Krumweide that night, but rather had talked "to a crowd." He could not remember the exact conversation with C. F. Peters since he was "quite . . . excited" by the time he got into Mr. Peters' house that night.[25, 26]

Julius had initially forgotten who S. T. Littleton was during the previous day's questioning, but after thinking about it he remembered. The two had talked while riding the Cedar Avenue streetcar, but it had been months since they had last spoken.

Julius said, "I never told anybody that I saw one shot fired as I was running towards the car; never told anybody that I only saw one man there."[27]

The testimony of Julius Heyn contradicted that of Henry Barrett on this key point. How could both Tim and Peter have been present with Henry if only two men accosted Thomas? The story Henry had told of Peter running along with him from the scene into the cemetery while leaving Tim behind with the streetcar driver may have sounded believable as far as the prosecution was concerned, but Julius Heyn's sworn, presumably unbiased, eyewitness testimony proves otherwise.

The testimony of E. A. Mitchell somewhat corroborated the testimony of Heyn. On the night of the crime, Mitchell was walking up Cedar Avenue around midnight. Somewhere between 24th and 25th Streets he had heard a sound he described as a "roar" just before a scream, followed by a gunshot, more screams, two more shots fired in rapid succession—and then no more screams. Mitchell thought it had sounded like a woman's screams. Then came a streetcar. It passed him and at that point jumped the tracks. He ran to it, hopped on board the back of the car and met Heyn, who told him the driver had been shot. Mitchell, a nurse, quickly went up to check on the driver but found him dead, sitting on one leg, and leaned over.[28]

>─┼─◆>─O─<◆─┼─<

Police Officer Daniel Day was called forward as a witness for the defense during Peter's trial, even though he had testified on behalf of the State during Tim's trial. He replied to Erwin's questions concerning the search of Mud Lake in mid-November: "[We looked] for a tin box; there were four [officers] besides myself; we looked for a post that stood in the lake; understood that there was some tin deposited near there; found the post . . . [but] found no pieces of tin. Henry Barrett directed us [as to] what portion of the lake to examine; Mr. Hankinson, Sergeant Coscran, Levi Gorman and myself were the officers; we had two scoops [that] worked nicely. . . . [W]e looked [for] an hour and a half. . . . The men worked hard and continuously while we were at the spot."[29]

In consideration of the apparatus used and effort made, Bill Erwin asked, "If there had been any tin in the designated spot, should you not have found it?"

However, Davis objected and the Court sustained.

In cross-examination Daniel Day stated, "This lake covers thirty or forty acres; the bottom is very muddy and weedy; the mud is very thin and very deep; it froze up so we could not make further search."[30]

>─┼─◆>─O─<◆─┼─<

A. C. Silverthorn, a witness for the State during Peter's trial, identified himself as a "special police [officer] for [the] Milwaukee Railroad" who had been on the force for four years. He stated, "I lived at 2228 22½ Avenue South; on the night of July 26th I was near the corner of 28th Street and Fort Avenue; about [midnight] I heard a pistol shot in the direction of the turntable and then a scream and then another pistol shot; only two in all." (The Hub of Hell was located near 28th Street and Fort Avenue.)[31]

Bill Erwin questioned him: "[Were you] discharged from the police force, because you were neglectful of your duties as a policeman?"[32]

A. C. Silverthorn replied, "I guess not."[33]

It seemed a rather timid and unsatisfactory response. Was he hiding something?

Erwin then asked why he had been discharged. The State objected, claiming the question to be "incompetent, irrelevant, immaterial, and not cross examination." The Court sustained the objection.[34]

John Lally, a grocer who lived at 121 Cedar Avenue, was a character witness for the defense. He testified, "I know Henry Barrett; have known him for about three years; I know his general reputation in the community where he lives, for truth and veracity, is bad."[35]

In cross-examination Lally said, ""The people I have heard talk about him said different things; one said he was a hard ticket, others that he was a scoundrel, no good and such things."[36]

Bill Erwin pressed further regarding Henry's reputation. "How, generally, have you heard [people talk] about him in the community? . . . Is it not a fact that you have heard him so generally described as a hard case that you are not able to specify particularly at once and the times when you heard it? . . . How long has this reputation affected him in the community . . . ? [A]t the other trial, did you not answer, 'Oh, there [are] all the people in the vicinity in which he lived?'"[37]

Each question was abruptly halted by objection from the State as "incompetent, immaterial and irrelevant," and the Court sustained each one. Obviously, the prosecution did not want the reputation of its star witness to be considered by the jury when they decided the verdict.[38]

John H. Long testified on behalf of the defendant. He had once been Henry's attorney and had known him since 1884. He told the court, "I was acquainted with [Henry's] reputation, truth and veracity at the time; it was bad; I would not, on the reputation of his character, believe him under oath. . . . I was attorney in some liquor case in which he was interested and at that time I heard officers and the prosecuting attorney say that he was a liar; I did not know him before that; never lived in the neighborhood; lived about three miles from his place."[39]

Another brief testimony concerning Henry Barrett's character came from a painter named W. H. Farney. He "[had] lived at 2845 16th Avenue South [for] four years . . . [knew] nothing about the reputation of Henry Barrett, . . .[had] heard people say generally about him, and . . . he would not believe him under oath."[40]

Mary Barrett-Coleman took the stand and testified, "I am the daughter of Mrs. [Ellen] Barrett and of John Barrett; lived on the 26th of July, 1887, at 26th Street and Fort Avenue, live there now; was at home on that day; saw my brothers Timothy and Pete on that night at 11 o'clock; they came from the City; Timothy was drunk or under the influence of liquor; he came into the room and was telling about the fire; was noisy; I told him to go to bed."[41]

Erwin once again raised questions regarding Timothy's intellect: "What is [his] usual condition as to being simple or bright minded?" He asked Mary, "[Did the family consider that Tim bordered] on idiocy? . . . . [Had they] . . . talked about sending him to the insane asylum, and . . . [tried] to get him there?"[42]

Each question was objected to by the State, and each time the Court sustained.

Mary stated, "The boys talked about the fire when they came home that night; that was the first time I ever heard about the Boston [Block] fire; the boys came before the doctor. . . . I told the doctor to call them in; I told him they were my brothers; I was in bed until the 3rd or 4th of August with sickness; on the 28th of July, Henry and another man came up there with some pond lilies; I was in the room at the time; the man's name was Murphy; I learned it at the time; I did not pay much attention to him; my impression is that he is a tall man; Timothy was home a long time before they came; this stranger went away first, I suppose; he went away first; I think Timothy went out with Henry up to the saloon. I remember before Henry was married, his having trouble with my father, and shooting at him; it was two or three years ago, it may be four; that was before I was married; I lived at father's place at the saloon."[43]

The State objected "on the ground that it is incompetent and immaterial," and yet again the Court sustained the objection.[44]

Erwin quickly countered, "I do not think the State had any right to make this objection now; that he is stopped from making it, and I want to state on the record because he did not make the motion when it was inquired of Henry, and admitted to be asked of Henry by me, and examined on that subject, and got his version of, and having obtained his version he is stopped from shutting out my contradiction of that version; it is too late for the State to interpose this objection, having brought out from Henry a full description of this matter upon their own motion; I now move to strike out the entire explanation which Henry made to the State in relation to this matter."[45]

However, Erwin's motion was denied by the Court.

Erwin asked Mary about the incident in which Henry had shot at their father, John Barrett, during an argument. "[Had John] tried to get the revolver away from Henry, when Henry shot at him? . . . Did you, afterwards, ask Henry if he intended to kill his father?"[46]

Once again the State objected to his questions and the Court sustained.

Mary said, "I know my mother and Henry had trouble about the saloon and about other matters. There has been trouble between Henry and mother for years; I know of trouble as late as in August."[47]

Erwin proceeded to ask about the nature of the trouble between Henry and his mother, and how long it had gone on. Again the State objected, so Mary was unable to answer.

However, the direct examination resumed. Bill Erwin wasted no time loading his questions with information for the jury to ponder, even though, of course, each question was systematically objected to by the State:

"What acts [did] Henry [do] towards your mother, showing hostility or hatred?"

"Do you know of Henry [trying] to rob your mother?"

"[Did he] make an attempt to kill her, and [had] Peter interfered and protected her?"[48]

"You may state if you know [of] any acts [of] . . . Henry's hostility to Peter . . . within five years . . . four years . . . three years . . . two years?"

Mary was finally able to reply, "Since last July, they had a quarrel at the saloon and he abused Pete, and said that he was the cause of the quarrel, that he had no business here, that he ought to stay in Omaha, and he ought to be content there without coming here."[49]

The cross-examination by the State resumed at that point, and Mary's opening statements were, "Tim went away on the 27th about noon; I am pretty sure about that; he ate breakfast downstairs, and I ate breakfast upstairs; I heard my brother Pete swear [so] here."[50]

This brought up a somewhat tiring and tedious line of questioning by the State as to where Tim had eaten breakfast. Had he done so at Mary's place, or at Henry's? Who went away first, Peter or Timothy? Those questions aimed to cast doubt on the important aspects of the testimony given by Mary and her brothers simply because of irrelevant inconsistencies in their recollections about breakfast. Timothy had stated that he had eaten breakfast at Henry's, and Pete had testified that he had not seen Timothy until he went up to Henry's place. Mary replied that she did not know whether the two brothers had seen each other that morning. How could she have? She was, after all, sick in bed—and that is where she had eaten her breakfast that morning.

Breakfast certainly seemed to have been an important matter to Frank Davis!

The prosecutor then turned his questioning toward the dictation of a letter. Had Mary dictated "a letter to Chloe Betts to be sent to [her] sister in Council Bluffs?"[51]

"I am willing to write some on a piece of paper for you." And Mary was allowed to do so, dispelling any insinuation that she was unable to write.[52]

Had a letter been written by Chloe on account of Mary's illness?

What was the point of this question, and where would the prosecutor have gone with it if Mary had not been able to write?

Bill Erwin resumed his examination briefly by touching on key points of Mary's testimony. She had said, "On the 26th, 27th, and 28th of July, I was sick at my own house." Erwin mentioned the incidents of July 26th: the Boston Block fire; the doctor's visit; and Tim's noisy demeanor as her brothers both talked with her that night. He then turned to the events of July 28th: the water lilies Mary was given as she lay sick in bed and the "man named Murphy [who] was introduced to" her. He then concluded his examination of Mary.[53]

Mr. J. C. McCall was sworn in on behalf of the defendant and testified that "he [had] lived for five years in the neighborhood of Henry Barrett and that he knew his reputation for truth and veracity; that it is bad, and that he would not . . . believe Barrett under oath."[54]

Under cross-examination he added, "I have heard two men speak about his truthfulness; that was since the trial of Timothy Barrett." He also noted that Henry "had a reputation as to being a hard case prior to the trial of [Timothy]."[55]

The prosecution made a great effort to discredit McCall's opinion since it only had been formed on the basis of the talk of two other men who knew Henry Barrett personally. He reasoned that perhaps it was an unfair assumption, considering that a man's reputation took time to build. However, McCall stood by his claim that Henry Barrett had a bad reputation and was known to be a liar.

George Coleman, who had been sick with pneumonia during Tim's trial, was finally well and able to testify for the defense during Peter's. By that time, he and Mary Barrett were married. He was described as having a "rather good Irish face, . . . evidently a workingman"—which may have meant that he had a muscular build. George remembered the night of the Boston Block fire, how Mary was ill and Dr. Heflin had made a house call to her. He did not actually see the doctor but heard him talking. George had gone to bed early that night but knew "the boys came in about 11 o'clock." Tim came into his room and slept with him. George said, "[I] got up at 6 o'clock the next morning and

Tim was then sleeping soundly." He was also sure that Pete was in the house at that time.[56]

John Barrett took the stand in defense of his youngest son, Pete, and testified the same as he had during Tim's trial—mainly, that Henry had lied under oath.

At fifty-two years old, the Irish immigrant still spoke with a heavy accent, his voice so soft he could barely be heard. Looking down, he held one hand over his eyes, as though embarrassed. Understandably so, as he explained to the court about meeting with Henry on January 8 in the front room of the Gault House. About fifty other people were in the same room at the time, during which the two had a private conversation. Henry told him that both Tim and Pete had been physically intimate with Minnie and Chloe. He was outraged—as any husband would be—and told his father he would get revenge. Henry was also upset with his mother because she held the mortgage to the Fort Avenue property and had foreclosed on it that fall while he was in jail. Tim and Pete had been put in charge of running the saloon. Henry was obviously jealous, angered, and insulted at the thought of losing the saloon—something he had worked at and considered his own—to his younger brothers.[57]

On another note, Henry admitted that Julius Heyn "was a good man who could not be bought and that he would contradict [Henry's] story."[58]

During that same January conversation, Henry told his father about meeting Patrick McLaughlin on the night of July 26. John relayed the information to Erwin, and that is how the defense was tipped off to secure McLaughlin as a witness. (Of course, Henry later denied having met McLaughlin on that night.)[59]

One other important point of John's February 13 testimony concerned Peter Barrett's age. John said his son would turn seventeen in 1888.

Was Peter only sixteen years old at the time of his trial?

Peter Barrett in the Hennepin County Jail.

Source: *St. Paul Daily Globe*, March 17, 1889, p. 1,
Library of Congress, Chronicling America, http://chroniclingamerica.loc.gov
image provided by Minnesota Historical Society, St. Paul, MN.

PETER: IN HIS OWN WORDS

FOLLOWING ARE the somewhat jumbled, but nonetheless exact words of Peter Barrett, as recorded in the transcripts of his trial at the Hennepin County Courthouse in the winter of 1888. (Added or changed words, done strictly for clarification, appear within brackets.) Peter testified,

[I was] arrested in Omaha; Kinney, Hoy and Howard, I think, brought me here. [It happened] about noon, [as I was] eating my dinner; I had some liquor on the way here; I did not drink, but they offered it to me; Kinney and Howard had the whiskey and offered it to me; I am 16 years old past; came on a night train [from Omaha], got here about 8 or 9 o'clock in the morning; I am not acquainted with this city; on the way up here they had some cigars and gave me some, and offered me whiskey, and kept talking to me about this

murder, what I knew about it; they offered to turn me loose
in Omaha if I would tell them; they had a story they [were]
telling me, if it was so, if it was something just as Henry
told here; they told me that Henry told them that it was me
that shot Tollefson; they said if I would tell them how it was
done they would turn me loose; on the train they offered
me money; I think it was Kinney that first mentioned it;
they said they would give me money to tell him who done
this; when I got here I was taken out to the police station;
I got there about 9 o'clock; they brought me in there, and
there were more fellows there; there was a big crowd,12 or
15 in there; they took me into the back room, sat down, and
all started talking to me, one at a time, talking about the
murder, and how it was done, saying that Henry said it was
me and Tim; they told me to tell it and they would turn me
loose, if I did not, I was going to be hung, there was a mob
outside going to hang me; there was noise around there; it
appeared to be upstairs; it appeared to be the rattling of
shovels and jumping round—men's feet on the floor; I believe it was Howard who told me they would take me out
the back window, if I would tell, and let me go; I was not
in a cell room; there was a table and chairs in where I was;
they said the mob was trying to get in, or trying to find out
whether I was in there or not; Pretty near all that was in
there, I guess talked to me; Howard and Jamison, that is all
about whose names I know; they did not take me before the
Court before they talked to me; they did not send out for a
lawyer, or for a friend to stay with me the time they talked
with me; they did not have any authority from anybody to
talk to me that I know of; I got here on Saturday; I was taken
before the Court at 9 o'clock Monday morning; all day on
Saturday they kept talking to me until about 1 o'clock, then
they gave me dinner and locked me up; I saw Mr. Donahue

that evening, Saturday evening, with my father, about 5
o'clock; there was not a witness produced against me at the
Municipal Court; they called me up and read something
and put my hearing for trial for 10 days; Mr. Jamison done
that; I was indicted before the 10 days expired; I never had
a hearing before a Justice; the first time either Timothy or
myself was tried was the last month; I was born in Mills
County, Iowa, about 30 miles below Omaha, on this side
of the Missouri River; I have lived in Omaha [six] years
with my mother; my father has been in Minneapolis most of
the time; Henry has been here during that time; father and
mother were divorced and I remained with mother; Henry
went with father; when Henry left I was so small I could
not remember anything about him hardly; we have never
associated much together as brothers until I came here this
spring; I don't think I was here over a month before this in
all my life; I came up in June the first time; stayed here two
or three weeks; I went down to Omaha, and I returned on
the 8th of July, I think; Mrs. Coleman is my sister who lives
here; mother sent me up here; she said she was coming up
shortly afterwards, that she was coming to take this place
from the old man, and to give it to us.[1]

Bill Erwin questioned Peter regarding the taking of his father's
place of business.

Peter explained,

We were talking about the subject, and we got a letter
from mother a short time after we came up here; after we
talked about it, the old man gave us two boys the place and
Henry and the old man had a little quarrel about the place;
Henry was mad at us on account of coming up here and father giving us the place; he said he did not think it was right;

I stayed at Mrs. [Mary Barrett] Coleman's when I came here; she was running a boarding house when I came here; Henry was working in the saloon for father.[2]

Bill Erwin asked, "Did your mother have a claim on the property?"[3] Peter replied,

> Yes, my mother had a lien on the property; it was for $1,000.00, I believe, I don't know exactly; Timothy and I went back to Omaha; the letter to Henry was the second time we came up; Henry was mad at my father and mad at me and Tim, both; I did not go around town a great deal between the 8th and the 26th of July; I was at Henry's place part of the time, and Mary's part of the time, and up town some of the while; I do not know the streets of the city; have no general acquaintance of them; have not studied the map of the city; I remember of the Big Boston [Block] fire; I heard Henry testify against me; I heard him testify that at a place near the corner of 29th and Cedar Avenue we boys talked about stopping a car for the purpose of robbing; that is not true; the first time I have heard of it, was when he got up on the stand against Tim; it is not true that we three came up to Lally Brother's and went down Second Avenue; went around the block and then came out on Washington Avenue, and took a Blooming-ton Avenue car and rode out to Franklin Avenue; no part of it is true . . . nothing he says in reference to Tim and me, being connected with the homicide, is true, not a word of it; I was not on Cedar Avenue and Lake Street that night.[4]

Erwin asked, "Do you know any reason why you should not be believed as well as that man Henry?"[5]

Frank Davis objected to the question, claiming again that it was "immaterial, incompetent and irrelevant."

And the Court sustained the motion.

When Erwin continued to ask Pete whether he had any hatred for Henry, or whether he thought Henry had made statements based on his own hatred toward Pete and the family, these, too, were met with objections that were sustained.

So Erwin tried one more angle: "Was there any other foundation and cause, so far as you can see, for Henry's hate, or perhaps his desire to save himself?"[6]

However, Davis objected to that question as well, and the Court, again, sustained the motion.

Peter's final comment at that time was, "I had no hand in or was I present or had any knowledge, or in any way aid, or assist in the plot or . . . contrive or conspire in the murder of Thomas Tollefson; I did not know anything about it until the next morning."[7]

Peter had stated that ". . . it is not true that we three came up to Lally Brother's. . . ." Yet at a later point during his trial he recalled having done so and gave information that corroborated Timothy's testimony. Did he knowingly contradict himself? Did he intentionally lie? Or had he simply made a minor error, a slip of the tongue, in his earlier statement? That the brothers stopped in at Lally Brothers saloon on the evening of July 26, 1887, was vital information. Lally Brothers saloon was where, according to Peter's later testimony (and Tim's, previously), two men, identified simply as Murphy and Hart, had approached Henry.

Pete recalled, "Henry set up the beer. I told Tim I wanted to get some clothes." Tim agreed to go with him. "Before we went out, I noticed two men in there speaking to Henry; after we had drank this first beer the two men came up to Henry and said, 'good evening Reddy'; he said good evening and then set up the beer and five of us drank that time."[8]

Peter testified, "[I] did not take much notice of the [two] men . . . [but that one] was a big man and had a black mustache and the other was smaller."[9]

Tim and Pete finished their beer, told Henry they would be back, and left. Henry stayed there in the company of Murphy and Hart.

Pete was unfamiliar with the street names but told of how they walked a few blocks and he "bought a suit of clothes," which took about a half hour. When they returned to Lally Brothers saloon Henry was gone, and so were Murphy and Hart. Why didn't Henry wait? It is possible that the three men left together. Even if they had left separately within the half hour, they could have easily met up somewhere else. If so, they could very well have been Henry's accomplices in Tollefson's murder.

Since Henry had already gone, Tim and Pete left as well. The two walked over to watch the Boston Block fire for a while, dropped by a few saloons, and then rode a streetcar "on the river side and went home." Peter said they rode all the way to their sister's house.[10]

When he and Tim arrived they learned that Mary was sick. They went upstairs to her room to check on her and told her about the fire.

Pete admitted that they both drank some beer earlier that night. He recalled, "Tim was pretty drunk . . . Tim is easily affected with liquor. . . . [He] drank several times before [we boarded the streetcar to come home]."[11]

Pete continued, "[The] doctor came after we [were] there a while, it was about half an hour after I got there before I went to bed." Tim also went to bed, but the two brothers did not share the same room. "I think [Tim] slept with [George] Coleman."[12]

Once again, defense attorney Erwin addressed the matter of Tim's mental limitations: "[H]as he not always been regarded as a simple-minded boy?" He continued by asking whether Tim was considered "bright-minded or simple-minded" and "whether it is not possible for Timothy to go through one day and tell at the close of the day without great mistakes and many mistakes what happened to him that day. . . . [H]e cannot go through the events of this night coherently on account of a defect in his memory?"[13]

But each question prompted an objection from Prosecutor Davis, and each objection was sustained by the Court.

Bill Erwin persisted, telling Judge Lochren, "For the purpose of illustrating the character of the mistake made by Timothy in his speech, I ask the question whether Timothy was not mistaken in his testimony, that he did not eat breakfast there, this being one of the immaterial facts that he was mistaken on."[14]

But the Court would not hear the argument: "We will not waste anymore time with Timothy's testimony, it is entirely immaterial."[15]

Peter testified concerning the days following Thomas Tollefson's murder. "[On July 27] I got up about 6 or 7 o'clock . . . went to talk with [Mary] a while; went to Henry's place, down to the saloon. . . . Tim was there." He said that Henry and Tim had eaten breakfast there. Peter continued, "On the 28th I was at Mary's place part of the time and at Henry's place part of the time; I was there and Henry and Timothy came back from some place in the afternoon."[16]

At this point in the testimony, attorney Erwin brought up the subject of the water lilies and asked, "Did Henry say that he got them [from] the lake?"[17]

The State objected to this line of questioning and, again, the Court sustained the motion.

Peter continued,

> I saw two or three packages of streetcar checks after the 26th of July in the middle drawer behind the bar in the saloon, but I do not know who put them there; Henry had the possession of the drawer most of the time; I don't know how they got in the drawer; I heard Henry, on or about the last of July, in the presence of my father, John Barrett and Timothy curse my mother, call her bad names, and declare to us all that she was not going to give him any of her property, and then said she had put $1000 out of his pocket. He said he would kill her, if he had to go to Omaha to do so; on the same afternoon, while Henry and I were looking for four-leafed clover, he told me he would kill the old lady if he had to go to Omaha; that he would have the place only for her, and that she would not live to give me all her property; I have never spoke to Henry since I was arrested."[18]

Erwin asked, "Has [Henry] done anything . . . shown any brotherly affection . . . since you have been accused, or kindness of any kind? . . . Has there not been an entire absence of any attention to you on the part of your brother's family, since you were accused, evincing a hardened nature?"[19]

Frank Davis objected again, claiming that Erwin's questions were "incompetent, irrelevant, and immaterial." And Judge Lochren, again, ruled in the prosecutor's favor.[20]

Peter was then cross-examined by Frank Davis. He began by asking him about his age and where he had been born.

"I know where I was born, I knew that before the last trial. . . . I said I did not know exactly how old I was."[21]

Davis asked, "[When] you say you are [sixteen] years old, that is a guess upon the subject of age?"[22]

Pete replied, "Yes, sir. . . . [T]hey never asked . . . how old I was in the office of the sheriff."[23]

(The 1870 United States Census record for Oak Township, Mills County, Iowa, indicates that Peter was born in February 1870.)[24]

Davis persisted questioning Pete about whether he had told anyone that he was either seventeen or eighteen years old.

Erwin objected to the questions as "immaterial."

But Judge Lochren overruled defense attorney Erwin's motion.

Questioning then turned to the arrest in Omaha. Pete repeated his earlier testimony regarding the train ride back to Minnesota, when the officers drank whiskey and offered it to him. "[I] drank a little of it [but not] enough to affect my mind in any way . . . did not take it more than once on the way."[25]

Davis mocked, "Had a bar on board, did they?"[26]

Erwin objected, "[This is an] open attempt to ridicule the testimony and disgrace the Court." However, the Court overruled Erwin again.[27]

Peter continued, "[I was taken to the] North Side [Police] Station. [Officer James Howard] said if [I] would tell who committed the murder they would let [me] loose, also that there was a mob outside [who wanted to hang me] and that they would let me out of the window; this was all said in the presence of the other officers and Jamison; I heard no shouts outside or voices; other officers came in, but made no demonstrations, the only noises I heard were like shovels scraping on the floor above; we were in a basement."[28]

Peter then answered Frank Davis's questions regarding the days immediately following Tollefson's murder: "Sometime after July 26th, Henry moved to Northfield and Tim and I went with him; while in Minneapolis, Tim and I stayed at either my sister's or at Henry's. After [going] to Northfield I went to Omaha and stayed there until I was arrested. All the statements that I heard Henry make about mother and me were made before going to Northfield."[29]

Regarding the events of the night of the murder, July 26, Peter said,

> I know Cedar Avenue, Fort Avenue and Washington Avenue; know where the turntable on Cedar Avenue is; know the country between the turntable and Henry's house, the saloon. When we left the house that night, Henry had a stick, it was dark when we reached Cedar Avenue; Tim was drunk and noisy when we got to my sister's that night; on the other trial I did not describe the shorter man who we met in Lally Brothers saloon; when Tim and I were going to [Mary's] that night we met two men going in our direction and Tim spoke to them. Dr. Heflin came to see sister after we got home.[30]

Attorney Davis redirected his questions to the time Pete had spent at Northfield with Henry and about a quarrel the two brothers had while there. Pete claimed it was about boarding. Davis asked, "The trouble was about boarding and not about your mother's property, the way she would dispose of it?"[31]

Pete insisted, "[The quarrel had started about] boarding and then we got to talking about different things; he blamed it on me on account of him going . . . to Northfield; he said the old lady came up here, and he would have stayed [if it hadn't been] for me."[32]

Pete claimed that when he got up the morning after the murder Tim was not at Mary's house.

Attorney Davis then referred to a conversation involving Henry, John Barrett, Tim, and Pete that took place on the front porch of Henry's house. "In the conversation that you had there on the porch, Henry was talking to the old man; he said the old man did not do right, cursed the old man and said that he would kill the old lady, if he had to go to Omaha to do it; the old man walked around and talked to Henry, and Henry got mad at the old man and cursed the old man?"[33]

Peter replied, "Tim talked to him . . . and he quit then. I told [Henry] it was not a nice way to talk about his mother; told him she was not the cause of his moving out of the place."[34]

At that time Henry was also concerned about some furniture he had recently purchased on credit and feared it would be taken away, which added to his hostility. That same day Mrs. Barrett came and confronted Henry about the matter. Pete, Tim, Henry, and John were all present.

Pete said, "She was talking to [Henry] about . . . [the] furniture [which cost $100]. Henry only paid $25 down on it, and had signed Tim's name, and mother was afraid Tim would get into trouble about it and it would be Henry's fault. [But Tim assured her] it would be all right and that there would be no trouble about it." She disagreed and warned Henry that "he never would have the furniture if she could help it." Pete recalled Henry threatening that "[h]e would throw her out if she did not keep still."[35]

Frank Davis redirected his questions back to the statements Peter had made to the officers at the North Side Police Station in Minneapolis after he was arrested and brought back to the city. The officers present at the time were identified as Michael Hoy, James Howard, John Hoy, J. W. Hankinson, L. W. Kinney, and Jacob Hein; the group also included Davis's assistant Attorney Robert Jamison. Davis asked, "Did you not on the 26th of November, 1887 . . . state a response to the inquiry made . . . by Mr. Jamison, 'I was in the City of Minneapolis at the time Tollefson was murdered; I did not hear of the murder until the morning after it occurred, I remember where I was, and what I did the night of the murder'?"[36]

At this point Bill Erwin exclaimed, "I object, Your Honor, on the ground that it is already in evidence, and the defendant was under duress, and in such a condition under such surroundings, threats and intimidations, nothing extorted from him on that occasion under the policy of the law could be made testimony against him for any purpose." Peter had no lawyer present with him when the statement was written; regardless, Judge Lochren overruled Erwin's objection.[37]

Erwin responded, "Counsel for the defendant requests to cross-examine the witness as to the condition of the witness's mind, and from what was done and said there before the admission of the testimony, and what was said by the witness against himself."[38]

Judge Lochren replied, "The Court denies the right to cross examine; the Court allows the counsel for the State to go on."[39]

Bill Erwin responded by asking to call Robert Jamison to the witness stand. With the attorney under oath, his testimony could prove that several officers had surrounded and intimidated Peter during his interrogation at the police station. Jamison had been present and witnessed the scene. The police had a story—the one Henry had told—and did all they could to get Peter to admit guilt. They had already plied him with whiskey on the train, hoping for a drunken confession, but Peter would not drink more than a swallow. At the police station, they had passed the whiskey bottle among themselves, threatened that a mob was about to lynch him, and bribed him with freedom, but Peter made no confession. Attorney Jamison had even offered to show favor to Peter—*because he was so young*—if he would confess, but he refused.

Erwin stated that he also wanted to question officers Hein, Howard, Hoy, and Kinney, in order to expose their unethical tactics, such as the use of whiskey and their attempts to terrify Peter. He would demonstrate to the Court that, based on their testimony, any statements his client had made during the police interrogation should be considered "absolutely worthless and improperly obtained."[40]

Judge Lochren then asked Frank Davis, "[Have you] any objection to [Erwin's] offer to call them out?"[41]

Davis replied, "Yes, sir. I think it was out of order, we do not intend to prove a confession."[42]

Erwin countered, "I make the further objection that there is no proper foundation laid for the admission of any testimony of this kind; that it is irrelevant, incompetent, and improper."[43]

Once again, the Court overruled Erwin's objection.

Peter then replied to Frank Davis's previous questions. "I told [Jamison] I did not hear of the murder until the morning afterwards; I said most of what you have asked me, I think; I could not say how many men were there or what their names were."[44]

He also answered questions regarding the women who had been at Henry's place on the night of the murder and watched as the three brothers left together to go into the city. Peter identified them as Minnie Barrett, Chloe Betts, and Lottie Welch. Frank Davis tried to trip up Pete's testimony, to get him to alter his confession, in a manipulative manner. He suggested that there was yet another woman, a Mrs. McLeod, present that night at the Hub of Hell (she had not actually been there). He repeated the sequence of events in a different order, such as when the brothers viewed the fire and went "uptown," and even added their return to Henry's saloon that night (things Peter had not said). Davis even implied that Pete had stated, "When we started out that evening Tim had a revolver, a Smith and Wesson . . . revolver, single action, and. . . [that] before or after the murder . . . Tim cut his initials, 'T.B.' in the handle."[45]

However, Peter firmly denied all of this.

Davis persisted, "Did you not . . . in response to an inquiry by Mr. Jamison, say, 'At the time of starting out that evening Henry also had a revolver and the butt end of a billiard cue; the revolver that Henry had was one I bought downtown a short time before Tollefson was killed; it was a red-handled revolver and although Henry had it that night it was mine; he gave it to me after Tollefson was killed and I lost it riding on a freight car in Northern Nebraska'?"[46]

Pete answered, "No sir, I didn't."[47]

Davis continued, asking him whether he had told Jamison that he had heard "two shots on the night of the murder" while he was back at home "sitting in the house."

Pete denied this also.

Davis asked him whether he had told Jamison that he remembered how "the second day after the murder . . . Henry and Tim started away together; they were gone two or three hours, when they returned they had a large number of water lilies" like those found in the lakes in the area?[48]

"Not all of that, [though] I did say that they had some water lilies," Pete replied.

Reading through the court transcripts gave an exceptional view of the dramatic trial. Some may say that the ways in which Frank Davis wove deception into his questioning were nothing short of skillfully shrewd and cunning, enabling him to cast deep shadows of doubt all over Peter's testimony—marks of an experienced and polished attorney.

Maybe so . . . but then, the trial wasn't over yet . . .

ERWIN'S STRONG DEFENSE

ERWIN HAD watched somewhat helplessly as Davis blew holes in his client's testimony. He had waited for the State's witnesses to testify, and in time they were sworn in. Eventually came the time for cross-examination, and Erwin was ready. He claimed that both Police Captain James Hankinson, who was the head of the Detective Department, and fellow Detective James Howard were not only lax in their duties, they had been manipulated and baited by the informant, Henry Barrett.

Detective Howard testified that Captain Hankinson, Assistant Prosecutor Jamison, and he had been with Henry at the house on Fort Avenue. (The Barrett's house had been built to replace the original one that had burned down. The cellar had been partly filled in, and what remained was little more than a hole beneath the floor, accessed by a narrow passageway near the stairs.) The men followed Henry down into the cellar. Detective Howard said they found a half-dozen streetcar checks, or tickets "on the ground . . . scattered around a circle of about two and a half feet."[1]

Erwin called attention to what he considered a serious error in judgment; Henry should not have gone down ahead of them, perhaps should not even have been present at all during the search.

Henry informed the detectives that he had placed one check in a certain corner of the cellar, but although they searched, the men could not find it. A couple of days later they went back down into the cellar to take another look and found the check, even though it was not where Henry had first indicated.

Concerning the second search, Erwin asked, "Did you search [Henry] before he went into the cellar?"[2]

They had not.

"Do you call that good detective work, in this case?" Erwin continued, "Is it not sometimes too much of a habit of detectives to believe readily without much proof, the story of some informer, and unwittingly lend themselves to brace and fix up a story? Would it not have been better to have searched [Henry] before he went down cellar, to see that he had no checks about him, to scatter underneath the house before you three came down? Is it not the practice of you detectives to credit informants rather than to discredit them in their story? . . . I ask if it is not too much the habit of detectives, and are they not too prone to lend themselves to, the story of an informer and treat him as a man who may be trying to absolve himself from guilt and give him his own sweet will?"[3, 4]

Naturally Frank Davis objected to Erwin's questions, and the Court sided with the prosecutor once again. In fact, according to the court transcripts I have reviewed, it appears that this happened the vast majority of the time; rarely did the Court allow the objections made by the defense to stand. Yet Erwin seemed more determined than ever, and he and his defense team built momentum as the final days of Peter's trial ensued.

One reporter commented, "The defense is beginning to show its hand and the case looks decidedly interesting. For the first time some of the ground seems to be cut from under Reddy, and the witnesses are people who will be readily believed."[5]

These witnesses included carpenter Patrick McLaughlin, a Civil War veteran. At the time of the crime, he lived near the intersection of 32nd Street and 21st Avenue, but moved to Hopkins (thirteen miles from Minneapolis) in mid-August of 1887. Although he had kept quiet about what he knew until after Tim's trial, he was considered to be the second most important witness for the defense during Peter's trial. Bill Erwin suggested that he had remained silent because he was afraid of Henry Barrett. Patrick knew Henry well, had often patronized the Hub of Hell saloon over the course of four years and often talked with him over a beer . . . but he had never uttered a word about the night of the crime.

Patrick McLaughlin, a veteran of the Grand Army of the Republic, testified that on the night of July 26, 1887, he had attended a meeting of the C. C. Washburn G.A.R. post. While on his way home from that meeting he had stopped briefly for a glass of beer at Brown's saloon, which sat at the corner of Franklin and Cedar Avenues.

Afterward, he had walked down the left-hand (east) side of Cedar Avenue toward Lake Street and when he reached the turntable at the corner there, he started across the prairie toward his house. Somewhere between the turntable and the bandstand he met three men and passed within a few feet of them. Apparently McLaughlin had cast too long a glance in their direction, and one of the men remarked, "[W]hat is the damned fool looking for?" while another quickly replied, "shut up"—and McLaughlin was sure that man was Henry Barrett.[6]

McLaughlin further testified,

> [This occurred about] 11 o'clock; I know Henry Barrett;
> I have known him for four years [thought] I saw him . . .
> near the turntable . . . a little off Lake and a little east of Ce-
> dar; there were two people with him; could not tell who. I
> was about five feet, I judge, from him; I thought it was him
> and I think so yet. One of the men with him was taller than

[Henry], the other was not as big. He was not as big as either of the other two. I do not think either of the other men was Peter Barrett. I went home after seeing these men. . . . [I]t was [twenty] minutes past 11 [o'clock] when I got home. My wife was in the house. I lit my pipe and sat on the steps to have a smoke; my wife sat alongside me. [We] sat there about two minutes, [and] a wagon passed, [after that] I heard a shot, and a little while after there was three shots. I heard a howl between the first shot and the three shots. I am sure I heard four shots altogether.[7]

He added, "I had known Henry Barrett four years; knew Tim and Pete slightly . . . had often been at the house, 2830 Fort Avenue and talked with Henry . . . never said anything to anyone about this until a short time ago. [On the night of the crime it was] dark . . . [I was only a] few feet from the men." Although he believed one of the men to have been Henry, he could not swear it was him.[8]

McLaughlin's comment concerning the size of the men was significant. Henry Barrett was considered a very tall man. His brother Tim was not as tall, and young Peter was described as being small in stature. As Bill Erwin would later point out during closing arguments, "Foster and McKinnon both [spoke] of the same tall man. . . . Henry Barrett is so tall that he would attract attention."[9]

Under further examination McLaughlin told the court that because of his wartime experience he knew the difference between the sound of "a shot [and] an echo." This likely referred to the ongoing dispute about the number of shots fired that night.[10]

Bill Erwin finally asked, "Are you afraid to positively identify Henry for fear of his vindictiveness?" However, the State objected, the Court sustained the objection, and Patrick McLaughlin's testimony ended.[11]

Another witness for the defense during that final week was George Robinson. He testified that he had been at William Petman's saloon on the night of July 26 when an alarm had sounded for the Boston Block fire. He and Petman went to watch the commotion and stayed for about forty-five minutes, then walked into a saloon ". . . [O]n Washington Avenue between Seventh and Eighth Avenues South," Robinson said. He saw both Barrett brothers there. "Tim was drunk and wanted to go back up town." However, Pete was sober and wanted to go home. He finally convinced Tim to go home, so they both boarded a streetcar.[12]

William Petman was immediately sworn in, and his testimony mirrored George Robinson's—but with one additional, interesting bit of information. A few days earlier Petman had been engaged in a private conversation about the Barrett boys and what he knew. He was interrupted by a police officer, who warned him, "If [you know] anything about them, [you] had better keep it to [your]self or [you will] get into trouble."[13]

As soon as William Petman stepped down from the witness stand, his wife, Mary, was called. She told the court that when she heard about the officer's threat she urged her husband to go and tell the Barretts' attorney what he knew. Mary Petman said, "I told him, it would be wicked to let the boys be tried for murder when [you know] they [are] innocent." However, he was afraid to. If neither he nor George would come forward to tell, she warned him, "I would . . . and I did."[14]

The prosecutor "tried to confuse" Mary Petman during the cross-examination, but his efforts failed.[15]

Another witness for the defense, C. A. Smith, had lived at 2930 Fort Avenue for ten years. Since Barrett's Hub of Hell saloon was located at 2830 Fort Avenue, they were practically neighbors, and Smith claimed that he knew Henry very well. He flatly called Henry a liar, saying, "Henry Barrett kept a bad place; there was fighting and shooting going on there nearly all the time as long as he was there."[16]

George B. Horton was the last passenger to leave Thomas Tollefson's streetcar and testified about what he had seen the night of the murder. At the very moment he stepped off, he noticed "three men advancing toward the car." Shortly after heading toward his home at 3040 22nd Avenue, he heard the sound of two pistol shots, immediately followed by the sound of people running toward Minnehaha, the street that ran parallel to Fort Avenue. Those streets were just east of the cemetery at the corner of Lake and Cedar and in the same direction in which eyewitness Julius Heyn had seen the men run.

A newspaper article titled "Drawing Toward the End" reported the brief, yet shocking statement given by Mrs. Sarah Welch, the mother of Lottie Welch. (Remember that Lottie had visited with Minnie and Chloe on the front porch of the Hub of Hell saloon the night of the murder and watched as the three Barrett brothers left together early that evening.) Mrs. Welch testified, "I was in the kitchen with my daughter when Mr. Jamison was talking with her about testifying in the case against the Barrett boys. I heard him tell her that *the Barrett boys would hang, guilty or not guilty* (emphasis added)." [17]

Was there a conspiracy to convict the Barrett brothers? The idea may not be far-fetched.

That same day defense attorney John T. Byrnes testified concerning his own experience just days earlier. He and two other men named Stevens and Alberty had gone to "E. Thompson's saloon that Monday evening between five and six o'clock." Byrnes explained, "We went down there to see what Thompson and his barkeeper would have to say *before* they were seen by the [city] detectives." Neither Thompson nor his barkeeper, Jacob Peterson, could recall who was in the bar on the night of July 26, 1887. [18]

An obviously upset Prosecutor Davis heatedly exclaimed, "You went down there to block the prosecution, did you?" [19]

"We went down there to block your game, and we succeeded, by finding out what they knew before you saw them," Byrnes replied confidently. [20]

During the trial that same day, the prosecution tried to smear the reputation of George Robinson, a witness for the defense, in order to discredit his testimony. Robinson was a horse dealer and the prosecution had found a couple of disgruntled customers who claimed he was dishonest.

However, the defense countered by securing a greater number of witnesses who verified the integrity of George Robinson. Four men, J.

B. Brouylette, James Manly, Matt Everton, and J. C. Carl, swore that he was a trustworthy businessman.

Was this ploy by Davis's team an example of hitting below the belt?

There was also an interesting twist regarding G. A. Chamberlain (he had testified during Tim's trial about an incident in which he had been accosted by two strangers and lost his rusted pistol in the struggle). A discussion between the attorneys and Judge Lochren determined that his testimony bore no relevance in the case against Peter, so he was never questioned during Peter's trial. Was his testimony truly relevant in Tim's case, or should this determination have had an impact concerning his trial—and its outcome—as well?

At the end of Peter Barrett's trial and during his own testimony, Bill Erwin once again addressed the manner in which Peter had been interrogated at the police station. "State [the] way the facts were put at you, whether they were asked so you could answer yes or no." He continued, "Were you permitted to speak freely, give statements?"[21]

Peter replied, "They told me a story and then asked me if that was so; I told them 'no,' and then they would say a little more, any part of it, and would ask me in all kinds of shapes, all kinds of questions; I saw whiskey that was passed around while Mr. Jamison was there; I saw men there take a drink in his presence."[22]

DAVIS'S STRATEGY

FRANK DAVIS called up various witnesses for the State during Peter's trial, including Officer Henry Krumweide, one of the first officers on the scene. He testified, "Julius Heyn told me on the night of the murder, near the turntable, that he heard two or three shots and showed me a place near the corner and said that the men disappeared all of a sudden and he thought they jumped the fence at that point." He recalled that the grass was short at that location and added that he had thoroughly examined the area the next morning but could find no tracks.[1]

This was in opposition to the testimony of Julius Heyn, who denied talking directly to Officer Krumweide that night. Heyn had stated that he talked to a crowd of people gathered there that night. Although Krumweide had been present and may have heard what Heyn said to the crowd at the time, Heyn had not spoken specifically to him.

Krumweide also told of examining the grassy area the next day to see whether there were any tracks, stating that he found none. However, it had rained on the night of the crime. Had the footprints been washed away?

G. W. Fassett also took the stand on behalf of the State. He testified that he knew Julius Heyn and was in the crowd that night when Julius spoke about the crime. Fassett claimed, "[Julius said he] saw one man run from the front end of the car towards the cemetery and that he thought he heard someone talking in the cemetery." However, Fassett also admitted, "I read the accounts of the testimony taken before the coroner's inquest, published in the daily papers."[2]

The Court seemed unconcerned that this witness, as well as some others, may have acquired the information for their sworn testimony from reading a newspaper article. Apparently there was no inkling that perhaps some of these people were more interested in getting attention than in getting to the facts. There also was no concern about the prosecutor leading his own witness as attorney Davis proceeded to question Fassett, "Do you recollect reading there that Mr. Heyn testified that he heard four shots?"[3]

Various other witnesses were called on behalf of the State, including Sophia Disper, Adam Disper, Frank Story, and S. T. Littleton, whose testimonies were somewhat inconsistent. Sophia and Adam Disper both claimed that on the night of the murder Julius Heyn had told them he had heard only two shots. According to Frank Story, Heyn heard three or more shots and saw at least two men running from the car.

S. T. Littleton testified, "Julius Heyn said to me, 'I . . . heard one shot and then screams; I ran towards the turntable; when I got within twenty feet of the street car I heard another shot; then I saw one man running towards the cemetery and I thought I heard someone over in the cemetery."[4, 5]

When Assistant County Prosecutor Robert Jamison took the stand, he gave a lengthy opening statement aimed at disputing Peter Barrett's testimony. He said,

I heard the testimony of Pete Barrett. I was present at the interview at the North Side Station, spoken of by Peter. No one said there that if he would tell who committed the murder he would be allowed to go—no one said that there was a mob outside and that they were going to hang him. Neither did anyone say that we would put him out of the window. His entire testimony in relation to threats and inducements at that interview is wholly false. No threats were made of any kind and no inducements or offers were held out or made to the defendant. There was some whiskey there; one of the officers who had just come in from Omaha had a bottle and several of the persons drank. My attention was called to the whiskey only once and that was when an officer asked Pete if he wanted a drink and I said he could have no liquor—I was there to see that the statement was made voluntarily and in a proper manner, and under proper and legal circumstances. A mob was spoken of there in the way, Pete wanted to hear why he was taken off the train before arriving at the depot and taken up there. Officer Hoy simply said that the streetcar men were a determined set and that they might be at the depot to give him a warm reception and that it was done for his protection. I asked most of the questions and the conversation was in an ordinary manner. There were no noises around the place, no offers of money or anything else were made to him.[6]

After this, Jamison's law partner, Frank Davis, questioned him regarding Peter Barrett's statement that night. It supposedly had been made in the presence of officers Michael Hoy, James Howard, John Hoy, J. Hankinson, L. W. Kinney, Jacob Hein, and himself—but with no attorney present to advise Peter.

Davis coyly introduced Peter's statement to the Court (even though he had refused to produce Henry's statement when Erwin had requested it). He strategically asked Jamison,

Did Peter say, in substance . . . :

"I was in the City of Minneapolis at the time Tollefson was murdered. I did not hear of the murder until the morning after it occurred. I remember where I was, and what I did the night of the murder. . . [?]"[7]

"About dark that evening, my brothers Tim and Henry, started with me from the saloon [at] 2830 Fort Avenue [Henry's place]. When we left the saloon Miss Betts, Mrs. McLeod, Henry's wife, and Lottie Welch were there, and saw us go away together. . . . [W]e went directly up town and went over near the fire, known as the Big Boston [Block] fire which occurred that night; we stopped and looked at the fire for a while and then started back on foot towards Cedar Avenue. . . [?]"[8]

"When we [Henry, Tim, and himself] reached the avenue we went out on the avenue to within a short distance of the H & D track, we then turned south in the direction of Henry's saloon, 2830 Fort Avenue, and went directly to it. . . . When we got to the house it was after 12 o'clock [?]" "When we started out that evening Tim had a revolver, Smith & Wesson, which he took from a man he undertook to hold up one night. . . . [I]t was a 38-caliber revolver, single action. Either before or after the murder of Tollefson, I do not remember which, Tim cut his initials 'T. B.' on the handle. . . . [T]hat same revolver was afterwards taken from him by an officer at Northfield. . . . [A]t the time of starting out that evening, Henry also had a revolver and the butt end of a billiard cue [but] I was not armed. The revolver that Henry had was one I bought downtown a short time before Tollefson was killed, it was a red-handled revolver, and although Henry had it that night, it was mine. . . . [Henry] gave it to me after Tollefson was killed and I lost it riding on a freight car in northern Nebraska. I remember hearing two shots on the night of the murder, that was after I got home that night, while I was sitting in the house. . . . I remember the second day after the murder that Henry and Tim started away together. . . . [T]hey [were] gone two or three hours when they returned, they had a large number of water lilies. During the evening when we were out together Henry gave me the stick, but I threw it away near the sidewalk somewhere on Cedar Avenue[?]"[9]

Jamison affirmed that Pete had, indeed, said all of these things.

Bill Erwin repeatedly voiced objections to Frank Davis's questions, calling them "incompetent, immaterial, irrelevant and no foundation laid for it; on the further ground that defendant was under duress at the time and under arrest and influenced by fear and promises of reward and not rebuttal."[10]

Judge Lochren overruled each time.

It is worth noting that the vocabulary and forms of expression in the statement (as read by Davis during the questioning of Jamison) do not seem to reflect the vocabulary used by Peter as revealed in the actual court transcripts. Words such as "undertook," clauses and phrases such as "we reached the avenue;. . . we went out on the avenue to within a short distance;. . . started away together;. . . afterwards taken from him by an officer at Northfield" seem a bit flowery, too poised and proper for the country boy Peter Barrett. Was Peter's statement of confession written verbatim? And if it was not, is it not possible—and even likely—that this rendition was not only inaccurate, but could be considered a false statement?

Officer James Howard had been among those present at the North Side Police Station on November 26, 1887, when Peter Barrett was brought in for questioning. He stated, "Mr. Jamison, Mr. Hankinson, Mr. Kinney and others were there. I was one of the officers who brought Peter Barrett to the City [in] the company [of] Officers Kinney and Hoy."[11]

Davis asked Howard, "Did you . . . while on the train, tell Peter Barrett [a] long statement in reference to the Tollefson murder, then

[ask] isn't it so, and say to him 'you know it is so and it is no use for you to deny it,' and then say to him, 'if you will say it is, we will let you go?' . . . that [if] he 'would tell you who killed the driver, you would let him go . . . and give him some money?'"[12]

"No sir, I did not," said Howard.

"Or that Henry and Tim had told you that it was he, Peter that had done it and if they had done it, meaning Henry and Tim, if Peter would tell you so that you would let him go?"[13]

Erwin objected on the grounds that this was "improper and leading."[14]

Judge Lochren advised, ". . . [I]f it is simply for the purpose of denial it is not leading." Attorney Davis affirmed that had been his intention.[15]

Howard's reply was informative, "Officer Kinney did say something of this sort to Peter."[16]

Officer Howard testified further, "When we arrived [at] the city we took Peter to the North Side Station, the train stopped on Washington Avenue, we got on a street car and rode up there. About 9 o'clock in the morning when we got up there . . . Mr. Jamison, Captain Hoy, and I think Chief [of] Police Hein, were there. Hankinson came afterwards. Kinney and I went up together. No one there offered Peter money to tell about the murder, no one offered to let him out through the back window. No one told him there was a mob outside and that they were going to hang him. There were no unusual noises about the building. No threats were made against him. No offers or promises were made him. There was some liquor there, one bottle that Kinney brought with him from Omaha; some of the officers drank, Pete had none of it."[17]

Frank Davis resumed his questioning based on Peter's statement at the police station. He read, "When we got to the house it was after 12 o'clock. I stayed around upstairs until after 1 o'clock. I don't know where Henry and Tim [were] while I was sitting around, but when I went to bed Tim was there."[18]

Officer Howard agreed that Pete had said this.

The last people to testify in Peter's trial were witnesses for the defense. Among them was Ed Stevens, who, along with a man named Alberty, had accompanied Defense Attorney John T. Byrnes that Monday to visit Thompson's saloon. This was Stevens's third time on the stand. After that the time for testimony ended.

A short recess was called before the Court would hear closing arguments on that Thursday, February 16, 1888. Peter's trial had lasted three weeks. More than 230 people had been directly involved with the trial, including the judge, attorneys, jury, court clerk, and sheriff's deputies. Of the one hundred witnesses, sixty-one testified on behalf of the State and thirty-nine testified for the defendant.

$$\text{23}$$

CLOSING ARGUMENTS OF PETE'S TRIAL

P ETER'S ATTORNEY, Will Donahue, was the first to speak during closing arguments that Thursday afternoon. Will conducted his oratory over the span of an hour and with methodical, attention-gripping precision utilized his voice and mannerisms. First off, he reached out to the jury, commending them for their responsibility and acknowledging the difficult task before them. He then spoke briefly, yet sympathetically, of Thomas's murder. However, when he turned his attention to the arrests of the Barrett brothers, he spoke emphatically about the mistreatment his clients had received—which he described as unmerciful. Donahue "reviewed the evidence . . . [and] argued that the detectives and police were bound to secure the reward and to do this they had to convict someone and Peter and Tim Barrett were *their victims* (emphasis added)."[1]

He strongly criticized Henry Barrett, describing him as "the most depraved and infamous of God's creatures." Looking directly at the jurors, he asked, "Why [should] so base a man . . . be believed against the innocent boy, Peter, and his loving sister? . . . Henry was the murderer, the red-handed murderer who perjured his soul to gain immunity from the just punishment for his crime."[2]

Again he pointed to the detectives handling of the case.

"Great God!" he exclaimed, "Has it come to this that justice cannot be meted out in our fair city? The county attorney stands as a bulwark between the accused and accusers. Everything has been concealed and hidden from the defense. Their practices have been infamous and their work is against a weak and innocent boy. Peter comes here with every presumption of innocence and it is your duty to find him guiltless and send him forth to the world."[3]

After Will Donahue had finished his argument, Frank Davis began his. He spoke for four hours that afternoon, until court was adjourned, but he still wasn't finished.

The Hennepin County Courthouse was crowded by 9:00 a.m. the next morning—just as it had been nearly every day of the Barrett brothers' trials. As seats were taken in the courtroom, it quickly became a standing-room-only affair, and people stood wherever they could in order to hear.

Frank Davis resumed his closing argument that Friday morning by ripping into the key witness for the defense. "If Heyn is right about the number of shots fired," stated Mr. Davis, "they all came from the same pistol and they were all at the same height. He testified that all the shots were fired directly at the car. Now these shots must necessarily have struck Tollefson or the car, if these shots were four feet from the ground. That was about the point [at which] Tollefson was shot in the leg. If Heyn was right Thomas Tollefson would be alive today. The shots did not strike the car. John McKinnon so testified. We do not need the testimony of Henry Barrett to show the error in Heyn's statement. His own words and words of Tollefson contradict it."[4]

Davis then turned to the ongoing family feud within the Barrett family. He suggested that all of the detail had been made up by defense attorney Bill Erwin and claimed that every time the subject was brought up in testimony it was only done so with Erwin's leading of the witness.

He spoke of his own key witness, Henry Barrett, stating, "The corroboration of Henry's testimony . . . all the witnesses and . . . circumstances proved beyond a shadow of a doubt that his story was true."[5]

Davis concluded with emphatic eloquence aimed to lasso the jurors' sympathetic hearts:

> Beside the scene of his untimely death rest the ashes of Thomas Tollefson. It is but a step from the busy street where up and down the mighty currents of life, in all its varied forms, go to and fro, to the solitude of this city of the dead. To him the wants of material life bring no more cares, the joys of life, no sweet, serene, and soft repose. No fireside shall call him master again, no home its lord, no wife her husband, no mother her son. The flight of days shall be unmarked by him. Spring shall bring its bursting life of flower and foliage; Summer with its tragic breath shall win Nature to mature luxuriance; Autumn shall brown meadow and forest and bear forth her golden treasure of fruit and grain; Winter shall sift his snows and blow in his wild rage, his storms across the land and sea, but all the change of seasons shall be changeless to the silent dead. For him there is no call of duty. Within the bosom of his mother earth, his form moulders into nameless dust; his soul, I trust, finds everlasting peace in Christ's sweet bosom. But law lives, justice reigns, and through your verdict may God's eternal fiat grow more clear and solemn—'Thou shalt not kill!'[6]

Everyone present seemed captivated by Davis's speech to the very end. The courtroom was silent for a moment, disrupted only by the sound of the prosecutor's footsteps as he returned to his seat.

One reporter wrote, "It was so still in the crowded courtroom that a whisper could be heard when Mr. Erwin began his argument—one of the ablest he has ever delivered. . . . The Lone Pine Tree arose slowly and moved to the clerk's desk. He spoke a few complimentary words to the [C]ourt, and then turned his face to the jury."[7]

That face had grown pale, its lines seemed more prominent than before, but "there was suppressed fire" in his eyes. His voice was low, each word carefully chosen as his speech fluctuated from tender to emotional to piercing.[8]

"You associate my client with me," Erwin said. "You watch me, my face, my manner to see how I look upon the truth. So in a measure my client is tried through me. I would to God I could peril my life, my limbs to save him. I would like to sit with you . . . in your homes and talk over the evidence in this trial and see who was to be believed in this case."[9]

He continued, "What a responsibility rests upon your heads. Oh, beware, lest over haste, over zeal cause you to take from Peter Barrett that which no man can return to him, to carry out the revenge and feed the hate of one who should have died to protect him. If Peter Barrett is an ascertained murderer, he has no rights, but until he is an ascertained murderer, by the Bill of Rights, by our laws and customs, his personal liberty is as inviolable as that of a judge who sits upon the desk crowned with honors and dignity."[10]

Bill Erwin recalled the way Peter had been treated when he was arrested and the attempts of the officials to bribe him and obtain a statement from him.

He advised the jurors against allowing sympathy to guide their decision when making the verdict, urging them to intelligently decide whom to believe.

The entire day, before court was adjourned, was spent hearing the arguments of both Frank Davis and Bill Erwin. On Saturday Erwin resumed his closing argument, a lengthy one that totaled nine-and-a-half hours.

It was 4:30 p.m. that Saturday, February 18, when Judge Lochren dismissed the jurors with some final words of advice:

> With regard to the statements of Peter Barrett, at the North Side Police Station in the presence of Mr. Jamison and others, you will consider the circumstances under which they

were made. If you should find from the evidence that such statements were made under the influence of fear of threats or because of hope of advantage there held out to him, you will disregard such statements altogether; but if you find that such statements were there voluntarily made by Peter Barrett simply in answer to questions put to him by Mr. Jamison, then it is proper that you should consider those statements and compare them with the testimony of Peter here upon the stand, to enable you to determine as to his truthfulness, and as to the amount of credit to be given to his testimony here; and in so far as it may aid you in arriving at the real facts of this case.[11]

The jury members quietly filed out of the courtroom at that time. Deputy Sheriffs Rouen and Lucker were assigned to guard the deliberation room where the jury gathered to discuss the case and reach a decision.

OBSERVATION AND OPINION

A YOUNG LAWYER named Charles B. Elliot had closely followed the Barrett trial and wrote of it in his diary of 1888. He described William Erwin as a prominent St. Paul criminal lawyer who had made a "magnificent effort to save the neck of his worthless client." Elliot wrote, "I am inclined to think that the jury will disagree owing to their hesitancy in believing the evidence of an accomplice who turns states evidence and thus attempts to hang his brother."[1]

Such seemed to be the popular opinion of the day. Many people considered Henry's testimony against his own brothers in order to save himself extremely cowardly. Henry already had a poor reputation when it came to the truth and was described as a violent man with a bad temper. Some people questioned the very legality of the prosecutor's offer of immunity to Henry; a man who had admitted to taking part in the crime and then turned informant.

According to the Minnesota Statutes of 1878, article 104, section 94, in regard to the "uncorroborated testimony of [an] accomplice[, a] conviction cannot be had upon the testimony of an accomplice, unless he is corroborated by such other evidence as tends to convict the defendant of the commission of the offense, and the corroboration is not sufficient if it merely shows the commission of the offense or the circumstances thereof." However, a supplement was added at some point during 1888 (which may or may not have been prior to Peter Barrett's trial), stating that in order for such evidence "to establish the guilt of the accused . . . it need not be sufficiently weighty or full as standing alone."[2]

The State depended heavily, if not solely, on Henry's testimony, but was his testimony corroborated by any other witness? Was it supported by evidence? Were the jurors even aware of the statute? Would it have any bearing on their decision?

Thomas Tollefson had been senselessly murdered, and his young bride had suffered a tremendous loss. It was time for justice.

How long would it take for the men of the jury to reach a verdict? Apparently not long. Two hours and forty-five minutes from the time the jury began deliberating "a momentous rap was heard on the door of the jury room"—the verdict was in.[3]

25

THE VERDICT

JUDGE LOCHREN and the attorneys were contacted, called back to court, and had returned by 8:30 p.m. Accompanied by deputies, Peter stepped through the doorway, his shoulders back and chin up as he looked around the courtroom. He smiled when he saw his supportive father, John, and older brother Frank. Various newspaper reporters sat near the front, poised and ready with their notepads.

Jury Foreman R. Mills solemnly handed the court clerk a folded piece of paper. After Judge Lochren had looked at it, he gave it back to the clerk, who read, "We the jury . . . find the defendant, Peter Barrett, guilty of the crime of murder in the first degree as charged in the indictment."[1, 2]

"Peter raised his head with a frightened look. Then he turned pale, trembled violently, and dropping his head upon his breast sobbed," wrote one reporter.[3]

John Barrett leaned close to his youngest son and whispered in his ear. Whatever he said must have helped. Pete raised his head, squared his shoulders, and even managed a brief smile, until the crushing verdict pressed against him and he sank back, tears flowing. Frank Barrett appeared to be frozen in shock, except for his narrowed eyes, which he eerily fixed on Frank Davis, following his every move.

At the request of County Attorney Davis, and by order of the Court, the jury members were duly polled, and each juror responded accordingly. The verdict was unanimous.

Pete's lawyers requested that the sentencing be delayed, and the Court agreed to wait until March 1, 1888. The defense wanted more time in order to prepare an argument that they hoped would convince the Court to grant their client a more favorable penalty. They planned to base their argument on "exceptional circumstances."[4]

Shackled and still shaken, Peter was escorted back to his jail cell, where he remained until he was brought back into court, as scheduled, on March 1.

At that time Attorney Erwin requested a "further stay of sentence," which Judge Lochren granted until the following day. This same scenario occurred on March 2.

Finally, on March 3, Peter faced the inevitable day of sentencing. Judge Lochren called him forward, then said: "It is considered that you, Peter Barrett, as punishment for the crime of murder in the first degree, for which you have been convicted, be taken hence to the common jail of this County of Hennepin and there confined, and that thereafter and after the lapse of the period of three calendar months from this day, and at a time to be fixed by the Governor of the State of Minnesota, and designated by his warrant, you be taken to the place of execution, and there hanged by the neck until you are dead. . ."[5]

The court transcript includes a summary of the judgment concerning this murder case, parts of which follow:

> "[O]n the 6th day of December, 1887, the Grand Jury
> was duly empanelled and sworn; which Grand Jury, on the
> 7th day of December 1887, returned into Court an indict-
> ment against Timothy Barrett and Peter Barrett, charging

them with the crime of murder in the first degree. . . [The accused] were given until December 9th,1887, to plead, and [on that date] each entered a plea of not guilty, and on December 19th, 1887, the defendants demanded separate trials. And on the 30th day of January, 1888, a jury was duly empanneled and sworn to try said Peter Barrett, one of said defendants, for the offense charged in the indictment; which jury, on the 18th day of [February], 1888, returned the following verdict . . . guilty of the crime of murder in the first degree, as charged. . .[6]

The document was filed by Clerk E. J. Davenport and Deputy George G. Tirrell and endorsed by the District Court of Hennepin County on March 3, 1888.

The final page of the court transcript for the trial of Peter Barrett is a "Bill of Exception" signed by Judge William Lochren on April 14, 1888, at the request of the council for the defendant. It simply states that all of the preceding pages of the transcript include ". . . all the evidence offered and received, and introduced; all the objections of the Council thereto, and all the rulings of the Court thereon, and the exceptions of the Council to said rulings: and all the proceedings had during the trial of . . . the defendant. . ."[7]

However, Bill Erwin filed an appeal later that spring.

Regardless, on May 11 the warrant for the hanging of Timothy Barrett was issued. Nearly one month later, on June 4, Governor McGill signed the warrant for the hanging of Peter Barrett. The execution, scheduled for Friday, July 13, 1888, would be carried out under the direction of Hennepin County Sheriff Swenson. [8]

One month later, the *St. Paul Daily Globe* reported that Attorneys Erwin, Donahue, and Byrnes had "made an application to Judge Dickinson for a stay," alleging numerous errors had occurred during the trials. Subsequently, Chief Justice Gilfillan and Judge Dickinson of the Minnesota Supreme Court held a hearing the following week that included all three defense attorneys as well as the "attorney general and Robert Jamison on behalf of the state." The Court granted a stay of execution pending the appeals and the final determination of the Minnesota Supreme Court regarding "the judgment and sentence of the district court." This gave the needed boost of encouragement for Bill Erwin's team of attorneys, who remained convinced of their clients' innocence; they worked tirelessly over the following months.[9]

26

REWARD MONEY

EVERAL MONTHS after the convictions of the Barrett brothers, an Omaha newspaper printed the story about two local officers, Turnbull and Cormick. They had arrested Peter Barrett in Omaha and then delivered him to Minneapolis yet were "cheated out of the reward." The reward had instead been given to "the so-called Minneapolis detective" who took the prisoner from their custody, and he refused to share any of the $2,200 with either of them.[1]

That Minneapolis detective was Chief of Detectives James W. Hankinson—an appointee of Mayor Ames. Hankinson had "brought Tim Barrett into the Central Police Station November 15, 1887, four days before Reddy Barrett confessed." At the time he had told the other officers present, "Boys, that is the man who killed Tollefson, and I will prove it to you before I get done with this."[2]

Hankinson's comment occurred four days before Henry Barrett made his confession to Assistant Prosecutor Robert Jamison. It was Hankinson, along with Officer James Howard and Attorney Robert

Jamison, who followed Henry down into the cellar to search for the streetcar checks stolen from Tollefson during the crime. And Hankinson, Jamison, Howard, and Hoy were all present when Peter Barrett was brought into the police station on the night he was interrogated—and intimidated—by the authorities.

It is also interesting that within weeks of the Omaha newspaper story, by January 1889, Hankinson was no longer the chief of detectives.

Some people thought Hankinson fully deserved the $2,200 reward money, but others were "skeptical."[3]

**Hennepin County Jail and sheriff's residence
Fifth Street South and Chicago, Minneapolis.**

Hennepin County Jail and sheriff's residence, Fifth Street and Eighth Avenue, Minneapolis.

Source: Photograph Collection, Stereograph 1870,
Minnesota Historical Society, St. Paul, MN.

Sheriff James Ege.

Sheriff Ege

Source: *St. Paul Daily Globe*, March 17, 1889,
Library of Congress, Chronicling America http://chroniclingamerica.loc.gov
image provided by Minnesota Historical Society, St. Paul, MN.

Ada "Addie" Boyd, Pete's girlfriend.

Source: *Minneapolis Evening Journal*, March 16, 1889,
Minnesota Historical Society, St. Paul, MN.

27

ℌENNEPIN ℭOUNTY ℑAIL ℑIME

WHILE THE Barrett brothers were held at the Hennepin
County Jail, the sheriff in charge was James Henry Ege. Born in Cumberland County, Pennsylvania, on March 20, 1844, he was in his
mid-forties.

According to the family history recorded by Barbara Gable Duffy,
his great-granddaughter, James Ege was a man of integrity with a
strong work ethic. He landed his first job at the age of fifteen, working
on a Pennsylvania farm where he was responsible for various chores
and earned $4 each month. James worked there until he had saved
enough to afford a train ticket to Illinois and arrived there with only
twenty-five cents in pocket change—but he wasn't broke for long.
Soon he had found work on another farm, where he earned $16 per
month. He worked that job full-time during the summer and attended
the local country school from autumn until spring. In 1862 he finished school and turned eighteen years old. The Civil War was on,
so he enlisted and served in Company F, the 93rd Illinois Infantry.

After the war, he returned to Illinois and married Margaret Catharine Quick on September 4, 1867. They settled into married life and
soon began a family. Their first child, Joseph, was born in July 1868,
and two years later, in August 1870, their son Benjamin was born.
The joy of parenting both a newborn and a toddler was clouded in
grief one short month later when little Joseph died at the tender age
of two. The following March the family moved to Minneapolis, where
James became a horse dealer. The change was good, and in 1875 the
couple welcomed the birth of a daughter, Mary Jane. In 1881 another
son, Edgar Geddes, was born.

The city directories of that era often listed a person's occupation
along with their address. In 1870 James Ege was listed as a horse
dealer. Ten years later he was the owner of a livery and stable. By
1885 he had changed professions and was serving as a deputy sheriff for Hennepin County, and by 1889 he had become the sheriff of
Hennepin County.

As the records prove, James Ege was a self-made man with ambi-
tion and a strong sense of duty. He was also a family man. In those
days the Hennepin County sheriff's residence was located in a private
section attached to the structure of the jail. Therefore, the Ege children were very much aware of the prisoners who were held there. In
fact, young Benjamin Ege was about eighteen years old by the time his
father became the sheriff, and he helped tend to the Barrett brothers.
(Benjamin later followed his father's footsteps and in 1895 became a
Hennepin County deputy sheriff.)

Sheriff Ege was a respected man in the community and well known
in various social circles. He was a member of the Royal Arcanum,
Knights of Pythias, and the Modern Woodmen of America, among
other social groups, and held various offices in each of them. Sheriff
Ege served from 1889–1890 and again from 1893–1894 (Peter Swen-
sen served as sheriff from 1887–1888 and 1891–1892).

It is interesting to note the relationship between Sheriff Ege and the
Barrett brothers. Later on we will learn more about the role he played
and his attitudes toward them. During their time in his jail, he got

to know them well, and I imagine he may have been a bit amused by some of the attention the brothers received . . . especially from some rather flirtatious young ladies.

Timothy and Peter Barrett were young and handsome. The trials had given them a lot of publicity. They had been the talk of the town for months . . . and the girls had noticed. The brothers soon realized a kind of fame, almost as though they were rock stars of the Wild West, and they were routinely visited by many of these smitten young ladies. Both Tim and Peter enjoyed the attention, but Peter soon became the more popular. One girl, who was employed at one of the local flour mills, even referred to herself as Peter's fiancé—until her infatuation passed. But then along came Addi Boyd, a teenaged schoolgirl. She had watched Pete closely during the trials and developed a strong crush on him.[1]

Born in 1872 in Minnesota, Ada Boyd was only fifteen years old during the trials. She lived with her family in an apartment at 3233 Third Avenue South, an area of Minneapolis known as the Bohemian Flats. Her father, Charles Boyd, was a veteran of the Grand Army of the Republic and a cooper by trade. Mariah Jarushah, a homemaker, was her mother. Both parents had been born in Pennsylvania. It is not known when they moved to Minnesota. (Addie had an older sister named Minnie and a younger brother named Mark.)

The newspapers described Addie's appearance as pretty, small, thin, and "waif-like," with a pale complexion and "bright black eyes." She had dark, curly hair and delicate facial features and often wore a "jaunty little soldier's cap . . . [and] short skirts." However, the reporters were not so kind when describing her behavior toward Pete, writing that she was silly for falling in love with him and hanging around the jail.[2]

But Addie was undeterred. She made friends with Detective Bassett, who allowed her to visit Pete regularly. The visits were strictly guarded, however, and Addie was required to stand at least two feet away from the bars of Peter's cell at all times. She didn't seem to mind the restrictions and often brought him treats of baked goods.

When Tim and Pete were first jailed, neither could read or write, and their language was crude and often vulgar. Another prisoner, who happened to be well educated, taught them both to read and write. Tim and Pete also learned to express themselves more graciously, even to the point that the jailers claimed "they could talk like gentlemen."[3]

As for those who firmly believed in Peter Barrett's innocence of the murder of Thomas Tollefson, an incident in mid-January 1889 may have caused them to reconsider: Peter attempted a jail break.

On that particular morning turnkey James Riley brought breakfast into the room where the prisoners of the second tier of cells ate. Jailer Kelly locked the door after Riley and stood guard behind it in the outer corridor, waiting for him to finish.[4]

They had no idea that three prisoners, George Day, William Barnes, and Peter Barrett, had hidden in the nearby water closet.[5]

It was about 7:30 a.m. As Riley leaned over the table he was attacked from behind by Peter, who jumped on his back and tried to choke him. William Barnes then struck Riley over the head with a heavy towel bar, knocking him to the floor.

When Jailer Kelly saw the commotion, he ran to get help.

The outnumbered Riley grabbed hold of the large knife he had used to cut the butter—it was apparently quite sharp—and lashed out at his assailants. Peter Barrett received a cut above his right eye, and Barnes was cut as well. When George Day saw their wounds he cowered back and "retreated to his [own] cell." Riley managed to get both Barnes and Barrett back into their cells and had them all locked up by the time Jailer Kelly arrived with help.[6]

Peter was, of course, a convicted murderer. What about the other two prisoners? George Day had been jailed and was awaiting trial for larceny. William Barnes was serving a sentence for stealing a cow. All three prisoners refused to talk about the incident to the press, but it was presumed by both jailers that the prisoners had planned to attack Jailer Kelly as well, had he opened the door to assist turnkey Riley. However, Kelly had out-smarted them and Riley simply out-whooped them.

On January 19 the *St. Paul Daily Globe* wrote that a still sore and rather pale turnkey James Riley had reported back to work less than a week after the incident. Riley commended his partner, Kelly, "Say, old man, you did all right when Barrett and the others made the attack on me. If you had rushed in, as they expected you would, we would have both been done up."[7]

Why did the prisoners do it? We will never know, but their failed attempt may have had deeper implications.

THE REPUTATION OF THE BARRETT BROTHERS

TWO MONTHS after the attempted jail break, the *Omaha Bee* reported that both Tim and Pete were "extensively known in police circles, having on various occasions been arrested for larceny and highway robbery." However, there were several factual errors regarding the crimes and arrests in that newspaper article. For instance, it incorrectly stated that Tim was arrested in Omaha, when that was actually Pete. The article also falsely claimed that Tim was eighteen years old. And perhaps the strongest example of false information within the article was the statement that Tim had admitted to having been present when Thomas Tollefson was murdered. In truth, Tim had firmly denied any knowledge or involvement.[1]

Another newspaper reported that both Pete and Tim were "familiar" to the Omaha police and known for their involvement in "a succession of drunken brawls, fights, thefts, imprisonments . . . [and] recognized as troublemakers. . . [though] not considered dangerous."[2, 3]

Other newspapers claimed that while the brothers were in Omaha they'd had "nightly excursions" with a group of young men. They would venture out "at nightfall and always return before dawn." During those escapades they might steal a harness or rob a hen house—crimes considered a nuisance but not serious. Another rumor claimed that Tim Barrett had been imprisoned at Fort Madison twice. Earlier in this book we learned that, in fact, young John, the brother who died of a gangrene infected gunshot wound, had served time in prison in Iowa.[4]

Unfortunately, inaccurate reporting seems to have been a problem back then, just as it often is today. The stories and rumors may have been partly true: the Barrett brothers admitted that they were no angels. We should not excuse any crime as simple mischief, and one thing can lead to another. But did their dalliance with petty crime escalate to the point of murder? Would they have accosted a streetcar driver at the end of his nighttime shift for the meager sum of whatever a ticket fares box may have held? Why would they have murdered a man like Thomas Tollefson? Did he unexpectedly resist? Did they specifically target him for personal reasons? Given their reputation for getting into trouble late at night, it may be believable that they *could have* committed the crime—but *did* they?

One newspaper reporter wrote about a conversation he'd had with a man from Omaha who knew the Barrett family well. When asked about their character, the man replied, "There isn't a child in the neighborhood that wouldn't do anything they asked them to. They were always giving [the children] nickels and little things, and I think anyone who was so kind to a kid, is as good as the people who like to say a bad word about them . . . and you won't hear anyone around here say a bad word about them. Everybody is sorry that this thing happened . . . . I remember little Pete. It was a surprise to us to hear that he was wanted for murder, because he didn't seem built that way. He had lots of sand in him though."[5]

Other news accounts suggested that the brothers had committed other crimes on the same night as Tollefson's murder. A man who worked with the Pioneer Fuel Company had been robbed of a gold watch and money, and another man had lost his silver watch and pocket change. A few days after that Tim had supposedly shot at a telegraph operator in Minnehaha because he had grown impatient waiting for him to close up so that he could "rifle the till" after the operator had left the office. The same article claimed that both Tim and Pete were members of "the notorious McCarty gang in Omaha." There must have been a reason this connection was made. Another report stated that "the Barretts claim kinship with the McCarty's on account of their notoriety and . . . the McCarty's disowned the Barretts because of their pettiness"—the Barretts were apparently not hardened enough. There was no comparison to the crimes committed by the McCartys.[6, 7]

The "McCarty gang" consisted of four brothers who lived in a small town called Bellevue in Sarpy County, Nebraska. They were known as tough, hardened criminals.

Vic McCarty had once quarreled with a companion as the two "chopped cord wood." Vic ended that quarrel with one strong-armed blow of his axe blade against the neck of the other man—which *decapitated* him. Vic faced a courtroom trial over the incident, but the jury was said to have been so intimidated and afraid of the McCarty gang that they dared not deliver a guilty verdict. So Vic McCarty walked away a free man.[8, 9]

An 1887 newspaper account told of a series of store burglaries and that of a train depot in Springfield. Sheriff Weymouth of Papillion County went to the Omaha police for help in tracking the perpetrators. The Omaha police immediately suspected that the McCarty gang was involved due to their reputation and obtained a search warrant to look for the stolen goods at Ellen Barrett's house "on 20th Street on the Bellevue road." Instead, Deputy Sheriff Nightingale and his posse passed by Ellen Barrett's home and rode straight toward the McCarty brothers' place.[10]

One of the brothers caught sight of the approaching lawmen and alerted the others. Armed with shotguns, they rode off on horseback toward Papillion County.

The lawmen were already close enough to notice that the McCartys wore new boots. At one of the stores several pairs of new boots had been stolen and old, worn boots left behind. Deputy Sheriff Nightingale assumed that this was evidence enough to conduct a search of the then abandoned McCarty mansion. He proceeded to do so, found many stolen goods there, and confiscated them.

In a bizarre twist the McCartys later charged Deputy Sheriff Nightingale with larceny. The case went to court, and the four McCartys showed up. They were armed with double-barreled shotguns and loudly debated among themselves whether to shoot Nightingale "on the spot or wait until after the trial." Shamefully, the other law enforcement officers who were present in the courtroom did nothing and said nothing to the McCarty brothers.

Nightingale was acquitted of the charges and left the next day on a train back to Omaha. The McCarty brothers boarded the same train and surrounded him, threatening to shoot "the top of his head off" unless he did as they wanted. As soon as the train reached Omaha, Nightingale slipped off and got to a telephone, where he called his department for assistance. But by the time the backup arrived, the McCartys were nowhere to be seen.[11]

It was the opinion of the newspaper reporter that the McCarty gang were able to "have their own way in Sarpy County, and the authorities [were] apparently afraid to attempt to arrest" them.[12]

Was there any kinship between the McCarty gang and the Barrett family? Maybe, or maybe this was just a good story for the reporter.

We do know that Ellen Barrett was adamant that her sons were innocent of the Tollefson murder and was convinced that they would receive a new trial.

She was also extremely bitter toward her son Henry, claiming that "When my boys are given a new trial . . . Henry will either leave the country or be shot, for there are plenty of people in Minneapolis who would as soon kill him as a dog."[13]

Those were rather harsh words coming from a mother.

APPEALS

M EANWHILE, DEFENSE attorneys Erwin and Donahue
worked tirelessly to gather solid new evidence to convince the Minnesota Supreme Court that their case was worthy of appeal. Erwin's
documentation cited twenty-eight "assignments of error" made by
the trial court pertaining to jury selection, admission, denial of testimony, and various other issues. He also submitted new evidence
on behalf of Tim and Pete that was corroborated by the affidavits of
several witnesses: Julius Heyn and his wife, Gertrude; Adolph and
Louisa Heyn (Adolf was Julius's brother and neighbor); Patrick Mc-
Laughlin; Mary Strong; and E. A. Mitchell.[1]

Time passed, and everyone involved earnestly waited for news
about the Minnesota Supreme Court's decision. By late January word
finally arrived.

The Court responded, "We find no error in the case, the judgment
and order denying a new trial are affirmed." They admitted that in
regard to upholding the conviction of Peter they had relied mainly on

the testimony of his brother Henry—even though Henry had admitted his own guilt in the crime. "In order to convict . . . it was essential that this witness be corroborated by evidence which tended in some degree to establish the guilt of the accused."[2]

Apparently the Court believed that there was sufficient evidence to back up Henry's testimony yet disregarded the testimony of several witnesses who had declared him a liar.

The Minnesota Supreme Court acknowledged that the actions of only one person may have actually led to the death of Thomas Tollefson, yet stated, "[A] person may be guilty of a murder actually perpetrated by another, if he combines with such other party to commit a felony . . . and death . . . [results]. . . all are alike guilty of the homicide."[3]

According to the Minnesota Statutes of 1878, the testimony of a witness of, or an accomplice to, a crime must be "corroborated by such evidence as tends to convict the defendant of the commission of the offense." However, the same source advised that it is "not sufficient [evidence] if it merely shows the commission of the offense or the circumstances thereof." In 1888 a supplement to the statutes states that in order for the testimony of an accomplice to be used to convict the accused, that testimony does not need to be "sufficiently weighty or full as standing alone."[4, 5]

Those statutes loosened the requirements and granted more power to jury members and district courts to exercise their own judgment when they rendered a verdict.

In spite of all the information, documentation, and new affidavits, nothing Bill Erwin had presented was sufficient to convince the Supreme Court. The chances for new trials and further review of the Barrett brothers' convictions were dashed. Timothy and Peter Barrett would die by hanging . . . unless a higher power were to intervene. That higher power was the governor of the state of Minnesota.

Governor William Rush Merriam, the Republican candidate elected in autumn of 1888, had recently been sworn in to office. The treasurer of the Hennepin County Republican Committee back in 1888 would most likely have been on friendly terms with candidate

Merriam. A fact worth mentioning is that this same treasurer was also familiar with the trials of the convicted Barrett brothers. The treasurer of the Hennepin County Republican Committee was Hennepin County Prosecutor Robert Jamison.

>─┼─◀▷──◯──◁▶─┼─◀

During suppertime on that cold January night, Deputy Sheriff Sorias and Jailer Riley called Tim and Peter into another room, away from the other prisoners, to tell them the news of the Minnesota Supreme Court's decision. Riley had tears in his eyes as he told them that the Court had refused Erwin's appeal for new trials.

After a brief moment of stunned silence, Tim angrily accused Riley of lying, even as the brothers were immediately handed new "suits of clothes"—complete with underwear—and told to strip down and dress. Pete willingly complied, but while Tim changed, he "expressed a desire to see Riley and nearly everyone else in a much warmer climate."[6]

Freshly dressed, Timothy and Peter were given supper. After they had finished eating, they were removed from the familiar jail cells they had occupied since the trials and led upstairs to the top tier of the jail. They were placed in separate cells and kept under a round-the-clock "deathwatch."[7]

Relocating the brothers effectively separated them from the other inmates, but further action was required. So, in accordance with the law, Sheriff Ege ordered alterations that created such dungeon-like darkness for Tim and Pete that they could barely "see an inch before their faces, even at midday." The iron bars of each cell door had to be spaced a mere one-and-one-half inches apart, and the surrounding cell walls were completely covered with "plates of boiler iron." The ironclad cells were stuffy, smelly, and overheated due to hot air rising from the floors beneath. Each brother was allowed one candle for light. Their view through the cell door was that of the "iron of the outer corridor" and the white wall of the jail.[8]

To make matters worse for Pete, his head hurt. The cut he had received over his right eye in the scuffle with Jailer Riley a few days earlier had become infected, and the environment of his cell didn't help matters.

Tim spent that night pacing nervously in his cell.

The day after hearing the Supreme Court's decision Bill Erwin and Will Donahue visited their clients to discuss the situation and devise a new strategy.

"There is no use in our giving up all hope," asserted Tim. "We may yet be pardoned." [9]

><+>–O–<+><

Weeks later, on Wednesday, March 20, 1889, Attorney Bill Erwin was spotted talking with an unidentified man at the Hotel Ryan in St. Paul. They discussed the Barrett case, and finally the man asked Erwin whether there was any hope of saving Peter Barrett from execution. Erwin replied, "Hope? Of course there is. The governor wouldn't hang a mere boy would he?" [10]

Ellen Barrett visited her boys at the jail that same morning. They talked for about a half hour, and she told them that Levi Gorman had made a sworn affidavit that would be shown to Governor Merriam. Gorman's statement should prove to the governor that it had been Henry, not Pete, who was involved in the crime and shooting. She encouraged them that the truth would come out and claimed that she would get Henry "to put it in writing" in order to back up Gorman's statements, certain that this would effect the governor's decision. By the time Ellen left, her sons expected they would escape execution. [11]

Early that afternoon Mary Barrett-Coleman visited her brothers. She also spoke about Levi's affidavit and told them she was "sure . . . their sentences would be commuted to imprisonment." [12]

Father Henry McGolrick and Father Corbett arrived next and the priests spent two hours talking and praying with Peter and Tim.

><+>–O–<+><

Even young schoolgirl Addie Boyd made an effort to help. She had fallen in love with Peter and visited him countless times at the jail. Likewise, Peter asked to see her during the week leading up to the execution, at a time when visitors were limited. Addie visited Ellen Barrett earlier that week about her petition to save the lives of Peter and Tim. She even told a reporter about it, saying that with the help of others she had acquired 5,000 signatures (quite possibly an inflated number). Addie made several attempts to see the governor in order to present her petition to him but was turned away by Secretary Elliot.[13]

Whether the efforts of so many would have been enough to convince the governor to reconsider the Barrett executions, one certain issue seemed most likely to get his attention: Peter Barrett's age. Federal Census records clearly show that Peter had been born during the early months of 1870. At the time of Thomas Tollefson's murder in July 1887, he was only seventeen years old.[14]

PLEAS TO GOVERNOR MERRIAM

AS THE execution date drew ever closer, concern intensified, and several people wrote letters to the governor claiming that the Barrett brothers were innocent and should not be hung.

With only days to spare, Mary Barrett-Coleman wrote a letter to the public, making an appeal for Peter's life. In the letter she stated that she regarded the "whole thing as the culmination of Henry's hatred for the rest of the family because [their] mother would not assist him in money matters."[1]

According to at least one newspaper reporter, the popular opinion was that Peter would, indeed, be pardoned and that only "one man [would] be hung on Friday."[2]

Erwin's team remained convinced of their clients' innocence of the crime and were determined to save the necks of both Tim and Peter. The Minnesota Supreme Court had denied their appeal, but they were not about to give up.

On Saturday, March 16, Will Donahue had already hand delivered a petition to the governor's office, which read:

> Honorable William R. Merriam,
> Governor of Minnesota:
>
>   In view of the youthfulness of Peter Barrett, now condemned to be hung at Minneapolis, Minn., and having in view the interests of the state and of society, and not forgetting those of humanity; and in view of the facts and circumstances attending the commission of the crime of which he stands convicted, and the manner of his conviction, we, the undersigned citizens of said city, petition and respectfully request Your Excellency to commute the sentence now resting upon Peter Barrett to imprisonment in the state penitentiary for life.[3]

More than 300 people had signed that petition, and nearly one-third of them were attorneys or judges.

A reporter for the *St. Paul Daily Globe* spoke with Governor Merriam at his home that same evening about the petition. Governor Merriam said, "[It] was handed to me this morning. I have been engaged . . . with legislative committees and have not had an opportunity to even look at the document. I will do so Monday."[4]

Monday came and went—with no word from the governor.

With no time to waste, Attorney John T. Byrnes and his assistant, David B. Johnson, both members of Erwin's team, left the city on Tuesday morning. They planned to visit each of the jury members in order to secure their signature on yet another petition. This would be a challenging task, since they would have to travel up to 200 miles to reach various towns and remote rural areas throughout Hennepin County.

A reporter for the *Minneapolis Tribune* wrote about a conversation he'd had with Governor Merriam at his residence on Wednesday night, the 20th of March. By then the execution was only two days away, and he asked about the fate of the Barrett brothers. The governor was blunt: "I have no reason to change my mind in the matter. . . . I expect the boys will hang. . . . The boys have had a fair trial, so far as I have been able to learn, and it only remains for me to perform my duty as the chief executive of the state. It would be unbecoming in me, and a stretch of the power reposed in me, to extend clemency in their cases. Nothing but the gravest consideration between now and Friday can influence me."[5]

If the petitions were not enough to persuade the governor, there were new affidavits. At 11:00 a.m. the following morning, Thursday, March 21, Defense Attorney Will Donahue brought Officer Levi Gorman and Chloe Betts to the capitol to meet with Governor Merriam. Levi and Chloe had filed separate affidavits that not only addressed Henry Barrett's admitted guilt in the Tollefson murder but proclaimed Peter Barrett's innocence. Chloe's affidavit was published in the *Minneapolis Tribune*:

> State of Minnesota,
> County of Ramsey } ss.
>
> Chloe Betts came before me personally and being duly sworn, says: That I am the sister of Minnie Barrett (Henry Barrett's wife) and lived with said Henry Barrett almost continually from May 1, 1887, to Feb. 4, 1889; that at some time in the month of March, 1888, at Henry Barrett's residence, 740 Third Street north, in Minneapolis, I heard a conversation between Henry Barrett and Minnie Barrett, his wife, in which Henry Barrett said in substance: "Don't tell Chloe," meaning thereby this deponent, "that I took the part in the murder of Tollefson that I swore my brother Peter took." Said Henry Barrett said: "[I] fired the first shot, which struck the car driver in the leg, and Tim remained and shot him in the breast." Deponent further avers that

after the conviction of said Peter Barrett, said Henry Barrett in deponent's presence said: "That he was sorry for his brother Peter, and if he (said Henry Barrett) had to testify again he would tell the truth about Peter, but at the time he first swore, and at Peter's trial, that Peter shot Tollefson in the leg, he was afraid to tell the truth.

(signed) CHLOE BETTS[6]

Levi Gorman's affidavit, dated March 20, 1889, appeared in the *St. Paul Daily Globe* :

State of Minnesota,
County of Hennepin } ss.

Levi Gorman came before me personally and, being duly sworn, says: I was deputy sheriff in charge of Henry Barrett and family for the period of fourteen and one-half months, extending from November 1887 to Feb. 4, 1889: that at No. 740 Third Street north, in the city of Minneapolis in the night . . . about March 1, 1888 I overheard a conversation between Henry Barrett and Minnie Barrett, his wife, in substance as follows:

"Have you told Chloe Betts (meaning thereby his wife's sister) how the murder was committed?" (meaning of the car driver, Thomas Tollefson.)

She, Minnie Barrett, answered, "No, I do not know it all myself."

Henry Barrett then said: "Don't tell her for the world that I took the part that I swore my brother Pete took. *I fired the fatal shot* (emphasis added). Pete did not want to rob the street car driver, but he called him a coward and told him (Pete) that he was afraid and to come on. Then we wanted him to catch the mules by the head, but he refused and Tim and me then went up to the car and I fired the first shot and struck the driver in the leg. After the first shot was fired Pete ran and I ran after him and overtook him, and after we both got a block away we heard another shot: then Tim came running after us with the car driver's box under his arm."

(signed) LEVI GORMAN[7]

Both of these sworn affidavits had similarities, however, according to Chloe, Tim was guilty of murder! Levi claimed Henry had admitted that he fired the fatal shot as well as the first shot, then insinuates that Tim murdered Thomas Tollefson. Were Tim and Pete present during the crime after all? Did John Barrett, Dr. Heflin, Mary Barrett Coleman, and George Coleman all lie? On the other hand, why would Chloe and Levi have lied under oath?

There was also a third affidavit. We can assume the person was impartial, since there was no mention of any relationship between him and any of the Barrett brothers. William Barry, also a prisoner at the Hennepin County jail, was nearby when Henry Barrett, accompanied by Father Corbett, called on Peter one day in August 1888. William overheard Henry say to Peter, "I am sorry that I testified that you fired the shot. If a new trial was granted, I would swear to the truth."[8]

Based on the new evidence revealed in the affidavits, Governor Merriam decided to hold a meeting at 3:00 p.m. that Thursday afternoon with Will Donahue, yet insisted that Prosecutor Robert Jamison be present as well. Jamison arrived ten minutes early, followed by Attorney General Clapp, and they both met privately with Governor Merriam for about thirty minutes before Will Donahue and Levi Gorman were allowed to join them.

Will Donahue presented the affidavits once again, and then he "made a most eloquent appeal." He started with the facts, stating that Henry's claim that Peter had shot Thomas Tollefson in the leg was a lie, because Henry himself had shot Tollefson, and the three affidavits proved it. He asked the governor to grant him just two more weeks so that the newly acquired evidence could be presented to Judge Lochren.

Donahue reminded the governor that the evidence, from two of the State's own witnesses in the case, was "voluntarily, unsolicited, and only impelled by the horror of a man being executed for a crime of which he was not guilty."[9]

Donahue then turned to Jamison and asked whether he had offered Peter a manslaughter plea before the trial began. He had not.

Donahue continued compellingly and dramatically,

> We are so near the grave now that there is no time for misrepresentation. The whole truth as is known by counsel on both sides should be shown to Your Excellency. In the name of the living God I proclaim before the world that I believe Peter Barrett did not fire a shot at Thomas Tollefson, or take any hand, act, or part, in the consummation of that fearful crime. In the name of humanity, justice, and mercy, I ask you now to exercise the power which is in you vested by the people of this great commonwealth [on] behalf of an unfortunate boy who was raised amid adverse circumstances, to save him from the untimely death which he has been condemned to suffer.[10]

However, the governor appeared unmoved. He remarked that he simply was not ready to make a decision on the matter and then dismissed Donahue.

When Will Donahue left, Robert Jamison and Levi Gorman remained. The governor questioned Gorman about his affidavit. He wanted to know why he had made the statement, whether it was true, and why he had waited so long to come forward.

Gorman made it clear to the governor that he had no personal concern for any of the Barretts but that his statement was true. He had believed that the truth would come out during the trials. "My conscience wouldn't let me keep still and see Pete Barrett hanged when I know he isn't guilty," Levi added, "I didn't tell it before because I didn't want to make enemies of Frank Davis and Bob Jamison. . . . I have told the truth now, and I will stand by it to the end of time." He added, "If the evidence would have been good then, is it not good news now?"[11, 12]

Jamison, who was still in the room, asked Gorman, "When you got ready to make the statement why didn't you come and tell me of it first?"[13]

"I did tell both you and Mr. Davis the day after I heard 'Reddy' make the admission, and you laughed it off and said it didn't amount to anything," Levi answered boldly.[14]

Jamison made the excuse that if he had been told he had simply forgotten.

Did Jamison have no concern for justice, or even consider the possibility that the State was about to execute an innocent person? The cases had been closed and resulted in notable victories for both the outgoing county attorney and the incoming county attorney.

Levi Gorman pressed on. He told the governor that he had told his story to the *St. Paul & Minneapolis Pioneer Press* reporter Joe Mannix one month earlier. So Governor Merriam sent for Mannix and dismissed Gorman.

Levi Gorman left that meeting disappointed, but without regret. He later told a newspaper reporter, "I told the straight truth. . . . I don't clamor for notoriety. . . . I have traveled and worked for the last four days at my own expense. It is not likely I would take so much trouble to invent a story for the benefit of men whom I hold in no higher esteem than the Barretts." He added, "County Attorney Jamison does not recollect my telling him of it, I am just as positive that I did tell him."[15]

By 4:00 p.m. that afternoon defense team Attorneys John T. Byrnes and David B. Johnson arrived at the capitol, likely rather disheveled and exhausted from having traveled 200 miles of rustic backroads.

Their mission to contact the twelve Hennepin County jurors from Peter's trial had been quite successful. They had managed to locate ten of those men, and each had signed the petition without reservation. In fact, two of them even wrote a personal message to Governor Merriam on the petition. Jury foreman R. Mills, who lived in the town of Independence, wrote, "I do most earnestly request that Your Excellency grant the commutation of Peter Barrett's sentence on account of his extreme youth and on account of his being led to crime by his older brother." Juror John Russell of Hassan wrote a similar message.[16]

Soon after Defense Attorneys Byrnes and Johnson had left, Joe Mannix arrived. He not only verified Gorman's affidavit but stated that Peter Barrett had told him the same story in a private conversation. What was said is uncertain, but the governor's meeting with Mannix was brief.

(*St. Paul & Minneapolis Pioneer Press* reporter Joe Mannix later wrote about the events of that Thursday, and in regard to the jurors' petition he recalled how immediately after the jury announced their verdict he had interviewed at least half of the jury members. He learned that the men had taken a vote amongst themselves "on a motion to recommend [Peter] to the mercy of the Court." Nine of the twelve jurors had favored a sentence of life imprisonment, not the "extreme penalty." When someone suggested that the Court "would doubtless consider the prisoner's youth, and deal with him accordingly," it was deemed unnecessary to express their opinion to Judge Lochren. In Mannix's opinion the jurors made a serious error by not voicing their concern, an error that could "cost Peter Barrett his life."[17])

Once Mannix left the governor's office, only Attorney Jamison remained.

It seemed as though none of the efforts made by the brothers' family, friends, or lawyers had any impact on the governor—until he carefully reviewed the petition signed by the jurors. At that point, Governor Merriam became concerned about Peter's age. However, when Attorney Jamison assured him "that Pete [was] not less than twenty-one years old," he was convinced that there was no basis for commuting his sentence to life in prison.[18]

Another hour passed. The two men parted ways as Governor Merriam left his office at the capitol and headed home.

Daylight had ended by the time he arrived at his mansion, but the governor's workday had not ended. He was visited there by Mrs.

Mary Barrett-Coleman and her friend, Mrs. Abbie Bryant, who was a reputable socialite. The two women tearfully pled for the life of Peter. Abbie Bryant also told the governor that John W. Arctander, an assistant to County Attorneys Frank Davis and Robert Jamison during the Barrett trials, had admitted to her that they all knew that Peter had not fired any shots, contrary to Henry's testimony.

Earlier that same day Governor Merriam had ordered that a telegram be sent to Frank Davis (at that time involved with a murder trial in Benson, Minnesota), requesting that he come at once to meet with him. By late evening Davis still had not arrived. . . . Thoughts about the petitions, the affidavits, and the various meetings stretched well into the evening. Governor Merriam had a lot to contemplate that night. Public sentiments regarding the executions were quite divided. Many thought of Henry Barrett as the ultimate betrayer of his brothers, while others, although few, sympathized with him. Some thought of the Barrett brothers as guilty criminals, but others believed they were actually victims.

That same day the *Minneapolis Tribune* had published an open letter written by Rev. J. B. Wright of Monticello, Minnesota—another plea to the governor. The reverend boldly requested "the commutation of the sentences of the Barretts in order that an 'atrocious murder' may not be carried out." [19, 20]

Many people expressed concern for the Barrett brothers, yet where was the concern for Thomas Tollefson, the murdered streetcar driver; for his widow, Lena; or for his family? Would the execution of the Barrett brothers truly bring justice or simply create more victims? Would a murder be avenged, or would an act of legal homicide occur? Would the actual murderer(s) remain free and possibly kill again?

We can only imagine that Governor Merriam must have contemplated all of those questions and more long after his final visitor left that evening. It was likely a long and restless night at the governor's mansion.

Governor Merriam.

Source: *St. Paul Daily Globe*, November 5, 1888,
Library of Congress, Chronicling America http://chroniclingamerica.loc.gov
image provided by Minnesota Historical Society, St. Paul, MN.

Hennepin County Attorney Robert Jamison.

Co. Atty. Jamison

Source: *St. Paul Daily Globe*, March 17, 1889,
Library of Congress, Chronicling America http://chroniclingamerica.loc.gov
image provided by Minnesota Historical Society, St. Paul, MN.

31

FINAL PREPARATIONS

WHILE GOVERNOR Merriam contemplated the situation, the Hennepin County Jail underwent various preparations for the executions and became quite a spectacle for the morbidly curious. The Barrett brothers were the talk of the town, and the newspapers printed stories about them almost daily. It was as though the people just could not get enough information. The reporters were eager to oblige, and the newspapers sold quickly.

On Thursday, March 21, photographer John E. Bodley became a prisoner at the Hennepin County Jail. Ironically, he had photographed the Barrett brothers in jail during the summer of 1888. Levi Gorman got ahold of the tintypes and showed them to artist Herbert Conner. Conner then sketched a more accurate likeness of each brother than had been done before and the *Minneapolis Evening Journal* published those sketches on March 22.

(Bodley, a forty-one-year-old, ran a city newspaper stand and lived in a boardinghouse at 243 Third Avenue North. This man of questionable character had allegedly been an abusive husband, and his wife, Lizzie, had divorced him. A license inspector named Mr. Ray arrested him for selling and possessing "indecent pictures." Bodley had the distinction of being the first person arrested for such a crime in the city—which carried the stiff penalty of either a "$500 fine or one year in the penitentiary."[1])

Other news of the week concerned the county's cost for the Barrett trials—about $8,000, which was a hefty sum back then. The expenses included $500 to County Attorney Jamison, $1,052.40 to Court Stenographer G. F. Hitchcock Jr., and, as one reporter referred to it, the "hospitality" bestowed upon Henry Barrett. "Instead of giving [Henry] the scaffold he was protected and fostered by the county for several months," wrote the reporter. At a total cost of over $1,000, Henry received various benefits as the prime witness for the State; among those itemized expenses were $22 for home repairs, $220.85 for groceries, $146.48 worth of meat, and at least one check written to Dr. W. F. Nye for Minnie Barrett's medical care. Henry and Minnie had lived under the protective custody of Officer Levi Gorman, who received $406.20 for room and board. Room and board at the county jail for Peter and Timothy Barrett, from the time of their arrests through March 1889, totaled about $800. So the expenses incurred, although meager by today's standards, made for another sore point, and it is likely that some citizens were eager to put an end to both the spending and the Barrett brothers.[2, 3]

During the mid-1800s execution by hanging had become an almost circus-like event rather than a somber occasion, often drawing large crowds of spectators. In an effort to create a more serious and dignified atmosphere, the scaffold was erected inside the Hennepin County Jail rather than out in the open, which effectively limited the viewing to a select number of people who would be admitted only by formal invitation. Although Sheriff James Ege tried to downplay the excitement about the event, he sent out more than 100 of these invitations, primarily to other sheriffs around the country.

Unfortunately, a few people acquired invitations underhandedly.

Some men had posed as representatives of the Street Railway Employees Association, and Sheriff Ege (unaware the men were imposters) gave them invitations. Shortly afterward, the association learned of it and met to discuss the situation. According to spokesman Simon McNulty, Chairman of the Executive Board for the association, the men were not only unauthorized to represent the association they were not even members. McNulty did not identify the men, but the motive behind their deception was obvious; they had sold the invitations.[4]

A photocopy of an original invitation to the execution of the Barrett brothers, signed by Sheriff Ege, appears at the end of this chapter. Instructions were also printed on the back of the invitation: "Present this for admission at the rear door of the jail."[5]

Regardless of the sheriff's efforts to restrict gawkers, excitement only intensified among the townspeople, and the topic continued to dominate newspaper headlines daily. A special telegraph line was even installed at the jail and strung through "the window on the Eighth Avenue side"—the side that faced "out[side] from the room where the execution" would take place. Curious spectators of all ages—men, women (some with babes in arms), and even schoolkids—gathered near the stone fence and steps of the jail "from almost sun-up to sundown each day."[6]

Chris Spere oversaw the construction of the gallows, a project that took nearly a week for the carpenters to finish. Afterward, they tested the device by attaching a sandbag weighing about 175 pounds to each rope and releasing the trapdoors. Apparently all was in working order, so the day before the execution jail officials began to admit groups of up to fifty people at a time to view the scaffold and watch a demonstration of how the trapdoors would be sprung (minus the use of ropes and sandbags, however).[7, 8]

>–‹•›–O–‹•›–‹

At 5:30 Thursday evening Tim and Pete were allowed to order their final supper from the Tremont Hotel, which provided much tastier food than the standard jailhouse fare. How well they actually ate depended on their appetite and is anyone's guess, since it must have been a rough night for the brothers. They might have wondered whether they would hear good news from Governor Merriam the next morning, or whether it would be their last. They might have imagined how it would feel to have a coarse hemp noose around their neck, to fall as the rope tightened under their own weight. Would they feel pain or be unconscious?

Tim and Peter had seen their mother during the day. She was heartbroken and made quite a scene, which only disturbed the brothers more. They likely would have welcomed a farewell visit from their soft-spoken father, John Barrett, but (according to one source) he had unexpectedly died in Sacramento, California.

Joe Mannix arrived and was allowed to remain long after other visitors had left.

Tim and Pete were visited by their priests, who stayed with them until the brothers seemed to be at peace. They left at 11:00 p.m.

It was very late that night when Peter called Jailer Riley over to his cell and the two talked. Riley held no ill feelings toward Pete, regardless of their January scuffle. Pete told him that he loved his brother Henry but felt betrayed. During his trial he'd hoped for a "life sentence, as he knew that 'Reddy' could not hold out for many years. . . . [The] truth would come out and [Pete] would be a free man once more." He said that Henry knew all about the shooting but did not say Henry was the shooter.[9]

Their talk ended, and Peter was alone. Was it hard for him to extinguish the flame of his only candle that night. . . to let the pitch black fall over him, filling the space where he lay between the ironclad walls? In the stillness of the hours when the living sleep came muffled, restless sounds from Tim's cell and the dull roar of the distant falls. . .

➤┼◆➤─○─◄◆┼◄

"Superintendent Brackett [had] detailed Captain Ness and [thirty-two] policemen" to keep order during the execution. The next morning, ten of these officers were stationed throughout the Hennepin County Jail. The others, under the command of Captain Harvey and Lieutenant Bean, stood guard outside where an orderly crowd of nearly 5,000 people gathered. "The [area] between the courthouse and the jail entrance was railed off and the policemen had no trouble in keeping the sightseers outside the enclosure. . . . A few boys had climbed the trees on the north side of 8th Avenue, but their cries were hushed and they conversed with each other in awestruck tones."[10, 11, 12]

⊱┄⊰⊱┄●┄⊰⊱┄⊰

When Ellen Barrett arrived at the sheriff's office with Attorney John T. Byrnes it was mid-morning. She asked to see her sons one last time but was denied and became hysterical, "I want to see my boys. I want to see my boys." She turned to Byrnes and asked, "Can't I see my boys? Make them take me to them."[13]

"Yes, you can," Byrnes consoled as he led her out the door, "Hurry now, Mrs. Barrett, and we will go uptown and see the governor and he will fix it for you."[14]

In truth, she was turned away at the request of her sons. They feared that to see her once more would break them down and create a terrible scene, so Father McGolrick and Father Corbett advised Sheriff Ege not to admit her that morning.[15]

⊱┄⊰⊱┄●┄⊰⊱┄⊰

Out of all who had been invited to witness the hangings, none had more right to be present than the widow of Thomas Tollefson. What had become of her?

The young woman who felt the brunt of loss and heartbreak, Mrs. Thomas Tollefson (whose first name had been recorded as "Christina" on their marriage license and in the city directory, also went by the name "Lena," as recorded in the newspapers), had worked (before their marriage) at the White Sewing Machine Company, located on

Nicollet Island. The superintendent of that company was Frank W. Barrett—of no relation to the Barretts in jail. He and his wife, Katharine, lived at 3336 Clinton Avenue with their three children, Richard, Edward, and Mary. The young widow Tollefson was naturally devastated by the news of her husband's death and became a close friend of Katharine. In fact, the family was so sympathetic toward Lena that they invited her to stay with them, which she did, for months at a time. (It was a strange irony that she was befriended out of the kindness of one Barrett family, while another was responsible for her suffering.)

It was during this difficult time that she met Morris T. Lunsburg through a mutual friend. Morris was a recent widower with two young children. They became well acquainted and eventually fell in love. On March 20, 1889, Morris and "Lena" Tollefson were married in Polk County, Wisconsin.

Just two days later, on March 22, the papers reported that the newlyweds were back in Minneapolis. They had gone to the Hennepin County Jail to witness the executions of the killers of Thomas Tollefson, but there was a problem. Lena had no formal invitation by which to be admitted. In fact, at that time women were barred from entering a room of execution. Although Sheriff Ege could have granted a special concession in her case, he could not be located at the time.

Thomas's widow, Christina Tollefson Lunsburg—who deserved admittance to the executions more than anyone else—was turned away.

The gallows inside the Hennepin County Jail.

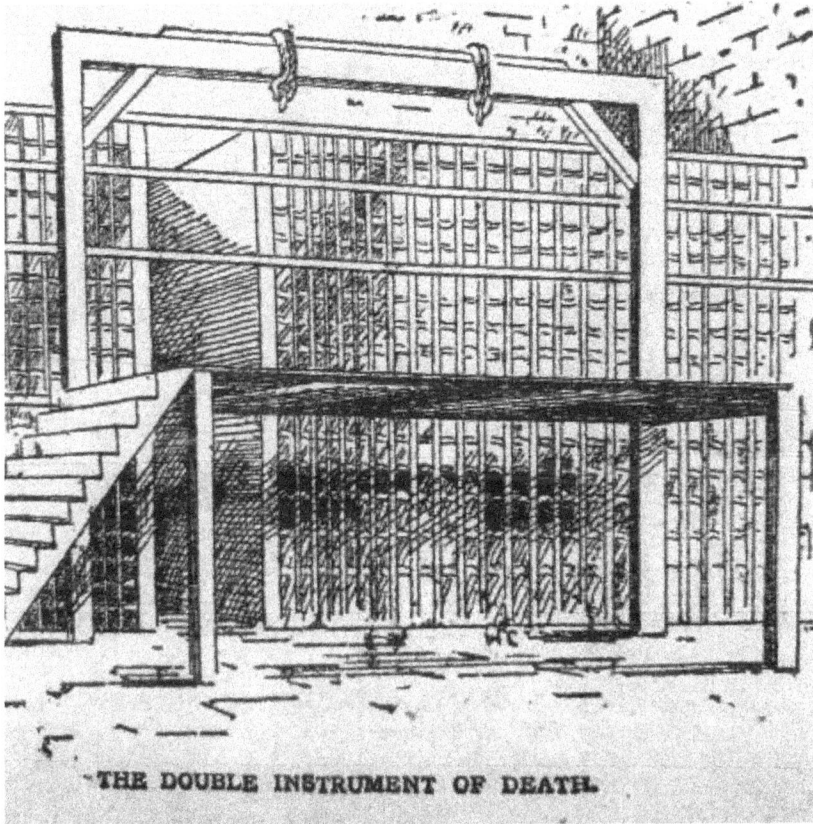

THE DOUBLE INSTRUMENT OF DEATH.

Source: *St. Paul Daily Globe,* March 17, 1889,
Library of Congress, Chronicling America http://chroniclingamerica.loc.gov
image provided by Minnesota Historical Society, St. Paul, MN.

Invitation to the execution
of Timothy and Peter Barrett.

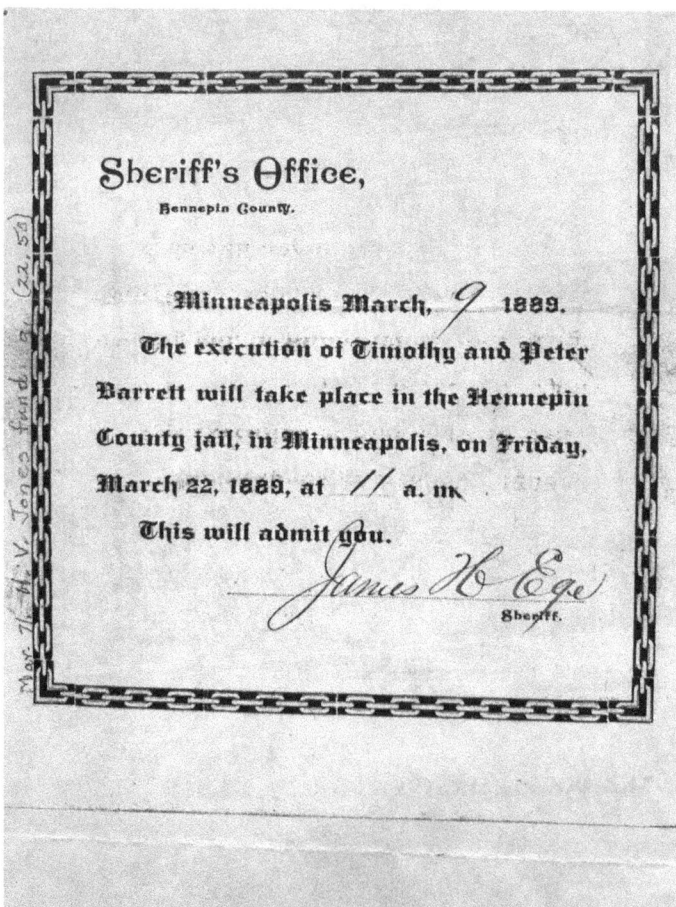

Sheriff's Office,
Hennepin County.

Minneapolis March, *9* 1889.

The execution of Timothy and Peter Barrett will take place in the Hennepin County jail, in Minneapolis, on Friday, March 22, 1889, at *11* a. m.

This will admit you.

James H. Ege
Sheriff.

32

Friday, March 22, 1889

AT 6:30 A.M. Father Corbett arrived at the jail to meet with the brothers. Father McGolrick arrived a half hour later. Moments spent with their spiritual advisors brought a much needed measure of serenity to the brothers.

Breakfast was delivered around 7:30 a.m. and was the heartiest meal ever served to them in jail. As they had requested, there were plates of fried eggs and toast, cranberry sauce, bananas, pie, jelly cake, and coffee. Tim ate well, but Peter could only force down some fruit and coffee.

Benjamin Ege, the sheriff's teenaged son, had often seen the brothers and chatted as he helped with various minor tasks at the jail. He visited the brothers one last time that morning, but they were withdrawn, deep in thought, and neither had much to say.

Peter nervously awaited news from Governor Merriam. Both brothers hoped for either a stay of execution or commutation of sentence, but no word came. The reality of what was about to occur grew louder with each silent cry of their hearts.

Sensing their final moments of life, they asked to see all of the deputies so they could say goodbye. When they met, each man shed a tear or two. In fact, Tim Barrett was so greatly affected that he wept bitterly.

By 9:00 a.m. the Reverend Father James McGolrick, a brother of Father Henry McGolrick who was already there, arrived at the jail and was escorted to the Barrett brothers' cells. The three priests administered rites and prayers for Timothy and Peter. At this point, the brothers could scarcely speak as a wave of fear and grief overwhelmed them.

Sometime shortly after, the brothers' attorneys showed up at the jail. When Pete heard that they had arrived, his face suddenly brightened, hoping for good news from Governor Merriam.

William Erwin, Will Donahue, and John T. Byrnes had made a strong but futile effort to save their clients. The three attorneys stopped briefly to view the gallows on their way to the brothers' jail cells. They met with Tim and Pete for about ten minutes. Little was specified as to what was said, but remorse and regret made for sad goodbyes.

With ashen faces, the attorneys somberly, quietly left the jail. This was the first time Bill Erwin had failed to save a client from hanging, and the burden weighed heavily on all of them.[1]

At 9:30 a.m. Governor Merriam staunchly told a reporter with the *St. Paul Dispatch*, "I shall not do anything. I do not intend to. I told [other] reporters that last night."[2]

Shortly after 10:00 a.m., with less than an hour to go before the executions, the brothers asked to see reporter Joe Mannix one last time and the three talked for about fifteen minutes. Whatever Tim's final statement was, it was meant to be kept private, so Joe simply wrote later that it was personal and not about the crime. However, Pete talked quite a bit and continued to claim he was innocent of the crime for which he was about to be punished. He was quoted as having said, "I am going to meet death like a man. I don't think I deserve this fate, but I must stand it. I now repeat as my dying statement that I did not take the part in the murder which Reddy said I took."[3]

It is interesting that the quote did not state that Pete *had no part* in the murder. In spite of all the evidence, all the effort made on his behalf, was this some admission of guilt, or simply the way Mannix reported it? On the other hand, if Peter were admitting guilt, wouldn't he have just said so? Both of these young men were about to die, they believed in God and had already met with their spiritual advisors, so wouldn't they have confessed their guilt? The mystery continues, in spite of the logical conclusion that they did not admit guilt because they were not guilty.

Sheriff Ege and Jailer James Riley also met with Tim and Pete in their cells. Father Corbett, Fathers James and Henry McGolrick, and Joe Mannix were all still there. Among the convicted brothers, reporter, law enforcement officers, and priests, there was not a single dry eye.

Although he didn't say much to the press about it, Joe Mannix learned that Sheriff Ege had furnished both Tim and Pete with brand new clothing to wear for the execution—suit coats made of black serge, a heavy twill fabric with diagonal weave, and crisp white shirts with high collars. The young men would at least wear clean, dignified clothing and appear at their very best despite their inner turmoil.

Strong, dignified, solid, yet tenderhearted, Sheriff Ege was more than a bit shaken by the whole matter, yet he understood that he had a job to do. As Sheriff of Hennepin County, his duty would be to pull the level that would release the trap doors of the gallows.[4]

With a firm handshake, Joe Mannix managed a final goodbye to the brothers he had befriended—a relationship that had begun shortly after the arrests. He believed Peter Barrett, whose story had never changed over the many times he'd told it. Joe Mannix, the reputable and seasoned reporter, was deeply moved and affected by the situation.

Meanwhile the examining board of physicians—Doctors Burton, Dunn, Kivington, Quinby, and Coroner Towers, along with Mayor Doc Ames—arrived just before 10:00 a.m. and settled into their seats at the gallows. It would be their authoritative duty to pronounce the time of death and examine the bodies. Other doctors were present to observe, including Coroner Willis Spring.

Police Superintendent Brackett had a simple, yet necessary task to perform in order to facilitate the gruesome deed: he rubbed bar soap over the rough surfaces of the ropes. The soap left a somewhat waxy, slick film that allowed the nooses to slide more easily and to tighten firmly. Final adjustments were also made to the length of each rope to ensure each body would fall properly through the trap door and hang at the correct level.

Former Sheriff Swenson stepped across the platform to shake hands with Sheriff Ege and the two spoke briefly in hushed tones.

The room was likely abuzz with multiple conversations when, with only minutes left to go before the execution, an assistant with the sheriff's office stepped to the front of the gallows and a hush fell over the waiting crowd. He announced, "May I have your attention, please. Sheriff James Ege has requested that as the prisoners enter, all gentlemen remove your hats and please refrain from talking until after the executions have been completed."

The priests stayed with the brothers throughout the remaining moments, calming them as best they could with prayers and the reading of the Holy Scriptures.

At 10:45 a.m. Sheriff Ege and his deputies approached the top tier of cells. One of the men carried neatly folded outer coverings for the condemned brothers to wear. Described as shrouds, the garments were straight, sleeveless coats made of "black facing cloth"—a fabric commonly used to line dresses in those days. The main purpose of the shrouds was to conceal the straps that were used to securely bind the legs and arms of the prisoners during execution. There were also matching black caps made of "heavy woolen goods with a deep roll to be turned down all around the head." A four-inch square piece of the black facing cloth was stitched to the front of each cap and would partially cover the face at the moment of execution.[5]

As the men entered the corridor just outside of the Barrett brothers' cells, Sheriff Ege stopped and loudly declared, "Timothy and

Peter Barrett, you have been previously informed that the death sentence passed upon you by the judge was affirmed by the governor of this state, and that the date of your execution was fixed for today. It now becomes my painful duty to carry out the sentence of the law." [6]

Sheriff Ege entered Tim's cell first and handed him one of the long shrouds to slip over his suit. He handcuffed him, then placed the black cloth cap on Tim's head. Ege entered Pete's cell, and repeated the procedure.

The officers had been waiting quietly just outside their cell doors and when Sheriff Ege led Tim and Pete into the corridor, they quickly lined up in the assigned order for the procession to the gallows. Sheriff Ege took the lead, with Father James McGolrick a few steps behind him. Then came Tim Barrett with Father Corbett beside him, accompanied by Deputies Jacob Rauen, Frank Ward, and George H. Johnson. Father Henry McGolrick walked with Pete Barrett while Jailer James Riley and Deputy John Peterson walked on either side, and Deputy John Servis followed. Frank Tickham and Joseph Shaw, "the faithful deathwatches, came up in the rear." The priests encouraged the brothers to have courage in spite of their fear and Father James McGolrick began to recite the Litany for the Dead. The group of fourteen men walked slowly through the jail, passing "forty [to] fifty prisoners in the second and first tier of cells [who] watched with breathless interest." They continued "down two flights of stairs, across the stone pavement, and through the hallway separating the two wings of the jail." [7, 8]

Muffled, monotonous sounds grew louder and more distinct to those who waited in the "death room." The procession finally entered a large room where hushed spectators stood rigid, the tense atmosphere oddly energized as anticipation mingled with dread. Leather soles scuffed against cold concrete, the wooden stairs leading up to the gallows creaked beneath each footstep, and the priests continued to recite the litany as the brothers responded, "God have mercy on us." [9, 10]

One observer noted that Tim's voice was strangely loud and methodical, his eyes dark-circled as he stared blankly from a colorless face. Peter was also pale, but he calmly rolled his eyes as though searching and effectively averted his gaze from the faces that glared judgment against him.

Outside the curious crowd spilled well beyond the front of the jail out into 8th Avenue South, filling the entire block between 4th and 5th Streets. A strangely sadistic block party, the mood was far less than somber. When news that the brothers had entered the execution room reached their ears, "a yell went up . . . which would do credit to a prize fight."[11, 12]

Pete ascended the gallows steps with no problem. However, Tim caught his foot in the ankle-length hem of the black shroud, stumbled briefly, and Deputy Rauen grabbed his arm to steady him. The deputies helped position the brothers, who were hindered by their shackles. Tim stood over the trap door near the window and Peter on the one nearer the entrance to the jail.

Father McGolrick stood between the two trap doors and began the Ceremony of Absolution for Tim; this lasted nearly ten minutes. Loudly and firmly Tim repeated, "Jesus, have mercy on us."[13]

At the conclusion of the ceremony on Tim's behalf, the deputies "commenced the work of pinioning the bodies with the straps. . . . Sheriff Ege adjusted the nooses over [the brothers'] necks." Those slight movements somewhat displaced the brothers' positions, and Sheriff Ege helped them inch back into place, which is as far as they were able to move at one time, so restrained by the tightened straps that bound their legs and arms.[14]

Sheriff Ege then lowered the black cap over Tim's face and he stood in that manner, slightly trembling, as he waited for the Ceremony of Absolution for Peter to be completed. In contrast to Tim, Peter spoke softly and fixed his eyes on the trap door at his feet.

At the conclusion the priest gave Peter a "parting kiss" and helped Jailer Riley pull the black cap down over his face. Peter moaned, then whispered emotionally, "Oh God, I am being punished too much for what I have done. . . . Oh Lord, I am innocent."[15, 16, 17]

The two brothers stood, awaiting the inevitable, bodies and faces covered in black, when a sudden glare shot through the window like a spotlight, momentarily illuminating their shrouded figures before it quickly disappeared. The dramatic, eerie display was later a topic of much speculation, but no one ever discovered the actual source of that beam of light.

Sheriff Ege quickly checked the brothers' straps, looked the ropes up and down, and cast one parting glance at the prisoners before stepping across the platform to complete his duty.

The priests continued reciting the Litany for the Dying, and the brothers were in the midst of responding when the trap doors beneath their feet fell open.

The last words ever spoken by Peter Barrett were "Oh, God, have—."[18]

At precisely 11:13:30 a.m. on Friday morning, March 22, 1889, Timothy and Peter Barrett were executed in the Hennepin County Jail.

Their suspended bodies hung rigid "for a moment, and then a convulsive quiver shook the entire frame of each. Tim made three spasmodic efforts to draw up his knees, after which his body remained [still] with the exception of a slight quiver." Timothy Barrett died within thirteen minutes. "Pete made several efforts to draw up his legs, and his body swayed slightly, the fingers of his hands twitching." Peter Barrett died within fifteen minutes. Ten more minutes passed before the officials pronounced them dead and at 11:47 a.m. their bodies were taken down.

The board of physicians completed their examinations and determined that both Tim and Pete had suffered dislocated necks. In their opinion, both brothers had lost consciousness almost immediately after the traps were sprung, in spite of the terrible spasms observed.

At 2:00 p.m. "the bodies were removed from the jail at a rear door so as to avoid the crowd" that still lingered outside. They were delivered to T. Connolly & Company, the undertaker, to be prepared for burial. Death certificates were filed by Coroner F. E. Towers, M.D., who wrote that the cause of death for both brothers was "strangulation by hanging."[19]

>–⊷–O–⊷–<

Father Corbett was "prostrated with grief," after the executions. Many people assumed that he believed that Peter was innocent of the crime and wrongly executed.[20]

The Minneapolis Evening Journal wrote that the Barrett brothers' execution was "one of the most dramatic stories in the criminal annals of Minnesota. . . . [F]rom the moment Reddy Barrett stepped upon the witness stand he was the central figure of the trial. All eyes were . . . upon him in mingled admiration and horror: admiration for the nerve of the man; horror that he could solemnly put the noose about his brothers' necks to save his own carcass." Several days later the April 4 edition printed, "The fact is, everything was thrown about that execution to give it a terrible solemnity. The solemn march of the procession to the scaffold, the loud chanting of the priests, and all that gave a dignity to the thing, though it could not conceal the fact that it was nothing less than legal butchery."[21]

>–⊷–O–⊷–<

On the morning of March 24 a funeral procession was led by ornately plumed horses that pulled two hearses. Carriages filled with the Barrett family and friends followed. The service for the brothers began at 9:00 a.m. at the Church of the Immaculate Conception in St. Paul. Father Corbett, who had been so grief-stricken, led the requiem high mass.[22]

On the very next day, Monday, March 25, Ellen Barrett returned to Omaha by train—the same train that had carried Peter to Minneapolis after his arrest, with the same conductor as well. Two pine box coffins containing the bodies of Timothy and Peter were loaded onto the baggage car. It was a bitterly difficult journey for Ellen, who wept and moaned the whole way, according to Tim Maquire, the baggage man. On her lap she carried a "small willow basket containing the shrouds" worn by her sons at the time of their execution.[23]

That evening a visitation was held in Omaha at Ellen's home. By then the pine boxes had been replaced with fine rosewood coffins, each embellished with a silver plate engraved simply "At Rest." Glowing taper candles surrounded each coffin during the wake, and the room was filled with friends and family who had come to pay their last respects and offer condolences to the family.[24]

At 10:00 a.m. on Tuesday morning, March 26, another funeral was held for Timothy and Peter Barrett, and they were buried in the family plot at St. Mary's Cemetery.

Diagram of the Hennepin County Jail showing the route to the gallows.

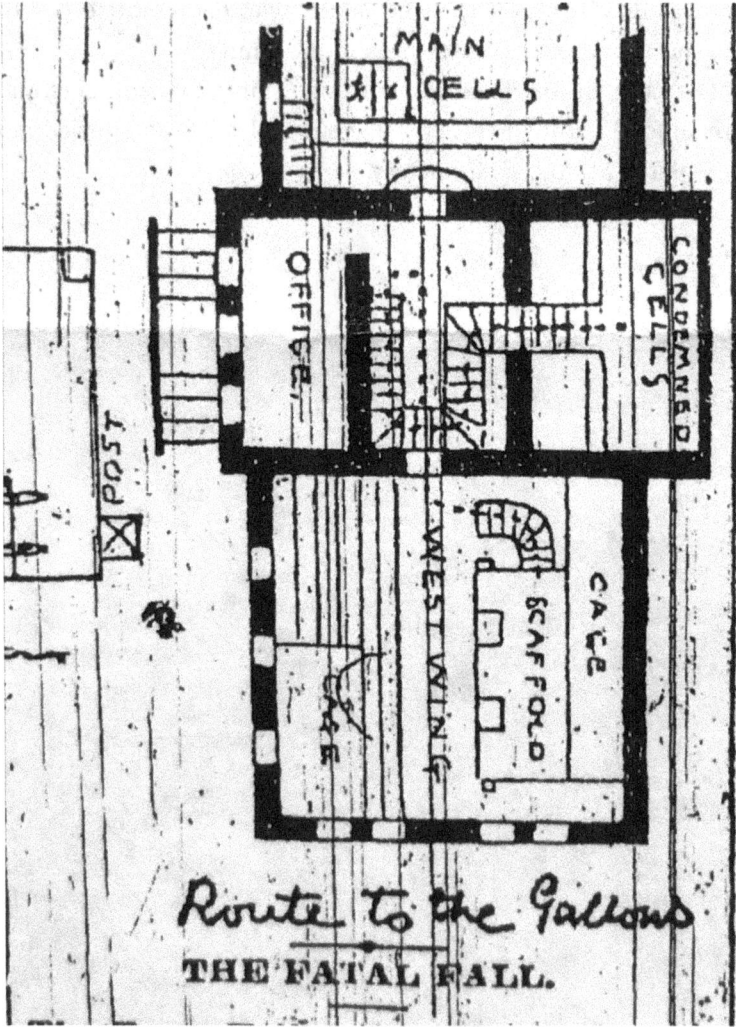

MAIN CELLS

OFFICE

POST

CONDEMNED CELLS

WEST WING

CAGE

SCAFFOLD

Route to the Gallows

THE FATAL FALL.

Source: *St. Paul & Minneapolis Pioneer Press*, March 23, 1889,
Minnesota Historical Society, St. Paul, MN.

The March to the Gallows.

The March to The Gallows

Source: *St. Paul & Minneapolis Pioneer Press*, March 23, 1889,
Minnesota Historical Society, St. Paul, MN.

"The Last Scene of Life—Pinioning Pete, while Tim Kneels in Prayer."

BEFORE THE DROP.

The Last Scene of Life--Pinioning Pete, while Tim Kneels in Prayer.
[From an Instantaneous Photograph, taken on the spot.]

Source: *St. Paul Daily Globe*, March 23, 1889,
Library of Congress, Chronicling America http://chroniclingamerica.loc.gov
image provided by Minnesota Historical Society, St. Paul, MN.

Father James McGolrick.

ᵁNEXPECTED ᴺEWS

I T DIDN'T take long before rumors started circulating and even made front-page headlines in the April 9 edition of the *St. Paul Daily Globe*:

Wild and Weird.
Are the Tales They Tell of Resuscitating Pete Barrett . . .

Undertaker Connolly and the
Physicians Scout the Strange Story.

Authenticated Cases in Which Gallows
Fruit Was Preserved.

Meanwhile Peter Barrett's Ghost
Terrifies the Car Drivers.[1]

The article reported that some of the streetcar drivers, among others, had supposedly caught sight of the Barrett brothers' apparitions near Layman's Cemetery. Oddly, more than a few people held the opinion that Peter Barrett was actually alive!

Could he have survived the execution? Apparently, there had been cases in which a condemned individual wore a special harness concealed under their clothing to prevent strangulation during the hanging.

Speculation about the possibility of Peter's survival may have been based on the newspaper story about a mysterious stranger who had visited the Barretts at the jail and attended the execution. (An invitation was required for admittance, the man had not been on the list, and Sheriff Ege had not invited strangers.) The man's demeanor was odd; he had never spoken to Tim or Pete, simply stared, and stared directly at their covered faces throughout the execution. When ". . . Undertaker Connolly and his assistants came to remove the dead . . . [the man] asked several questions . . . became annoying and was ordered away by the police." He left the jail but followed the hearses from the jail to the morgue, where officials turned him away.[2]

The newspaper reporter identified the strange man as "Dr. Patrick McMahon . . . a practicing physician at Omaha, [and] an intimate friend of the Barretts." The previous night he reportedly boarded a train for Chicago "accompanied by a heavily veiled old lady . . . [and] occupied a section of the sleeping car [he had] booked . . . under the name of 'Dr. McMahon and Mother.'" The reporter surmised that the old lady, who was "clad in deep mourning" clothing was actually Peter Barrett in disguise![3]

He then explained his conspiracy theory in detail. First, that Dr. McMahon had resuscitated Peter Barrett after the hanging and switched his body with that of a corpse. The pallbearers of Peter's coffin at the funeral the next day (who had refused to give their names) were actually medical students of Dr. McMahon at St. Joseph's Hospital back in Omaha and had come along in order to assist the doctor with his plan.

The reporter even ran this theory past some of the attending physicians who had been present at the execution, although he admitted,

"No one who knows Mr. Connolly could for a moment believe that he could be personally influenced or deceived in a way to render such an occurrence possible, and his assistants are also very honorable and trustworthy men. But, all things—humanly speaking—are possible, and they may have been successfully deceived."[4]

Another reporter interviewed Connolly and asked him about the possibility of such a thing having happened. The undertaker "at first appeared as much amused as he was surprised, but soon manifested annoyance and indignation of the inventor of 'such foolish gossip.'" Connolly assured, "I brought [those bodies] here directly from the gallows. They were stripped and carefully prepared for burial. They were in as fine condition as any that I have ever handled—Pete's especially. I do not think his neck was broken, but that he was strangled. I feel sure of it; but I am most absolutely certain that they were both 'as dead as a doornail,' as the saying is, and what's more, they'll never come to life again. They were in my charge until they were placed aboard the train for Omaha. All this gabble about their ghosts is worse than nonsense. It is not right."[5]

Dr. Quinby told the reporter, "I examined both of those bodies carefully and know that they were dead—of course they were dead. Their necks were dislocated, the respiratory center was displaced and they were beyond all possibility of resuscitation." Doctors Burton, Dunn, Kivington, and Coroner Towers were all in agreement and thought it was foolish to entertain such gossip, let alone dignify it by printing it in the newspaper. (Mayor Doc Ames was ill at the time and unavailable for comment.)[6]

The reporter added, "All however, agreed that a post-mortem examination alone could absolutely disclose the real cause of the death of the Barretts. Ought not the law require a thorough post-mortem be made in each and every instance?"[7]

The *St. Paul Daily Globe* reporter then alluded to a story the *Minneapolis Evening Journal* had published a few days earlier regarding a news report from Smithville, Tennessee. A stranger there had stopped at a "well-known farmer's house and stayed several hours. The farmer saw his guest arranging his handkerchief around his neck and saw that his neck was badly skinned and swollen. The man, on being closely questioned, confessed that he was Mark Francis, who had been hanged . . . at Lebanon, and that he had been resuscitated by his relatives. Francis's neck was not broken and as the rope slipped, he was not strangled. After his body had hung for twenty minutes the physicians pronounced him dead."[8]

The same article referred to yet another instance of a man who had been hung and then resuscitated: "Antonio Pallidino . . . was executed upon the gallows Oct. 8, 1888, at Bridgeport, [Connecticut] for the murder of his brother. The citizens believe (and the local newspapers published the facts) that the culprit was not dead when cut down, after having hung thirteen minutes, and despite the fact that the priest superintended the burial of the body, it was believed to have been exhumed quickly, under cover of darkness, hurried away to a secluded dwelling far out of the city and . . . received by a number of waiting physicians and students from Yale college, who at once set to work, applied electric and other means, which soon resulted in complete restoration. No intelligent physician or scientist will deny that such results are possible, and . . . if the neck of the victim was not broken, all the probabilities were in his favor."[9]

The story continued that after the execution the body had been cut down and examined by the doctors, none of whom could detect any heartbeat or "pulsation of the . . . temples." The implication was that they had missed the last smoldering spark of life—that the victim was merely unconscious, his heartbeat so slow and his breathing so shallow as to be undetectable.[10]

Apparently there were "at least some who [would] never be convinced that Peter Barrett was not secretly removed from the morgue . . . hurried away to the lone forest cottage back of the Lake of the Isles, and there brought back to life, nursed, nourished, strengthened, and . . . hearty as ever."[11]

Were such stories the result of a few overactive imaginations, or could they have been true? Only a couple of weeks had passed since the executions, and there remained so much interest about the case that there was talk of putting the gallows on display at the popular Dime Store Museum.

The notion that Peter survived would eventually die off without proof and the stories would end.

On Saturday, June 1, 1889, yet another story appeared. A reporter with the *Omaha Herald* had interviewed a woman named Mrs. Thomas. She was certain she had spoken to Peter months after the executions, his voice still hoarse from the incident. According to her, Peter admitted that his execution had been staged to look as though he were dead. The noose had been adjusted somehow so that it would not slip, and he had worn a special type of harness concealed beneath his clothing. Peter was rendered unconscious by the sheer force of his body falling through the trap door. The coroner pronounced him dead before handing his body over to friends of the Barretts. At that time, someone worked on him for three hours in order to revive him. After he had somewhat recovered, he left Minneapolis dressed as a woman and traveled to Chicago.

The story continued that a corpse had been taken from the morgue, was substituted for Pete's body, and was sent back to Omaha along with Tim's body. At the wake their mother had caressed the top of Tim's casket as she mourned over him. However, she quite noticeably ignored the other casket—odd, considering that Peter, the youngest, was known to be her favorite son.

Mrs. Thomas, a neighbor of the Barretts, had known the family for several years. She stated that she was willing to sign an affidavit that Peter Barrett was still alive. A young woman named Johanna Corbitt had lived with the Barrett family for two years and also claimed that Peter was alive. Peter reportedly had told both women that he would be leaving for California and would never return to Omaha. He had sent word for Johanna to come and see him before he left. An unidentified twelve-year-old neighbor boy had also seen Peter and said he had watched him leave the house in the early morning and return at dark each day.

William Raley was a traveling salesman from Cincinnati who told the same reporter about a common rumor he had heard circulating in Minneapolis: "Pete Barrett did not pay the penalty of the law" for the Tollefson murder.[12]

The reporter's story sounded convincing. But could it have been true?

At the time of the execution, Sheriff Ege and his deputy entered Tim Barrett's cell first and gave him the black shroud and cap to wear. They entered Peter's cell afterward. Could they have placed a special harness under Pete's clothing at that time and concealed it under the black shroud?

When the bodies were taken down after the hangings, it was determined that neither neck was broken. The bodies were taken from the jail using the back door to avoid the crowd. Could they have taken Peter's body to some Barrett family friends? Could there have been another corpse at the morgue that was substituted for Peter?

In order for Peter Barrett to have escaped death by the noose, the sheriff, deputies, examining physicians, coroner, and even the Catholic priests had to be willing to work together in order to disobey the law. How likely was that?

SEASONS OF CHANGE

A FEW DAYS after the executions of the Barrett brothers, one Minneapolis judge recommended a monument to honor the memory of crime victim Thomas Tollefson. "He was a brave man," the judge noted, adding that he was certain the donations for it could be raised, especially if Thomas Lowry were to take the lead "with his customary generosity."[1]

Whether or not the idea caught on, I know of no such monument in existence today. It would have been a fitting tribute for the young man whose grave was marked by a simple wooden shingle, roughly and briefly inscribed "Thomas Tollefson, July 26, 1887."[2]

Two months before the executions, on January 13, 1889, Henry and Minnie Barrett had another son and named him Theodore, after Minnie's father, Theodore Betts of Northfield, Minnesota. The baby was born in Hennepin County, so we know the family was still in Minneapolis at that time.

In February 1889 Henry passed through Council Bluffs, Nebraska, on his way to St. Louis to be with Minnie, who was ill. Reporters talked with him there and noted that he had not visited his mother or other family members.

This was probably due to the fact that they were all angry with Henry, even to the point that his brother Frank had threatened to shoot him on sight. As far as the Barrett family was concerned, Henry was a traitor. One can only imagine how the painful burden of family shunning, the guilt, must have weighed heavily on Henry's soul. He told an *Omaha Daily Bee* reporter, "I have told my story and it is on the court records in Minneapolis. I am sorry to say that it is true . . . for more reasons than one."[3]

Henry again repeated his version of the crime story: how it had been Tim who fired the shot that killed Thomas Tollefson and that he and Pete had run off into Layman's Cemetery. He blamed Tim for the whole thing. He had hoped that both of his brothers would receive a lighter sentence but wasn't overly concerned about Tim, whom he described as a "tough character." However, he was concerned about Pete, and had believed that he would be spared from execution by Governor Merriam.[4]

Henry complained about the hardships of his life under police surveillance during and after the trials and noted that because the Supreme Court had decided not to grant the appeal he was finally free to move on. He expressed a desire to settle down someplace where the terrible situation would "not stare me in the face."[5]

The reporter also wrote that Ellen Barrett and the grown children who lived with her were under constant police surveillance at that time. Ed Barrett had been arrested for larceny on numerous occasions, various family members were known by the Omaha courts, and Tim and Pete had bad reputations and were considered "dangerous characters by the authorities." Was all of that true, or was that simply according to an obviously disturbed Henry?[6]

Two months after Tim and Pete were executed, the May 30 edition of *The Worthington Advance* newspaper printed the following brief story:

Supposed Suicide of a Famous Witness.

A farmer driving into Winona the other day found the body of a man hanging to a tree in a pasture. People who had examined the corpse thought it was that of Henry Barrett through whose testimony his two brothers, Timothy and Peter, were hanged in Minneapolis last March for the murder of a street-car driver. Deceased was seen a day or two before, and appeared to be wandering around in an aimless fashion. Henry Barrett left Minneapolis about a month before his brothers were hanged.[7]

How tragic . . . except that the story was false!

Earlier news accounts had mentioned the possibility that Henry and Minnie had changed their names. While they lived under protective custody as witnesses for the State during the trials and stayed at the Lake House in Waconia, they went by the names of Mr. and Mrs. Smith. Considering the threats they had received, it is quite understandable, and even reasonable, to suggest that they might have decided to permanently change their names in order to have a fresh start.

There was no more information about, or reference to, Minnie or Henry in the city directories or local newspapers until autumn of 1889. Reddy Barrett sent a letter to Levi Gorman stating that he was financially "prospering and [had] a bank account, but wanted to get away from the Barrett family, and wanted to move to South America."[8]

▷–◆◇–O–◇◆–◁

The United States Census is a good source of family history, but, unfortunately, the census data for 1890 was largely destroyed in a fire. The Federal census is recorded every ten years, making 1900 the next year available. So other sources, such as Find a Grave, Family Search, Gen Forum, Gen Web, Heritage Quest, etc., had to be utilized to trace Henry and Minnie—another option was to search the names of other family members. For example, searching the names of Minnesota Betts's family members yielded information. Theodore Betts, the father of Minnie and Chloe, was admitted to the United States National Home for Disabled Veterans in Milwaukee in January 1908—almost twenty years after the executions. Only Chloe, of Minneapolis, was listed as his next of kin; there was no Minnie on the record.

Also, Chloe Betts had married Levi Gorman, and the couple had two daughters, Hazel and Minnie. Researching the names of Chloe's daughters led to the Find a Grave website, and vital information was found there—including actual photographs of both Henry and Minnie! They had changed their last name and moved to Chicago. (For the sake of protecting the identities of their children's descendants, the surname used will not be revealed here.) Fact checking dates of birth, next of kin, etc., confirmed that they truly were Henry Michael Barrett and Minnesota Betts Barrett.

Henry is listed in the Chicago city directory as early as 1889; however, he is not listed every year. This may be due to the fact that the couple moved so frequently. The city directories back then listed a person's occupation along with their address. Henry started his life in Chicago as a "canvasser" living at 23 Fry Avenue. One year later he was a "clothes wringer" and lived at 22 Bismarck. There is a five-year gap with no listing for Henry, but his name reappears in 1896—he had moved once again and lived at 1091 Hancock, and his occupation was listed as a "carrier" for the post office—a job he continued for at least four years and likely much longer. By 1900 he had moved again and lived at 1835 Augusta. After 1900 there is a fifteen-year span of time with no listing for him.

In one unexpected twist I found a brief notice regarding the arrest of Henry in May 1912. He had already been employed by the United

States Postal Service as a mail carrier for several years but was arrested when he allegedly "rifled mails." (The old news source titled "The Day Book" was an advertisement-free paper about Chicago happenings that was published by Edward Willis Scripps. Geared for the "working-class readership," it ran every day except Sundays from September 1911 through July 1917.)

Regardless, Henry and Minnie seem to have had a successful and happy life together after the executions of his brothers. They had several children after the tragic loss of their newborn Henry Jr. during the Barrett trials in 1888. As stated previously, in 1889 baby Theodore was born, and in the years following came the births of Arthur, Harry, Catherine, Alfred, Mary, John, and Eleanor. It appears that the couple took on the role of loving parents and responsible citizens. In later years Henry was employed in honorable positions as a postmaster, bank manager, and insurance broker. He eventually became a landowner as well and owned an entire section (160 acres) of land in the Humbolt Park area where they lived.

Did the couple ever long for what life might have been like had they not changed their last name and moved to Chicago? Did Henry ever have feelings of shame or remorse over the execution deaths of his brothers?

We don't know the answers to those questions, but Henry and Minnie did experience personal heartache and tragedy while in Chicago. Sadly, their eldest son, Theodore, died on July 26, 1904—the seventeenth anniversary of the murder of Thomas Tollefson. Was this an eerie coincidence—or something more?

Theodore was a fifteen-year-old "school boy" whose death was reported by Charles Espy, the neighborhood doctor. Since it was not reported by his parents, he may have been under the doctor's care when he died.

Six years after Theodore's death, Henry and Minnie lost another child, their daughter Catherine. And a few short years later Henry suffered another devastating blow when his sweetheart, Minnie, died in early January of 1913 at the age of forty-one.

Henry survived Minnie by more than three decades and spent some of his final years at the home of one of their sons. Henry was seventy-eight years old when he died on August 21, 1945. He is buried near Minnie, son Theodore, and daughter Catherine at Oakridge-Glen Cemetery in Cook County, Illinois.

Henry and Minnie were beloved by their children and grandchildren, who likely were unaware of the family's dark secrets or the connection with the Barrett family. The information recorded here is not intended to do harm. The situation of any ancestor's background may not be common knowledge among their descendants; however, the facts stand and are disclosed here according to well-documented and credible sources.

Many people were embittered by the deaths of Peter and Timothy Barrett. Some blamed Henry for the whole situation, even going so far as to say that Henry betrayed the lives of his brothers to save his own. Frank Barrett threatened Henry's life because of his testimony against them, and the Barrett family was forever torn apart.

Yet, there were others who believed Henry, sided with him, and sympathized. After all, he was young, newly married, and had a baby on the way at the time of the trials. The lives of Henry and Minnie were never the same from the moment they became protected witnesses for the State. Henry may have saved his life, but in a very real sense, he also lost it. The broken family ties were never mended.

Thomas and Christina Tollefson were newlyweds, as well. They likely had hoped to begin a family of their own—until Thomas's life was cut short. Regardless of who had committed this tragic crime, Thomas and Christina were the primary victims. They deserved justice, but did the executions of Peter and Timothy Barrett deliver justice or create more victims?

Corruption was rampant under the leadership of Mayor 'Doc' Alonzo Ames and his cronies. Unfortunately, there were some dirty cops, all of which made it extremely frustrating and difficult for honest and decent lawmen, leaders, and citizens who tried their best to perform their duties. We will likely never know the whole story of

Thomas Tollefson's murder, or of the Barrett brothers, this side of heaven. The one remaining, tragic truth is that the State of Minnesota sentenced an underaged prisoner to death.

John T. Byrnes, the assistant attorney for the Barretts, made the following statement after the executions:

> I assert that the hanging of Peter was a judicial murder. I think County Attorney Jamison went too far. The conviction was secured on very questionable evidence, but Mr. Jamison fought for it, going beyond the courts and using his influence with the governor to have the boy hung, even after the evidence of Levi Gorman and Chloe Betts, who say they heard Reddy Barrett say that it was he and not Peter who fired the shot. . . . Mr. Jamison's duty as an official was fully discharged when the case went to the jury, but he was present when this new evidence for the State that had been discovered subsequent to the trial was given the governor, and [he] disputed the truthfulness of Gorman and Chloe Betts, both of whom he had used as witnesses for the State. As to the governor, he should have given us [the defense counsel] the time to carry the new evidence to the courts, and not act upon the evidence of the prosecuting attorney. Another thing, the governor would not allow the counsel for the defense to be present when Levi Gorman told his story, but allowed Mr. Jamison, the prosecuting officer, to be there and dispute the witness' truthfulness.[9]

Regardless of whether we believe that the Barrett brothers were guilty or not, the fact is that Peter was only seventeen years old at the time of Thomas Tollefson's murder. Were he and Tim involved? Were they at the scene of the crime? Consider the witnesses who testified. Who had a motive to lie? Was there a cover-up? Was there evidence of corruption? Consider the reputation of the reporter who so easily gained the trust of the prisoners, even stayed with them during their final moments—would *he* have lied?

Governor Merriam chose not to intervene with the decisions the court had made before his election— in part due to County Prosecutor Robert Jamison's insistence that Peter was of age, despite the insistence of others that he was not. What convinced him to ignore the pleas of the brothers' sister, Mary Barrett-Coleman? To dismiss the reputable Addie Bryant? Or to question the testimony of Officer Levi Gorman? Why did he disregard Attorney William Donahue, who was so adamant about Peter's young age that he presented the governor with not just one but two separate petitions—one of which had been signed by hundreds of citizens, including 100 attorneys and judges?

Historically, Governor Merriam is regarded as a good man and a good governor. Did he ever regret his decision?

Ten days after the Barrett brothers were executed, a bill to abolish the death penalty—which had been postponed—was again debated. The Barrett case was cited as having had a profound impact on lawmakers at the time, and legislation to change the manner in which executions were carried out was passed. Decades later, on April 22, 1911, the death penalty was abolished in Minnesota.

Undeniably, there must be a deterrent in place for those who would commit the terrible crime of murder. There are convincing legal arguments for, as well as against, the death penalty. Whichever side of the issue you find yourself on, we should all be able to agree with these distinct words of wisdom: "Acquitting the guilty and condemning the innocent—the LORD detests them both" (Proverbs 17:15, NIV).[10]

Thomas Tollefson.

Source: *St. Paul Daily Globe*, March 17, 1889,
Library of Congress, Chronicling America http://chroniclingamerica.loc.gov
image provided by Minnesota Historical Society, St. Paul, MN.

AFTERWORD

❦ THOMAS TOLLEFSON:

His grave was relocated from Layman's Cemetery (aka Old Soldiers and Pioneers Cemetery) to the Hillside Cemetery on September 30, 1921. Aside from the information in this book, little is known about the young homicide victim.

❦ STREETCAR NUMBER 132:

Thomas Tollefson drove this streetcar on the night of his murder. The *St. Paul Daily Globe* published a story on September 13, 1903, titled "Makes His Home in the Old Street Car on Which Thomas Tollefson Was Murdered by the Barrett Boys in Minneapolis 16 Years Ago." The occupant, a nearly sixty-year-old Swedish immigrant named Peter Olson, was "employed by Barrett & Zimmerman to take charge of their horse pasture in the Midway district. . . . [H]e secured possession of the car . . . moved [it] over to one corner of the pasture, near the gate, and proceeded to fix it up as a residence." Located at Merriam Park, the one-room "house" included a cot, a small bureau, a table, and a cooking stove (apparently used for heat as well). The exterior was covered with multiple layers of tarpaper and had two front windows complete with lace curtains.[1]

❦ HENRY BARRETT:

According to his death certificate, Henry died on August 21, 1945, at 12:45 a.m. of "generalized carcinomatoid, primarily [of the] brain [and of the] prostate"; a condition he had suffered for one year. He was born on February 22, 1867, in Mills County, Iowa. He died at the age of seventy-eight years, five months, and twenty-nine days, in Chicago, Cook County, Illinois, where he had lived for over fifteen years.

A physician named M. V. Cook attended Henry and had last seen him alive two days before his death, which was reported on August 22. He was buried the next day at Oak Ridge Cemetery in Cook County. Henry died alone, was discovered the following day, and was buried less than twenty-four hours later.

❦ MARY BARRETT-COLEMAN:
She and George H. Coleman married September 28, 1887, with Timothy Barrett and Chloe Betts as witnesses, according to their marriage license. They had two children, George Jr. in September 1888 and Kate in May 1890. The family continued to live on Hiawatha Avenue (formerly known as Fort Avenue).

❦ CHLOE BETTS:
After the trials, she married Levi Gorman. They had two daughters, Hazel and Minnie.

❦ THEODORE BETTS:
The father of Minnie and Chloe was a Civil War veteran. In March 1913 he died at a home for disabled veterans in Wisconsin. He had a twin sister named Theodosia and several other siblings. His older brother William, who lived in McLeod County, Minnesota, is referenced in this book.

❦ ADDIE BOYD:
Peter's teenaged girlfriend was one of the few who formally identified his body. In the aftermath of the executions, the press seemed especially cruel and heartless when it mentioned how she suffered over Peter's death. In 1890 she married Alphonse Brinkman, and the couple raised two children. Alphonse and Addie moved to California in their later years, where he died in 1932 and Addie in 1940. Both are buried in Forest Lawn Cemetery in Los Angeles.

❧ ABBIE ROBINSON BRYANT:

The widow of James Bryant, the Register of Deeds for Minneapolis. The couple were respected and regarded as citizens of influence among their peers. She and James raised a large family: one son and six daughters, one of whom later married a son of Mayor Doc Ames.

Abbie was a personal friend of Mary Barrett-Coleman and accompanied her as she met with Governor Merriam on the night before the executions. She would have been about forty-two years old at that time. Abbie had a brother named George who was about seven years younger. (A twenty-eight year old horse dealer named George Robinson, lived on 22nd Avenue South according to the 1880 United States Census, and is likely the same George Robinson who testified for the defense during Peter's trial.) Abbie died at the age of seventy-two on November 11, 1919.

❧ WILLIAM DONAHUE:

A graduate of Hillsdale College and the University of Michigan Law School. The Barrett case was instrumental in his career, and he continued to practice as a criminal lawyer in Minnesota for several years. He later focused exclusively on civil law and eventually became a Hennepin County judge in 1909, appointed by Governor Johnson. Judge Donahue served for only a few months. That May, at the age of fifty-one, he died in Philadelphia after having surgery for cancer of the neck. He was survived by his wife, Mary, and five children. The train that carried his body back to Minneapolis was met by "more than fifty members of the Hennepin County Bar." A special memorial for Donahue was given by the "five judges who were [his] colleagues on the bench, held at the Hennepin County Courthouse, and attended by over 100 members of the Minneapolis Bar."

A memorial tribute adopted by the Hennepin County Bar Association lauded Donahue's "uncompromising honesty, deep sincerity, and fearlessness in the expression and advocacy of his convictions. He had high ideals for the legal profession, its dignity, its ethics . . . he furnished an example for all . . . an able lawyer . . . good mental capacity . . . sound knowledge . . . his judgment of human nature was keen and accurate." Most profoundly, "He was a good man, who loved justice and hated injustice."[2]

❧ WILLIAM ERWIN:

In March 1889 one newspaper reporter expressed his opinion that Erwin had "blundered," resulting in the brothers' deaths, claiming that the Barrett case was "Erwin's Waterloo." However, Erwin continued his career in law and became "a hero of the labor movement," according to information found on Placeography.org. In 1892 he traveled to Pittsburgh and defended the steelworkers against Andrew Carnegie, and in 1894 he defended the leaders of the Pullman Strike in Chicago.[3]

❧ THE HUB OF HELL:

One year after Thomas Tollefson's murder the Hub of Hell saloon where the Barretts had lived and worked sat abandoned and ruined, its floors torn up by the police search, its windows broken. By the 1890s the Hub of Hell was no longer a fierce, rowdy neighborhood. As the troublemaking inhabitants left—either by choice or under police escort—honest and reputable blue-collar workers moved in, and churches and schoolhouses were built there.

❧ ROBERT JAMISON:

Born in 1858, he died in 1922. In 1886 he was appointed assistant attorney to Hennepin County Attorney Frank Davis. In 1888 he was elected to the position of county attorney and served one term. He became a judge in 1893.

❧ JUDGE WILLIAM LOCHREN:

The judge who had presided over the Barrett brothers' trials was known for his quiet, levelheaded mannerisms and enjoyment of his long-stemmed pipe. He look a long family vacation to the coast of California after the Barretts were executed. He remained a judge until 1896, when President Grover Cleveland nominated him to fill a vacant seat in the United States Senate—he was confirmed the same day and remained a Senator until his retirement in 1908. William Lochren died on January 27, 1912.

❦ JOE MANNIX:

Joe continued his work as a reporter. In 1905 he became a Minnesota State Representative. During the winter of 1917, he was hospitalized for three months due to pernicious anemia. Eventually he became a world traveler and, according to his passports, visited such places as Japan, South Africa, Australia, India, Singapore, China, Korea, and the Dutch East Indies—sometimes for months at a time. He never married, and died in Hennepin County on March 2, 1932.

❦ POLICE OFFICERS AND DETECTIVES:

Michael Hoy, John Byrnes (the court officer who guarded the door while Mike Hoy beat the young burglary suspect, Sweeney), Daniel Day, W. Brackett, Henry Krumwiede, Jacob Hein, Charles Hill, James Howard, and others named in this book retained their positions on the police force for many years.

❦ DETECTIVE MICHAEL QUINLAN:

Born in Wisconsin in 1853, died on May 8, 1942, at the age of eighty-nine, in Minneapolis, Hennepin County, Minnesota. Quinlan was a former friend and detective agency partner of Norman W. King, but the two parted ways during the 1890s—to the point of engaging in a fistfight at a local bar. Michael Quinlan retained his reputation as "one of the shrewdest detectives that has ever served on the force."[4]

❦ MAYOR DOC AMES:

The corruption and graft under his rule continued unchecked for several years, until 1902, when the grand jury for that summer's term was formed from a group of ordinary citizens, with the exception of the jury foreman, Hovey C. Clarke.

Clarke had come to Minneapolis from New England in 1887. As a young man he had made his way into a successful career in the lumber business. The challenge to do something about the ruthless "Ames gang" spurred him on in spite of the attitudes of his fellow jurors. Even the county prosecutor had basically told Clarke not to attempt it.

Undeterred, Clarke led indictments against Ames's key players—and the mayor was furious. But Clarke did not back down. One day he confronted the mayor at City Hall and declared, "Yes, Doc Ames, I'm after you. I've been in this town for seventeen years, and all that time you've been a moral leper. I hear you were rotten during the ten years before that. Now I'm going to put you where all contagious things are put—where you cannot contaminate anybody else."[5]

It was a rough road paved with confrontations, threats, and attempted bribery, but Clarke stood his ground.

Eventually trials followed, men were convicted and sentenced, including Doc Ames. Ames appealed twice and was granted new trials, both of which were declared mistrials.

In the end, Ames never did time behind bars. He died in 1911.

ACKNOWLEDGEMENTS

THIS PROJECT began with one small newspaper article (*The Daily Call*, Greenville, MI, Wednesday, March 27, 1889), but my files are filled with copies of vintage newspaper articles that have been a tremendous source of information for this book. I am thankful for the reporters, sketch artists, and photographers from that era, whose diligence and skill created such informative records of the past. I'm also grateful for the organization and extensive work of archivists, faculty, students, librarians, volunteers, family historians, and history buffs. Their ongoing efforts to preserve various forms of documentation enable us to study our rich history.

I've encountered many helpful people over the years as I researched and gathered information to develop this project including: author, private investigator, and retired Hennepin County Sheriff's Captain Chris Omodt, the son of retired Hennepin County Sheriff Donald Omodt; Barbara Gable Duffy, the great-granddaughter of former Hennepin County Sheriff James Ege of this book; Pat Olive; Heidi Heller, Jennifer Huebscher, Steve Nielsen, Patrick Pfundstein, and Adam Taylor of the Minnesota Historical Society; Marilyn Rehling of the Catholic Cemeteries Archdiocese of Omaha; Jace Klepper, University of Texas Libraries; Ruthie Brock, Andy Herzog, Ben Huseman, Sara Pezzoni, and Cathy Spitzenberger of the Special Collections, Central Library of the University of Texas Arlington; Mike Maxin, Erin Schultz, and Kelly Worden of the Flat River Community Library; Susan Hunter-Weir and Dana Peterson of the University of Minnesota; Robin Butterhof of the Newspaper and Current Periodical Reading Room at the Library of Congress; Matt Piersol of the Nebraska

State Historical Society; the staff of the Carver County Historical Society, Waconia, Minnesota; the staff of the Grand Rapids Public Library; and others who helped in various ways over the years.

Thank you to my husband and family for your love and encouragement. Thanks also to my friends for blessing me with your time and friendship. Thank you to Tim Beals and Credo House Publishers for your encouragement and expertise. And ultimately, thanks to my Lord and Savior, Jesus Christ.

ƐNDNOTES

CHAPTER 1

1. *Fourth Street* by A. J. Russell, 1917, p. 18.
2. *History of the Fire and Police Departments of Minneapolis*, A. E. Costello, 1890, The Relief Assoc. Publishing Co, Minneapolis, MN, p. 279.
3. http://www.rootsweb.com/~ialee/data/census/1880pris.htm, Lee County Iowa GenWeb Project, Iowa State Prison, Ft. Madison, p. 2.
4. *The Omaha Republican*, Saturday, March 23, 1889, "Lassoed," p. 1, retrieved from Omaha Public Library.
5. https://FamilySearch.org, 1885 Minnesota Census, McLeod County, Hutchinson.

CHAPTER 2

1. "Minnesota, County Marriages, 1860–1949" database with images, https://familysearch.org, O. E. Brecke and Serianna Tollefson, 1886.
2. http://chroniclingamerica.loc.gov, *St. Paul Daily Globe*, January 31, 1886, p. 1, "The Street Car Drivers."
3. State of Minnesota, County of Hennepin, Fourth Judicial District Court, State of Minnesota vs. Peter Barrett, February 2, 1888, p. 32.
4. "Minnesota, County Marriages, 1860–1949" database with images, https://familysearch.org, Thomas O. Tollefson and Christina Nelson, 1887.
5. http://chroniclingamerica.loc.gov, *St. Paul Daily Globe*, July 27, 1887, "Fierce Flour City Flames."
6. Ibid.

CHAPTER 3

1. http://chroniclingamerica.loc.gov, *St. Paul Daily Globe*, July 28, 1887.
2. http://chroniclingamerica.loc.gov, *St. Paul Daily Globe*, July 29, 1887, p. 3, "No Clue."
3. http://chroniclingamerica.loc.gov, *St. Paul Daily Globe*, March 17, 1889, "The Murdered Man."
4. http://chroniclingamerica.loc.gov, *St. Paul Daily Globe*, July 30, 1887, p. 3.
5. http://chroniclingamerica.loc.gov, *St. Paul Daily Globe*, August 31, 1887, "Nearly $900 Placed in the Bank to the Credit of Mrs. Tollefson."

6. Ibid.
7. http://chroniclingamerica.loc.gov, *St. Paul Daily Globe*, Aug. 21, 1887, "A Clue to the Tollefson Murder."
8. Ibid.
9. Ibid.
10. Ibid.

CHAPTER 4

1. *History of the Fire and Police Departments of Minneapolis*, A. E. Costello, 1890, The Relief Assoc. Publishing Co, Minneapolis, MN.
2. Ibid; "Histories of the Dakota Co. Irish," by Shawne Fitzgerald. https://freepages.rootsweb.com/~friendsofthehighlandcemetery/genealogy/kevintoc.
3. http://chroniclingamerica.loc.gov, *St. Paul Daily Globe*, July 29, 1887, "Our Burglars and Their Recent Doings."
4. Ibid., "Benevolent Order of Burglars"
5. Ibid.
6. Ibid.
7. Ibid.
8. Ibid., "A Patrolman's Suggestion."
9. http://chroniclingamerica.loc.gov, *St. Paul Daily Globe*, Jan. 19, 1889, "Capt. Harvey on the Rack."
10. http://chroniclingamerica.loc.gov, *St. Paul Daily Globe*, May 26, 1887, "Charged With Cruelty, An Inspector's Alleged Method of Pumping a Prisoner."
11. Ibid.
12. www.minnesotalegalhistoryproject.org, Mark Neuzil, Ph.D, *McClure's Magazine*, January 1903, vol. XX, no. 3, "The Shame of Minneapolis" by Lincoln Steffens.
13. http://chroniclingamerica.loc.gov, *St. Paul Daily Globe*, July 29, 1887, "The Murderers Spotted."
14. Ibid.
15. http://chroniclingamerica.loc.gov, *St. Paul Daily Globe*, July 28, 1887, "For Twenty Dollars."
16. http://chroniclingamerica.loc.gov, *St Paul Daily Globe*, Aug. 21, 1887, "A Clue to the Tollefson Murder."
17. http://chroniclingamerica.loc.gov, *St. Paul Daily Globe*, June 5, 1884.
18. http://chroniclingamerica.loc.gov, *St. Paul Daily Globe*, July 17, 1887.
19. http://chroniclingamerica.loc.gov, *St. Paul Daily Globe*, September 7, 1887, p. 3.
20. http://chroniclingamerica.loc.gov, *St. Paul Daily Globe*, September 6, 1887, "Minneapolis Globules."
21. http://chroniclingamerica.loc.gov, *St Paul Daily Globe*, November 24, 1887, "May be Serious."
22. http://chroniclingamerica.loc.gov, *St Paul Daily Globe*, September 9, 1887, "Minneapolis Globules."

CHAPTER 5

1. http://chroniclingamerica.loc.gov, *St. Paul Daily Globe*, August 15, 1887, "Under the Old Reform."
2. Ibid.
3. Ibid.
4. Ibid.
5. Ibid.
6. Ibid.
7. Ibid.
8. http://chroniclingamerica.loc.gov, *St Paul Daily Globe*, Wednesday, September, 28, 1887, "Liquor Men Are Scared"
9. Ibid.

CHAPTER 6

1. http://chroniclingamerica.loc.gov, *St Paul Daily Globe*, November 16, 1887, "Tim Barrett's Methods of Robbery Excite the People About Minnehaha."
2. Ibid.
3. Ibid.
4. Ibid.
5. Ibid.
6. Ibid.
7. http://chroniclingamerica.loc.gov, *St. Paul Daily Globe*, November 18, 1887, "Still A Question . . ."
8. http://chroniclingamerica.loc.gov, *St. Paul Daily Globe*, Feb. 5, 1888, p. 10, "Reddy's Round-Up. "
9. http://chroniclingamerica.loc.gov, *St. Paul Daily Globe*, November 18, 1887, "Still A Question . . ."
10. https://en.wikipedia.org/wiki/Minneapolis_Police_Department.
11. http://chroniclingamerica.loc.gov, *St. Paul Daily Globe*, November 23, 1887, "The Police Have a Probable Murderer . . ."
12. http://chroniclingamerica.loc.gov, *St. Paul Daily Globe*, November 15, 1889, "For Sale or Rent" p. 7.
13. http://chroniclingamerica.loc.gov, *St. Paul Daily Globe*, January 6, 1888, "A County Expense."
14. http://chroniclingamerica.loc.gov, *St. Paul Daily Globe*, January 1, 1888, "The Testimony Is All In."
15. https://heritagequestonline.com, St. Paul City Directory for 1888, Heritage Quest, October 2016.
16. http://chroniclingamerica.loc.gov, *St. Paul Daily Globe*, Nov. 24, 1887, "Both are Free."
17. http://chroniclingamerica.loc.gov, *St. Paul Daily Globe*, November 29, 1887, p. 3, "Not Yet Ready . . . The Barrett's in Court. . ."
18. Ibid.

19. Ibid.
20. Ibid.
21. Ibid.
22. Ibid.
23. Minnesota Historical Society Collections, *St. Paul Dispatch*, Thurs., Jan. 5, 1888, "A Point Scored."
24. http://chroniclingamerica.loc.gov, *St. Paul Daily Globe*, May 19, 1889, "A Judicial Flush."
25. http://www.fjc.gov/servlet, Judges of the United States Courts.
26. Minnesota Historical Society Collections, *Minneapolis Evening Journal*, Wed., April 24, 1889, "A Story on Judge Lochren."
27. Minnesota Historical Society Collections, *St. Paul & Minneapolis Pioneer Press*, Tuesday, December 20, 1887, "The Trial of Tim Barrett."

CHAPTER 7

1. http://chroniclingamerica.loc.gov, *St. Paul Daily Globe*, December 10, 1887, p. 3, "The Barrett Murder Case."
2. Minnesota Historical Society Collections, *St. Paul & Minneapolis Pioneer Press*, December 20, 1887, "Tim Barrett On Trial."
3. Ibid.
4. Ibid.
5. Ibid.
6. Ibid.
7. Ibid.
8. Minnesota Historical Society Collections, *St. Paul & Minneapolis Pioneer Press*, Thursday, December 22, 1887, "The Story of the Murder."
9. Ibid.
10. State of Minnesota, County of Hennepin, Fourth Judicial District Court, State of Minnesota vs. Peter Barrett, February 2, 1888, p. 6.
11. Minnesota Historical Society Collections, *St. Paul & Minneapolis Pioneer Press*, Thursday, December 22, 1887, "The Story of the Murder."
12. Ibid., p. 2.
13. Minnesota Historical Society Collections, *St. Paul & Minneapolis Pioneer Press*, Friday, December 23, 1887, p. 1, "Turned State's Evidence."

CHAPTER 8

1. Ibid.
2. Ibid.
3. Ibid.
4. Ibid.
5. Ibid.
6. Ibid.
7. Ibid.

8. Ibid.
9. Ibid.
10. Ibid.
11. Ibid.
12. Ibid.
13. Ibid.
14. Ibid.
15. Ibid.
16. Ibid.
17. Ibid.
18. Ibid.
19. Ibid.
20. Minnesota Historical Society Collections, *St. Paul & Minneapolis Pioneer Press*, Tuesday, December 27, 1887, "Paragraphic Addenda."
21. http://chroniclingamerica.loc.gov., *St. Paul Daily Globe*, December 31, 1887, p. 3, "The Barrett Trial. . . Naughty Work."
22. Ibid.
23. Minnesota Historical Society Collections, *St. Paul & Minneapolis Pioneer Press*, Friday, December 23, 1887, p. 1, "Turned State's Evidence."
24. Ibid.
25. Ibid.
26. Ibid.

CHAPTER 9

1. Minnesota Historical Society Collections, *St. Paul & Minneapolis Pioneer Press*, Tuesday, December 27, 1887, "The State Rests and the Defense Puts Tim Barrett on the Witness Stand . . ."
2. Minnesota Historical Society Collections, *St. Paul & Minneapolis Pioneer Press*, Thursday, December 22, 1887, "Notes of the Trial."
3. Minnesota Historical Society Collections, *St. Paul & Minneapolis Pioneer Press*, Sunday, December 25, 1887, "Bracing Up Henry's Story."
4. Ibid.
5. Ibid.
6. Ibid.
7. Ibid.
8. Ibid.
9. Ibid.

CHAPTER 10

1. Minnesota Historical Society Collections, *St. Paul & Minneapolis Pioneer Press*, December 27, 1887, "Tim and Henry Don't Agree."
2. The District Court for the 4th Judicial District, County of Hennepin and State of Minnesota, State of Minnesota vs. Timothy Barrett and Peter Barrett, 1887.

Box 37, file 553, page 33, Minnesota Governor: McGill, records Minnesota Historical Society, State Archives.

3. Ibid., p. 34.

4. Minnesota Historical Society Collections, *St. Paul & Minneapolis Pioneer Press*, Tuesday, December 27, 1887, "...A Voice From Northfield."

5. Ibid.

6. Ibid.

7. The District Court for the 4th Judicial District, County of Hennepin and State of Minnesota, State of Minnesota vs. Timothy Barrett and Peter Barrett, 1887. Box 37, file 553, page 61, Minnesota Governor: McGill, records Minnesota Historical Society, State Archives.

8. Minnesota Historical Society Collections, *St. Paul & Minneapolis Pioneer Press*, Tuesday, December 27, 1887, "...Minnie Barrett, Henry's Wife, Among the Last Witnesses for the Prosecution—the Story of the Day."

9. Ibid.

10. Ibid.

CHAPTER 11

1. Minnesota Historical Society Collections, *St. Paul & Minneapolis Pioneer Press*, Tuesday, December 27, 1887, "The State Rests and the Defense Puts Tim Barrett on the Witness Stand as a Starter."

2. Ibid.

3. Ibid.

4. Ibid.

5. Ibid.

6. Ibid.

7. State of Minnesota, County of Hennepin, Fourth Judicial District Court, State of Minnesota vs. Timothy Barrett, December 1887, p. 111.

8. Ibid.

9. Ibid.

10. Ibid.

11. Ibid.

12. State of Minnesota, County of Hennepin, Fourth Judicial District Court, State of Minnesota vs. Timothy Barrett, December 26, 1887, p. 26.

13. Ibid., p. 4.

14. State of Minnesota, County of Hennepin, Fourth Judicial District Court, State of Minnesota vs. Timothy Barrett, December 28, 1887, p. 1.

15. Ibid., p. 2.

16. Ibid.

17. Ibid., p. 8.

18. Ibid.

19. Ibid.

20. Ibid.

21. Ibid., p. 9.
22. Ibid.
23. Ibid.
24. Ibid.
25. Ibid.
26. Ibid.
27. Ibid.
28. Ibid.
29. Ibid.
30. Ibid.
31. Ibid.
32. Ibid., p. 26.
33. https://www.glenwood.lib.ia.us, Glenwood Iowa Public Library, *Malvern Leader*, Thursday, October 9, 1884.
34. Minnesota Historical Society Collections, *St. Paul & Minneapolis Pioneer Press*, Wednesday, December 28, 1887, "Cross Examining Tim."
35. Ibid.

CHAPTER 12

1. Minnesota Historical Society Collections, *St. Paul & Minneapolis Pioneer Press*, Sunday, December 25, 1887, "This and That."
2. http://chroniclingamerica.loc.gov, *St. Paul Daily Globe*, Sept. 21, 1880, "A Couple of Rowdies Get a Handsome Sentence for Their Rascality."
3. http://chroniclingamerica.loc.gov, *St. Paul Daily Globe*, June 13, 1885, "The Rice Street Gang."
4. https://chroniclingamerica.loc.gov, *Omaha Daily Bee*, March 12, 1889, "Alleged Citizens Bank Robbery."
5. State of Minnesota, County of Hennepin, Fourth Judicial District Court, State of Minnesota vs. Timothy Barrett, December 28, 1887, p. 84.
6. Ibid., p. 85.
7. http://chroniclingamerica.loc.gov, *St. Paul Daily Globe*, September 28, 1887, "Liquor Men are Scared. Some Blind Pig Cases . . ."

CHAPTER 13

1. Minnesota Historical Society Collections, *St. Paul & Minneapolis Pioneer Press*, Thursday, December 22, 1887, p. 39, "Notes of the Trial."
2. Ibid.
3. Ibid., p. 27.
4. Ibid.
5. Ibid.
6. Ibid., p. 28.
7. Ibid., p. 29.
8. Ibid.

9. Ibid.

10. Ibid., 30.

11. http://www.rootsweb.com/~iamills/Places/iowainstitution.

12. Minnesota Historical Society Collections, *St. Paul Dispatch*, Dec. 30, 1887, "Minneapolis. The Barrett Case. Mr. Chamberlain's Revolver Plays an Important Part in the Trial."

13. Ibid.

14. Ibid.

15. Ibid.

16. Minnesota Historical Society Collections, *St. Paul & Minneapolis Pioneer Press*, January 1, 1888, "The Testimony's All In."

17. State of Minnesota, County of Hennepin, Fourth Judicial District Court, State of Minnesota vs. Timothy Barrett, December 28, 1887, p. 43.

18. Ibid.

19. Ibid., p. 41

20. Ibid.

21. Minnesota Historical Society Collections, *St. Paul Dispatch*, Wed., Dec. 28, 1887, "The Barrett Case."

22. http://chroniclingamerica.loc.gov, *St. Paul Daily Globe*, Dec. 29, 1887, p. 3, "The Cyclone Detective and the Mysterious Plotting He Heard at the Falls."

23. Ibid.

24. Ibid.

25. Ibid.

26. Ibid.

27. http://chroniclingamerica.loc.gov, *St. Paul Daily Globe*, December 10, 1887, p. 3, "Remarkable Narrative of Young Cyclone, the Detective, and Wild Frank."

28. Minnesota Historical Society Collections, *St. Paul & Minneapolis Pioneer Press*, Sunday, January 1, 1888.

CHAPTER 14

1. http://chroniclingamerica.loc.gov, *St. Paul Daily Globe*, January 3, 1888, p. 3, "Dissected by Davis."

2. Ibid.

3. Ibid.

4. Ibid.

5. Minnesota Historical Society Collections, *Minneapolis Evening Journal*, Wed., January 2, 1888, "Talking for a Life."

6. http://chroniclingamerica.loc.gov, *St. Paul Daily Globe*, January 3, 1888, p. 3, "Dissected by Davis."

7. http://chroniclingamerica.loc.gov, *St. Paul Daily Globe*, January 4, 1888, "The Plea Made by Mr. Erwin . . .'

8. Ibid.

9. Ibid.

10. Ibid.

11. Ibid.
12. Ibid.
13. Ibid.
14. http://chroniclingamerica.loc.gov, *St. Paul Daily Globe*, December 31, 1887, p. 3, "How the Prosecution Pumped Tim in Jail."
15. Ibid.
16. http://chroniclingamerica.loc.gov, *St. Paul Daily Globe*, January 4, 1888, "The Plea Made by Mr. Erwin . . ."
17. Ibid.
18. Ibid.
19. Ibid.
20. Ibid.
21. Ibid.
22. http://chroniclingamerica.loc.gov, *St. Paul Daily Globe*, January 4, 1888, p. 1.
23. http://chroniclingamerica.loc.gov, *St. Paul Daily Globe*, January 6, 1888, p. 3, "He May or May Not Hang."
24. Ibid.
25. http://chroniclingamerica.loc.gov, *St. Paul Daily Globe*, January 13, 1888, p. 3, "To Be Hanged."
26. Minneapolis Historical Society Collections, *St. Paul & Minneapolis Pioneer Press*, Friday, January 13, 1888, "Tim Barrett Must Hang."
27. http://chroniclingamerica.loc.gov, *St. Paul Daily Globe*, January 12, 1888, p. 3, "The Fate of Tim."
28. http://chroniclingamerica.loc.gov, *St. Paul Daily Globe*, January 13, 1888, p. 3, "To Be Hanged."
29. Ibid.
30. Ibid.
31. Ibid.
32. Ibid.
33. Minnesota Historical Society Collections, *St. Paul & Minneapolis Pioneer Press*, Friday, January 13, 1888, "Tim Barrett Must Hang."
34. Ibid.
35. http://chroniclingamerica.loc.gov, *St. Paul Daily Globe*, January 13, 1888, p. 3, "To Be Hanged."
36. Ibid.
37. Minnesota Historical Society Collections, *St. Paul & Minneapolis Pioneer Press*, Friday, January 13, 1888, "Tim Barrett Must Hang."
38. Ibid.
39. Ibid.

CHAPTER 15

1. http://climate.umn.edu/doc/historical/winter_storms.htm, "Famous Minnesota Winter Storms" p. 1.

2. Minnesota Historical Society Collections, *St. Paul Dispatch*, Sat., Jan. 14, 1888, "The Talking Machines," "A Joke on Mark Twain," "The White House Dinners," p. 2.

3. http://chroniclingamerica.loc.gov., *St. Paul Daily Globe*, Feb. 10, 1888, p. 3, "New Revelations Coming Out in the Defense in Barrett's Trial."

4. Minnesota Historical Society Collections, *The Minneapolis Evening Journal*, Monday, January 30, 1888, p. 1, "Pete Follows Tim."

5. Ibid., pp. 2, 3.

6. Ibid.

7. Ibid., pp. 3, 4.

8. Ibid.

9. State of Minnesota, County of Hennepin, Fourth Judicial District Court, State of Minnesota vs. Timothy Barrett and Peter Barrett, 1887, p. 6.

CHAPTER 16

1. Minnesota Historical Society Collections, *Minneapolis Evening Journal*, Friday, February 3, 1888, p. 1, "Reddy's Now Familiar Story."

2. Ibid., p. 59.

3. Ibid., p. 49.

4. State of Minnesota, County of Hennepin, Fourth Judicial District Court, State of Minnesota vs. Timothy Barrett, December 28, 1887, p. 52.

5. Ibid., p. 50.

6. Ibid., p. 56.

7. State of Minnesota, County of Hennepin, Fourth Judicial District Court, State of Minnesota vs. Timothy Barrett, December 28, 1887, p. 69.

8. http://chroniclingamerica.loc.gov., *St. Paul Daily Globe*, Jan. 2, 1888, p. 3, "Reddy's Nerve. He Declares War Upon Newspaper Reporters and Editors."

9. Ibid.

10. State of Minnesota, County of Hennepin, Fourth Judicial District Court, State of Minnesota vs. Timothy Barrett, December 28, 1887, p. 65.

11. Ibid., p. 66.

12. Ibid., p. 67.

13. Ibid., p. 68.

14. State of Minnesota, County of Hennepin, Fourth Judicial District Court, State of Minnesota vs. Timothy Barrett, December 28, 1887, p. 85.

15. Ibid.

16. Ibid., p. 87.

17. State of Minnesota, County of Hennepin, Fourth Judicial District Court, State of Minnesota vs. Peter Barrett, February 2, 1888, p. 7.

18. Ibid., p. 9.

19. Ibid.

20. Ibid.

21. Ibid.

22. Ibid.

23. Ibid., pp. 12, 13.
24. Ibid., p. 13
25. Ibid., pp. 13, 14, 15.
26. Ibid., p. 16.
27. Ibid., p. 17.
28. Ibid.
29. Ibid.
30. Ibid.
31. Ibid.
32. Ibid.

CHAPTER 17

1. Ibid., p. 19.
2. Ibid., p. 20.
3. Ibid.
4. Ibid.
5. Ibid.
6. Ibid.
7. Ibid.
8. Ibid.
9. State of Minnesota, County of Hennepin, Fourth Judicial District Court, State of Minnesota vs. Timothy Barrett and Peter Barrett, 1887, p. 6.
10. http://chroniclingamerica.loc.gov, *St. Paul Daily Globe*, Feb. 5, 1888, p. 10, "Reddy's Round Up."
11. Ibid.
12. Ibid.
13. Ibid.
14. Ibid.
15. Ibid.
16. Minnesota Historical Society Collections, *St. Paul & Minneapolis Pioneer Press*, Fri., Dec. 23, 1887, "Turned State's Evidence...Henry Barrett's Striking Testimony."
17. Ibid.
18. Minnesota Historical Society Collections, *Minneapolis Evening Journal*, Thurs., Feb. 9, 1888, "Frank Barrett's 'Breaks'."
19. Ibid.
20. Ibid.
21. Ibid.
22. Ibid.
23. Ibid.
24. Ibid.
25. Ibid.
26. Ibid.

CHAPTER 18

1. *Victorian America, Transformations in Everyday Life*, Thomas J. Schlereth, Harper Perennial, 1991, p. 272.
2. Minnesota Historical Society Collections, *St. Paul Dispatch*, Tues., Feb. 7, 1888, "The Barrett Case. The Jury Visits Mrs. 'Reddy' Barrett in Bed."
3. State of Minnesota, County of Hennepin, Fourth Judicial District Court, State of Minnesota vs. Peter Barrett, p. 37.
4. Ibid.
5. Ibid.
6. Ibid., p. 38.
7. Ibid., pp. 32, 38.
8. Ibid., p. 32.
9. Ibid., p. 38.

CHAPTER 19

1. State of Minnesota, County of Hennepin, Fourth Judicial District Court, State of Minnesota vs. Peter Barrett, February 2, 1888, p. 32.
2. Ibid., p. 35.
3. Ibid., p. 42.
4. Ibid.
5. Ibid.
6. Minnesota Historical Society Collections, *The Minneapolis Evening Journal*, Thurs., February 9, 1888, "Witness Heyn Describes Tollefson's Murder as He Saw It."
7. State of Minnesota, County of Hennepin, Fourth Judicial District Court, State of Minnesota vs. Peter Barrett, February 2, 1888, p. 44..
8. Ibid.
9. Ibid.
10. Ibid.
11. Ibid., p. 45.
12. Ibid.
13. Minnesota Historical Society Collections, *Minneapolis Evening Journal*, Thursday, Feb. 9, 1888, "Witness Heyn Describes Tollefson's Murder as He Saw It."
14. State of Minnesota, County of Hennepin, Fourth Judicial District Court, State of Minnesota vs. Peter Barrett, p. 46.
15. Ibid.
16. Ibid.
17. Ibid., p. 47.
18. Ibid.
19. Ibid.
20. Ibid., p. 51.
21. Ibid., p. 52.
22. Ibid., p. 54.

23. Ibid.
24. Ibid., p. 57
25. Ibid., p. 58.
26. Ibid.
27. Ibid.
28. http://chroniclingamerica.loc.gov, *St. Paul Daily Globe*, Feb. 10, 1888.
29. State of Minnesota, County of Hennepin, Fourth Judicial District Court, State of Minnesota vs. Peter Barrett, pp. 86, 87.
30. Ibid., p. 87.
31. Ibid., p. 40.
32. Ibid., p. 41.
33. Ibid.
34. Ibid.
35. Ibid., p. 87.
36. Ibid., pp. 87, 88.
37. Ibid., p. 88.
38. Ibid.
39. Ibid., pp. 88, 89.
40. Ibid., p. 90.
41. Ibid.
42. Ibid., p. 91.
43. Ibid., p. 91.
44. Ibid.
45. Ibid., p. 92.
46. Ibid.
47. Ibid.
48. Ibid., p. 97.
49. Ibid., p. 98.
50. Ibid.
51. Ibid., p. 99.
52. Ibid.
53. Ibid.
54. Ibid., p. 94.
55. Ibid.
56. Minnesota Historical Society Collections, *Minneapolis Evening Journal*, Monday, February 13, 1888, "For His Son's Life."
57. Ibid.
58. Ibid.
59. Ibid.

CHAPTER 20

1. The District Court for the 4th Judicial District, County of Hennepin and State of Minnesota, State of Minnesota vs. Timothy Barrett and Peter Barrett, 1887. Box

37, file 553, pp. 66, 67, 68. Minnesota Governor: McGill, records Minnesota Historical Society, State Archives.

2. Ibid., p. 68.
3. Ibid.
4. Ibid., p. 69.
5. Ibid.
6. Ibid., p. 70.
7. Ibid.
8. Ibid., p. 71.
9. Ibid.
10. Ibid.
11. Ibid., pp. 71, 72.
12. Ibid.
13. Ibid., p. 72.
14. Ibid., p. 73.
15. Ibid.
16. Ibid.
17. Ibid.
18. Ibid., p. 74.
19. Ibid.
20. Ibid.
21. Ibid.
22. Ibid.
23. Ibid.
24. https://familysearch.org, United States Census, 1870, Iowa, Mills County, Oak Township, provided by the Church of Jesus Christ of Latter-day Saints.
25. State of Minnesota, County of Hennepin, Fourth Judicial District Court, State of Minnesota vs. Timothy Barrett and Peter Barrett, 1887, p. 75.
26. Ibid.
27. Ibid.
28. Ibid., p. 76.
29. Ibid.
30. Ibid.
31. Ibid., p. 77.
32. Ibid.
33. Ibid., p. 78.
34. Ibid.
35. Ibid., pp. 80, 81.
36. Ibid., p. 81.
37. Ibid.
38. Ibid.
39. Ibid.
40. Ibid., p. 82.

41. Ibid.
42. Ibid.
43. Ibid.
44. Ibid.
45. Ibid., pp. 83, 84.
46. Ibid., p. 85.
47. Ibid.
48. Ibid.

CHAPTER 21

1. State of Minnesota, County of Hennepin, Fourth Judicial District Court, State of Minnesota vs. Peter Barrett, February 2, 1888, pp. 29, 30.
2. Ibid., p. 30.
3. Ibid.
4. Ibid., p. 28.
5. http://chroniclingamerica.loc.gov. *St. Paul Daily Globe*, Fri., Feb. 10, 1888, "New Revelations Coming Out in the Defense in Barrett's Trial."
6. Ibid.
7. The District Court for the 4th Judicial District, County of Hennepin and State of Minnesota, State of Minnesota vs. Timothy Barrett and Peter Barrett, 1887. Box 37, file 553, page 61, Minnesota Governor: McGill, records Minnesota Historical Society, State Archives.
8. Ibid.
9. http://chroniclingamerica.loc.gov., *St.Paul Daily Globe*, Feb, 18, 1888, p. 3,"The High-Up Oratory."
10. The District Court for the 4th Judicial District, County of Hennepin and State of Minnesota, State of Minnesota vs. Timothy Barrett and Peter Barrett, 1887. Box 37, file 553, page 61, Minnesota Governor: McGill, records Minnesota Historical Society, State Archives.
11. Ibid.
12. http://chroniclingamerica.loc.gov., *St. Paul Daily Globe*, Tues., Feb. 14, 1888, "They Corroborate Peter."
13. Ibid.
14. Ibid.
15. Ibid.
16. The District Court for the 4th Judicial District, County of Hennepin and State of Minnesota, State of Minnesota vs. Timothy Barrett and Peter Barrett, 1887. Box 37, file 553, page 61, Minnesota Governor: McGill, records Minnesota Historical Society, State Archives.
17. http://chroniclingamerica.loc.gov., *St. Paul Daily Globe*, Feb. 16, 1888, "Drawing Toward the End."
18. Ibid.
19. Ibid.
20. Ibid.

21. State of Minnesota, County of Hennepin, Fourth Judicial District Court, State of Minnesota vs. Peter Barrett, p. 86.
22. Ibid.

CHAPTER 22

1. Ibid., p. 101.
2. Ibid., p. 102.
3. Ibid.
4. Ibid.
5. Ibid., p. 103.
6. Ibid.
7. Ibid., p. 104.
8. Ibid.
9. Ibid., pp. 104, 105, 106, 107.
10. Ibid.
11. Ibid., p. 107.
12. Ibid.
13. Ibid., p. 108.
14. Ibid.
15. Ibid.
16. Ibid.
17. Ibid., pp. 108, 109.
18. Ibid., p. 110.

CHAPTER 23

1. Minnesota Historical Society Collections, *Minneapolis Evening Journal*, Thursday, Feb. 16, 1888, "Talking For a Life."
2. Ibid.
3. Ibid.
4. Minnesota Historical Society Collections, *Minneapolis Evening Journal*, Friday, Feb. 17, 1888, "A Strife of Minds."
5. Ibid.
6. Ibid.
7. Ibid.
8. Ibid.
9. Ibid.
10. Ibid.
11. State of Minnesota, County of Hennepin, Fourth Judicial District Court, State of Minnesota vs. Timothy Barrett and Peter Barrett, 1887, p. 111.

CHAPTER 24

1. Charles W. Elliott, Ed., page 124, copyright 1937, Minnesota Historical Society.

2. http://www.revisor.mn.gov, *Minnesota Statutes 1878*, Ch. 73, "Witnesses and Evidence" art. 104, sec. 94 and MN Statutes 1888 Supplement, art. 104, sec 94.
3. Minnesota Historical Society Collections, *Minneapolis Evening Journal*, Monday, February 20, 1888, "Pete is Guilty Too."

CHAPTER 25

1. Ibid.
2. http://chroniclingamerica.loc.gov, *Daily Inter Ocean*, Chicago, IL, Sun., Feb. 19, 1888, "In The First Degree."
3. http://chroniclingamerica.loc.gov, *St. Paul Daily Globe*, Sun., Feb 19, 1888, p. 1, "Pete Too Must Hang."
4. Ibid.
5. State of Minnesota, County of Hennepin, Fourth Judicial District Court, State of Minnesota vs. Peter Barrett, Verdict, 1888, p. II.
6. Ibid., p. III.
7. Ibid., p. 112.
8. http://chroniclingamerica.loc.gov, *St. Paul Daily Globe*, June 5, 1888, p. 3.
9. http://chroniclingamerica.loc.gov, *St. Paul Daily Globe*, July 11, 1888, p. 2.

CHAPTER 26

1. http://chroniclingamerica.loc.gov, *Omaha Daily Bee*, November 23, 1888, p. 8, "Cheated Out of the Reward."
2. http://chroniclingamerica.loc.gov, *St. Paul Daily Globe*, Jan. 29, 1889, "After Blood Money."
3. Ibid.

CHAPTER 27

1. Minnesota Historical Society Collections, *St. Paul Dispatch*, Friday, March 22, 1889, p. 1, "During Their Imprisonment."
2. Minnesota Historical Society Collections, *Minneapolis Evening Journal*, Saturday, March 16, 1889, "About Pete's Girl."
3. Minnesota Historical Society Collections, *St. Paul Dispatch*, Friday, March 22, 1889, p. 1, "During Their Imprisonment."
4. http://chroniclingamerica.gov, *St. Paul Daily Globe*, Jan. 14, 1889, "Jumped on a Jailer."
5. Ibid.
6. Ibid.
7. Ibid,

CHAPTER 28

1. Retrieved from Omaha Public Library, *The Omaha Republican*, Saturday, March 23, 1889, "Lassoed," p. 1.
2. https://chroniclingamerica.loc.gov, *Omaha Daily Bee*, March 23, 1889, provided by University of Nebraska-Lincoln Libraries.

3. Minnesota Historical Society Collections, *The Minneapolis Evening Journal*, Friday, March 22, 1889, page 2, "The Dark and Bloody History of the Barrett Family."
4. Ibid.
5. http://chroniclingamerica.loc.gov, *Omaha Daily Bee*, March 26, 1889, p. 8, provided by University of Nebraska-Lincoln Libraries
6. Ibid
7. Minnesota Historical Society Collections, *Minneapolis Evening Journal*, March 22, 1889, "A Dark Drama of Death."
8. Ibid.
9. http://chroniclingamerica.loc.gov, *Omaha Daily Bee*, Jan. 2, 1887, "Police Authority Defied."
10. Ibid.
11. Ibid.
12. Ibid.
13. Minnesota Historical Society Collections, *Minneapolis Evening Journal*, March 22, 1889, "A Dark Drama of Death."

CHAPTER 29

1. http://chroniclingamerica.loc.gov, *St. Paul Daily Globe*, Jan. 29, 1889, "After Repeated Delays the Supreme Court Refuses the Barretts' Appeal."
2. Ibid.
3. Ibid.
4. http:www.revisor.mn.gov, *Minnesota Statutes 1878*, chapter 73, "Witnesses and Evidence" article 104, Sec. 94.
5. Ibid., "Minnesota Statutes 1888 Supplement," article 104, Sec. 94.
6. http://chroniclingamerica.loc.gov, *St. Paul Daily Globe*, Jan. 29, 1889, "After Repeated Delays the Supreme Court Refuses the Barretts' Appeal."
7. Ibid.
8. http://chroniclingamerica.loc.gov, *St. Paul Daily Globe*, Feb. 2, 1889, p. 3, "The Torture Prepared for the Barretts Preliminary to Hanging."
9. http://chroniclingamerica.loc.gov, *St. Paul Daily Globe*, Jan. 30, 1889, p. 3, "The Barretts."
10. Minnesota Historical Society Collections, *The Minneapolis Tribune*, Thursday morning, March 21, 1889, p. 1, "The Two Must Die."
11. Ibid.
12. Ibid., "The Jail Opened to Visitors."
13. http://chroniclingamerica.loc.gov., *St. Paul Daily Globe*, March 18, 1889, p. 3, "It's Henry's Hatred."
14. https://familysearch.org, United States Census, 1870, Iowa, Mills County, Oak Township; Minnesota Death Records, provided by the Church of Jesus Christ of Latter-day Saints.

CHAPTER 30

1. http://chroniclingamerica.loc.gov., *St. Paul Daily Globe*, March 18, 1889, p. 3, "It's Henry's Hatred."
2. Ibid.
3. http://chroniclingamerica.loc.gov., *St. Paul Daily Globe*, March 17, 1889, p. 3, "Will Not Interfere."
4. Ibid.
5. Minnesota Historical Society Collections, *The Minneapolis Tribune*, Thursday morning, March 21, 1889, p. 1, "The Two Must Die."
6. Ibid., "A Fight for Life."
7. http://chroniclingamerica.loc.gov., *St. Paul Daily Globe*, March 21, 1889, p. 1,"To Save Pete."
8. Minnesota Historical Society Collections, *The Minneapolis Tribune*, Thursday morning, March 21, 1889, "A Fight for Life."
9. Ibid.
10. Ibid.
11. Ibid.
12. https://newspapers.mnhs.org., *The Minneapolis Tribune*, March 22, 1889, p. 2.
13. https://newspapers.mnhs.org., *The Minneapolis Tribune*, Thursday morning, March 21, 1889, "A Fight for Life."
14. Ibid.
15. https://newspapers.mnhs.org., *The Minneapolis Tribune*, March 22, 1889, p. 2, "Gorman is Disappointed."
16. Minnesota Historical Society Collections, *St. Paul & Minneapolis Pioneer Press*, Friday, March 22, 1889, p. 1, "Tender-Hearted Jurors."
17. Ibid.
18. Ibid., p. 1, "A Fight For Life."
19. Ibid., "An Open Letter Received."
20. Minnesota Historical Society Collections, *The Minneapolis Tribune*, March 22, 1889, "An Open Letter Received."

CHAPTER 31

1. Minnesota Historical Society Collections, *Minneapolis Evening Journal*, March 21, 1889, "Naughty Pictures."
2. Minnesota Historical Society Collections, *St. Paul & Minneapolis Pioneer Press*, Friday, March 22, 1889, "They Cost Over $8,000."
3. Minnesota Historical Society Collection, *The Minneapolis Tribune*, March 22, 1889, "They Cost Over $8,000."
4. http://chroniclingamerica.loc.gov, *St. Paul Daily Globe*, March 21, 1889, "Were Imposters," p. 1.
5. http://chroniclingamerica.loc.gov, *St. Paul Daily Globe*, March 12, 1889, p. 3.
6. Minnesota Historical Society Collections, The *Minneapolis Tribune*, Thursday, March 21, 1889, p. 1, "The Two Must Die."

7. Ibid.
8. Minnesota Historical Society Collections, *St. Paul & Minneapolis Pioneer Press*, Friday, March 22, 1889, p. 1, "Early Morning Hours."
9. http://chroniclingamerica.loc.gov, *St. Paul Daily Globe*, Saturday, March 23, 1889, p. 3 (continuation of p. 1) "Hempen Horror."
10. Minnesota Historical Society, reserve*HV 6248, .B27H4.
11. Minnesota Historical Society Collections, *Minnesota History*, "Minnesota's John Day Smith Law and the Death Penalty" by Michael Anderson.
12. Minnesota Historical Society Collections, The *Minneapolis Evening Journal*, March 22, 1889, "The Crowd Outside."
13. Ibid.
14. Ibid.
15. Minnesota Historical Society Collections, *St. Paul & Minneapolis Pioneer Press*, Friday, March 22, 1889, p. 1, "Early Morning Hours."

CHAPTER 32

1. Retrieved from Omaha Public Library, *The Omaha Republican*, Saturday, March 23, 1889, "Lassoed," p. 1,
2. Minneapolis Historical Society Collections, *St. Paul Dispatch*, Friday, March 22, 1889, p. 1, "Merriam Says No."
3. Minnesota Historical Society Collections, *St. Paul & Minneapolis Pioneer Press*, March 23, 1889, "Death's Discount."
4. Minnesota Historical Society Collections, *St. Paul & Minneapolis Pioneer Press*, March 22, 1889, "The Death Cloaks."
5. Ibid.
6. Minnesota Historical Society Collections, *St. Paul & Minneapolis Pioneer Press*, March 22, 1889, "The Death Parade."
7. Minnesota Historical Society Collections, *St. Paul & Minneapolis Pioneer Press*, March 22, 1889, "The Death Cloaks."
8. Minnesota Historical Society Collections, *St. Paul & Minneapolis Pioneer Press*, Saturday, March 23, 1889, "Death's Discount," p. 1.
9. Minnesota Historical Society Collections, *St. Paul & Minneapolis Pioneer Press*, Friday, March 22, 1889, "The Execution," p. 1.
10. Minneapolis Historical Society collections, *Minneapolis Evening Journal*, March 22, 1889, "Sprung in Plain Sight."
11. Ibid., "The Crowd Outside."
12. Minnesota Historical Society Collections, *St. Paul & Minneapolis Pioneer Press*, Friday, March 22, 1889, p. 1, "Strangled."
13. Ibid.
14. Ibid.
15. Ibid.
16. http://chroniclingamerica.loc.gov, *St. Paul Daily Globe*, March 23, 1889, "The Hempen Horror. Cell to Scaffold," p. 3.

17. http:///chroniclingamerica.loc.gov, *New Ulm Weekly Review*, March 28, 1889, "Two Lives Taken."

18. http://chroniclingamerica.loc.gov, *St. Paul Daily Globe*, March 23, 1889, "The Hempen Horror. Cell to Scaffold," p. 3

19. http://chroniclingamerica.loc.gov, *St. Paul Daily Globe*, March 23, 1889, p. 3, "Was He Innocent."

20. Ibid.

21. Minnesota Historical Society Collections, *The Minneapolis Evening Journal*, April 4, 1889.

22. http://chroniclingamerica.loc.gov, *St. Paul Daily Globe*, March 23, 1889, p. 3, "Was He Innocent."

23. Retrieved from the Omaha Public Library, *The Omaha Republic*, March 26, 1889, p. 1, "They Arrive,"

24. http://chroniclingamerica.loc.gov, *The Omaha Daily Bee*, March 26, 1889, p. 8, "Brothers in Crime."

CHAPTER 33

1. http://chroniclingamerica.loc.gov, *St. Paul Daily Globe*, April 9, 1889, "Wild and Weird."

2. Ibid.

3. Ibid.

4. Ibid.

5. Ibid.

6. Ibid.

7. Ibid.

8. Ibid.

9. Ibid.

10. Ibid.

11. Ibid.

12. http://genealogytrails.com/minn/hennepin/news_crimehang.html, transcribed for Genealogy Trails.com by Mary Kay Krogman, *Omaha Herald*, Saturday, June 1, 1889, "Rumors—Is Pete Barrett Living?"

CHAPTER 34

1. http://chroniclingamerica.loc.gov, *St. Paul Daily Globe*, March 25, 1889, "After the Execution."

2. Minnesota Historical Society Collections, *Minneapolis Evening Journal*, Friday, July 20, 1888, "The Story of a Year."

3. http://chroniclingamerica.loc.gov, *Omaha Daily Bee*, February 12, 1889, p. 8, University of Nebraska-Lincoln Libraries.

4. Ibid.

5. Ibid.

6. Ibid.

7. http://chroniclingamerica.loc.gov, *The Worthington Advance*, May 30, 1889, "Supposed Suicide of a Famous Witness."
8. http://chroniclingamerica.loc.gov, *St. Paul Daily Globe*, November 19, 1889, p. 9, "Minneapolis Globules."
9. http://chroniclingamerica.loc.gov, *St. Paul Daily Globe*, March 26, 1889, "Minneapolis. After the Execution," p. 3.
10. Holy Bible, New International Version®, NIV® Copyright ©1973, 1978, 1984, 2011 by Biblica, Inc.® Used by permission. All rights reserved worldwide.

AFTERWORD

1. http://chroniclingamerica.loc.gov, *The St. Paul Daily Globe*, September 13, 1903, "Peter Olson's Unique Dwelling."
2. Minnesota Historical Society Collections, *Minneapolis Evening Journal*, May 15, 1909.
3. Minnesota Historical Society Collections, *Minneapolis Evening Journal*, March 22, 1889, "Bill Erwin's Waterloo."
4. http://chroniclingamerica.loc.gov, *St. Paul Daily Globe*, January 29, 1891, "Police Changes."
5. www.minnesotalegalhistoryproject.org, Mark Neuzil, Ph.D, *McClure's Magazine*, vol. XX, no. 3, January 1902, "The Shame of Minneapolis" by Lincoln Steffens.

ABOUT THE AUTHOR

The author, in the office
where she writes.

BEVERLY J. PORTER has written numerous articles that have appeared in various publications over the years. A passion for history and research led her down a long path of discovery as she patiently developed this manuscript. More than a decade in the making, *The Hub of Hell: A True Story of a Nineteenth-Century Neighborhood, Murder, and Trial* is her third book.

Her previous books include . . .

One Amazing Night,
beautifully illustrated (by Jan Bower) Christmas book for children,
Storybook Meadow Publishing Company, 2018,
received the Dove Foundation Seal of Approval for All Ages.

Hills, Deals, and Stills,
the memoir of Tennessee businessman Hack Ayers,
Credo House Publishers, 2015.

www.ingramcontent.com/pod-product-compliance
Lightning Source LLC
Chambersburg PA
CBHW052121270326
41930CB00012B/2714